A Reference Grammar of Spol

M000288652

This is a reference grammar of the standard spoken variety of Tamil, a language with 65 million speakers in India, Sri Lanka, Malaysia and Singapore. The spoken variety is radically different from the standard literary variety, last standardized in the thirteenth century. The standard spoken language is used by educated people in their interactions with people from different regions and different social groups, and is also the dialect used in films, plays and the media. This book, a much expanded version of the author's *Grammar of Spoken Tamil* (1979) is the first such grammar to contain examples both in Tamil script and in transliteration, and the first to be written so as to be accessible to students studying the modern spoken language as well as to linguists and other specialists. The book has benefited from extensive native-speaker input and the author's own long experience of teaching Tamil to English-speakers.

Harold F. Schiffman has taught at the University of California (Davis), the University of Washington (Seattle) and is presently at the University of Pennsylvania. He has written and co-authored books on Dravidian linguistics, language standardization, diglossia, language policy and the sociolinguistics of South Asia. He has extensive experience of teaching Tamil to English-speakers, and has also undertaken research on the Tamil media and film industry.

A Reference Grammar of Spoken Tamil

Harold F. Schiffman

CAMBRIDGE
UNIVERSITY PRESS

CAMBRIDGE UNIVERSITY PRESS
Cambridge, New York, Melbourne, Madrid, Cape Town, Singapore, São Paulo

Cambridge University Press
The Edinburgh Building, Cambridge CB2 2RU, UK

Published in the United States of America by Cambridge University Press, New York

www.cambridge.org
Information on this title: www.cambridge.org/9780521640749

First published 1999
This digitally printed first paperback version 2006

A catalogue record for this publication is available from the British Library

Library of Congress Cataloguing in Publication data
Schiffman, Harold F.
A reference grammar of spoken Tamil = peeccut tamir nookk
ilakkaṇam/Harold F. Schiffman.
p. cm.
Includes bibliographical references and index.
ISBN 0 521 64074 1 (hardback)
1. Tamil language – Spoken Tamil. I. Title.
PL4753.S34 1999
494′.81182421 – dc21 98–53883
CIP

ISBN-13 978-0-521-64074-9 hardback
ISBN-10 0-521-64074-1 hardback

ISBN-13 978-0-521-02752-6 paperback
ISBN-10 0-521-02752-7 paperback

For my father,

Merl Schiffman

in celebration of ninety years

of grace-filled living

1909-1999

Contents

List of Tables

Figure 0.1: List of Abbreviations and Symbols Used

Abbreviation	Meaning	Abbreviation	Meaning
*(FORM)	Form is ungrammatical	LT	Literary Tamil
ACC	Accusative Case	LXP	Locative Expression
ADJ	Adjective	MALICE	Malicious Intent
AJP	Adjectival Participle	M	Masculine
AFFECT	Affectionate	N, NTR	Neuter
AM	Aspect Marker	NC	Nasal + Homorganic Consonant
ANIM	Animate	NECESS	Necessity
ASP	Aspect; Aspectual	NAJP	Negative Adj. Participle
AV	Adverb(ial)	NEG	Negative; Negation
AVP	Adverbial Participle	NEGIMP	Negative Imperative
BENEF	Benefactive	NBT	Non-Brahman Tamil
BT, BR	Brahman Tamil	NP	Noun Phrase
CAUS	Causative	PERF	Perfect
CC	Homorganic Consonants	PRES	Present Tense
CHGOFST	Change of State	PL, PLUR	Plural
COMPL	Completive	POL	Polite
COND	Conditional	POS	Positive
DAT	Dative Case	OBJ	Object
DEF	Definite	PEJOR	Pejorative
DEFER	Deferential	PNG	Person-Number-Gender
DEICT	Deictic	POSTP	Postposition
ECHOREDUP	Echo-word Reduplication	PRO	Pro-form (e.g. Pronoun)
EMPH	Emphatic; Emphasis	Q, Q-WORD	Interrogative
EPIC	Epicene	QT, QTV	Quotative
EXCL	Exclusive	REPORT	Reportive
EXDEIC	Exdeictic	§	Section Number
F, FEM	Feminine	SG, SING	Singular
FOC	Focus	SOV	Subject-Object-Verb
FUT	Future Tense	SIMULT	Simultaneous
FUTUTIL	Future Utility	s.o.	Someone
HON	Honorific	s.t.	Something
IMPAT	Impatience	SST	Standard Spoken Tamil
INCHOAT	Inchoative	ST	Spoken Tamil
INCL	Inclusive	TNS	Tense
INF	Infinitive	TXP	Time Expression
IMP	Imperative	TR, TRANS	Transitive
INAN	Inanimate	VB	Verb
INTERROG	Interrogative	VBSTEM	Verb Stem
INTR	Intransitive	VP	Verb Phrase
ITERAT	Iterative	WH-INTER	Wh-Interrogative
LOC	Locative Case	XPRESLT	Expected Result

Foreword

This grammar has been in preparation for many years, starting at least with the first classes of Tamil I taught at the University of Washington in 1966, when I began preparing grammar handouts for student use in class. Later I compiled these and expanded them into a grammar that accompanied the *Radio Play Reader* I edited in 1971. Eventually that grammar was revised and appeared as *A Grammar of Spoken Tamil,* published by the Christian Literature Society, Madras, in 1979.

Over the years I have very much benefited from the help and suggestions of S. Arokianathan, R.E. Asher, Norman Cutler, E. Annamalai, N. Kumaraswami Raja, V. S. Rajam, A. K. Ramanujan, and many others too numerous to mention who have contributed to my knowledge. I am very much indebted to them for their help and suggestions, particularly those who participated in the review of this grammar in manuscript form. In the production of this version of the grammar, the help of Prathima Christdas and R. Vasu have been invaluable, both in terms of the electronic formatting, correction of proofreading errors, and in providing linguistic examples to improve my faulty understanding of many fine points of Tamil grammar. I also thank Linda Ward for keyboarding in the 1979 manuscript, which formed the basis of this electronic version.

The final copy of this grammar has been photocomposed and typeset using the electronic document preparation system LaTeX, a subvariety of the so-called TeX system, developed by Donald Knuth. The Tamil fonts used in this system were devised by Dr. Thomas B. Ridgeway, former Director of the Humanities and Arts Computer Center (HACC) at the University of Washington, using the METAFONT font generation system, also devised by Knuth. This Tamil TeX font is in the public domain.

Chapter 1

Phonology and Transliteration

1.1 Introduction

1.1.1 Background

1.1.1.1 Standard Spoken Tamil

This grammar assumes that there exists a variety of spoken Tamil that is 'standard' alongside the long-since standardized LT variety (LT). This is a somewhat problematic assumption. Many linguistic scholars have approached the issue and have various conclusions to offer; the consensus seems to be that a standard spoken Tamil, if it does not already exist, is at least 'emerging' and can be described as that variety that one hears used in the Tamil 'social' film, and on the radio and in the production of 'social' dramas, both live and, on radio and television, in situation comedies. It is the variety that is used when speakers of various local and social dialects meet in college and university hostels in Tamilnadu and must, perhaps for the first time in their lives, speak a variety of Tamil that is understandable to other Tamils from vastly different parts of Tamilnadu. An attempt to be comprehensible to the largest number of speakers means avoiding regionalisms, caste-specific forms, rustic or vulgar forms, or anything stereotypical of a particular place or community. In recent years this kind of inter-caste, inter-regional dialect has most typically resembled higher-caste, educated speech of non-Brahman groups in Tamilnadu; according to some it is neither from the far north (i.e. Madras) or from the southernmost reaches of Tamilnadu (e.g. Kanniyakumari District), but rather from urban areas in the more 'central' districts of Tamilnadu such as Thanjavur, Trichy or Madurai. In cases of doubt as to whether a form is acceptable or not, speakers apparently tend to lean more toward LT, and may choose a form that is not actually found in any spoken regional or social dialect, but is known from LT. Since LT is the form that all educated speakers know, it can be a repository from which general forms can be chosen; this is another aspect of Labov's maxim (1971:450) ccording to which non-standard languages in contact with a standard one will vary in the direction of the standard. Here it is not in a formal context, but in a context of avoiding stigmatization.[1]

For some, including both researchers and speakers of Tamil, Tamil is not 'standardized' because it has not been codified by a committee or a board or an eminent person, or because a standard has not been declared and disseminated by the school system or whatever; or because a 'book' has not been written called *A Grammar of Spoken Tamil.* In fact, I claim (Schiffman 1998) that Spoken Tamil (ST) has become standardized by a process of informal consensus, in the same way that other diglossic languages that possess ancient standard literary languages have evolved modern spoken koinés. It is in fact quite easy to get Tamil speakers to agree that certain forms are preferred and others are dispreferred; there is remarkable unanimity in this area, wherever Tamil is spoken, with the exception of Sri Lanka. The film, and spoken drama groups before it, have been responsible for the evolution and dissemination of this consensual standard.

For example, speakers may model their choice of the past neuter form of verbs on the LT past அது *adu*, e.g. வந்த்-அது *vand-adu*, rather than the form found very commonly in many non-Brahman dialects, i.e. *-cci* or *-ccu*, e.g. *vandu-cci* 'it came' (which is not found per se in LT with this verb, but has spread from Class III verbs, or from the prototypical pasts in -ற்று of verbs like போ *poo* 'go' and ஆகு *aa(hu)* 'become', which have spoken pasts *pooccu* and *aaccu* (from LT போயிற்று and ஆயிற்று, respectively). Other speakers may choose the *ccu/i* forms unequivocally, so that no hard and fast rules can be given for many forms.

In fact even though we conclude that some consensus may exist as to what ST entails, the situation must be described as being variable and fluid. Individual speakers may vary considerably in their own speech, depending upon whom they are talking to, their gender (or the gender of their interlocutor) or what the topic of conversation is. These phenomena have been noted by many linguists working in the field of sociolinguistics, and are not

[1] It is interesting to note that though some writers deny that ST is standardized in any way, the variety they describe in their writings is extremely close to what is described here. For example, the variety Asher (1982) describes, though he claims it is not possible to say it represents a standard, happens, not by chance, to resemble closely what I would call standard.

limited to Tamil. Speakers may vary depending on social characteristics such as their place of birth, their community of origin, their level of education, their socio-economic status, their sex, their age, their occupation, whom they are talking with, and any other social markers one may isolate.[2]

Given this kind of fluidity, we have made our own decisions about what form might be given that would be acceptable to most speakers, forms that would be neutral as to most social characteristics (except that they would not be typically Brahman, nor from the lowest non-Brahman usage.) This is based on our own observations of Tamil usage, and in particular from close study of the Tamil film and the Tamil radio play.

1.2 Phonetics of ST

There are a number of descriptions of the phonetics of ST available in various sources (Asher 1982, Rajaram 1972, Firth 1934 (in Arden 1934)); it is useful to point out where many of them lean in the direction of LT pronunciation, even when they profess to be describing ST. Thus, though we would like to concentrate on describing ST, we must often do it by contrasting it with LT, in order to emphasize the differences, which do not often get adequately described.

1.2.1 Tamil Vowels

ST has a ten-vowel system with long and short இ *i* ஈ *ii*, எ *e* ஏ *ee*, அ *a* ஆ *aa*, ஒ *o* ஓ *oo*, and உ *u* ஊ *uu*.[3] We use throughout this grammar the double-letter representation of long vowels, except where we are being explicitly phonetic. That is, ஆ will be transcribed as *aa* except when a purely phonetic representation is wanted; then it will be [a:].

[2] Many people have contested the notion that the Tamil social film is in 'standard' spoken Tamil because of the variety of dialects, some of them deliberately used for humorous or other effect, found there. To this I would reply that in most of these films, the main characters (hero, heroine, perhaps other friends or kin) speak SST; other characters around them are 'character actors' and use the non-standard, rural, rustic, or other dispreferred varieties of speech, for deliberate effect of some sort. (In fact, many films deliberately *lampoon* the non-standard forms; certain character actors, such as the famous Nagesh, specialized in this.) Thus the film provides not only a model of standardness or correctness (the main characters) but also a model of speech to be avoided.

[3] The diphthongs ஐ *ai* and ஔ *au* found in LT are not usual in ST; a few loan words contain ஔ *au*, but often these can be represented by அவு *avu* as in பவுண்டு *pavuṇḍu* 'pound.'

1.2.1.1 Initial Position

All vowels may appear in initial position in both ST and LT, but there is one major difference between LT and ST in that high short vowels (இ *i* and உ *u*), when followed by a single consonant and the vowel அ *a*, are replaced by எ *e* and ஒ *o* respectively. That is, the high vowels are *lowered* to mid-vowel position if they occur in the first syllable. (They may be preceded by a consonant, but are not required to be.) This means that there are *no* words in ST that now begin with short high vowels followed by a single consonant and the vowel அ *a* or ஐ *ai* (which in ST usually is replaced by எ *e*).

- LT இடம் *iḍam* ⟶ எடம் *eḍam* 'place'
- LT உடம்பு *uḍambu* ⟶ ஒடம்பு *oḍambu* 'body'
- LT இலை *ilai* ⟶ எலெ *ele* 'leaf'
- LT குழந்தை *kur̤andai* ⟶ கொழந்தெ *kor̤ande* 'child'
- LT நினை *niṉai* ⟶ நெனெ *nene* 'think'

Note that in these forms, LT final ஐ *ai*'s all become எ *e*.

1.2.1.2 Final Position

In ST all 'words' now end in a vowel (unlike LT where words could end in sonorants and glides) so a number of phonetic changes have taken place in final position.

1.2.1.3 Words Ending in a Vowel plus Nasal

Words of more than one syllable ending in a vowel plus the nasal consonants ம் *m* and ன் *n* change to nasalized vowels, and the nasal segment is deleted.[4]

Generally, long vowels retain their same quality, but add nasalization. Short vowels may change, e.g. undergo rounding, fronting or some other phonetic process.

- Thus words ending in அம் *am* such as மரம் *maram* 'tree' are pronounced [õ] in final position, i.e. *maram* is phonetically [mərõ].
- Long ஆ *aa* before ம் *m* retains the low-central quality: போகலாம் *poohalaam* 'let it go' is phonetically [poːhəlãː].

[4]This does not occur with final retroflex ண் *ṇ*; such items have an epenthetic உ *u* added (cf. §1.2.5 below).

- Long ஓ *oo* before ம் *m* retains the tense mid back position: இருக்குறோம் 'we are' *irukkroom* is [irʉkrõː].

- Long ஏ *ee* before ன் *n* retains the tense mid front articulation: இருக்குறேன் *irukkreen* 'I am' is [irʉkrẽː].

- Short உ *u* after ம் *m* remains high, back and rounded: போகும் *poohum* 'it will go' is [poːhũ].

- Short அ *a* before ன் *n* is fronted in the dialects of many speakers, to [æ] or [ɛ]: அவன் *avan* 'he' is [avæ̃] or [avɛ̃].

- Short எ *e* before ன் *n* occurs mainly in the item என் *en* 'my', where it is pronounced [ʸɛ̃].

- Short ஒ *o* before ன் *n* occurs mainly in the item ஒன் *on* 'your', where it is pronounced [ʷɔ̃].

- There are few if any occurrences of ஊ *uu*, or of short இ *i* before nasals in final position; LT ஊன் *uun* 'gum' follows the pattern of adding உ *u*.

- Pronouns that end in nasal consonants, such as நான் *naan*, என் *en* etc. behave differently from other words; they undergo nasalization (to [nãː], [ɛ̃], etc.) irrespective of syllable count or vowel length, but other words like மீன் *miinu* 'fish' do not; epenthetic உ *u* is added instead.

1.2.1.4 The Epenthetic Vowel உ *u*

When all other methods have been exhausted, Tamil can always make a word end in a vowel by adding the so-called 'epenthetic' (or 'enunciative') vowel உ *u* to any word that does not already have a final vowel. This 'fleeting' vowel is often present only in isolation, i.e. before a pause. If the word is joined to another, this vowel then disappears. Phonetically, this vowel is usually an unrounded high back lax vowel [ɯ], [ʉ] or [ɨ]. In fact, Tamil pronounces all orthographic *u*'s as [ʉ] after the first syllable of a word, except for final உ *u*'s in some names, chiefly male nicknames.[5] Furthermore, many *i*'s are also pronounced [ʉ] or [ɨ] in similar positions, so words like சாப்பிட்டுகிட்டிருக்கு *saappiṭṭukiṭṭirukku* 'it is eating' is actually phonetically [saːpṭʉṭṭrʉkʉ], i.e. all the vowels after the first syllable are identical, or in

[5] This is also a pattern in some Indo-Aryan languages, and may be borrowed. Thus பாலசுப்பிரமணியம் *baalasubramaṇiyam* may be shortened to பாலு *baalu*, ராஜேந்திரன் *raajeendran* to ராஜு *raaju*, etc.

some cases have been deleted. This vowel has been unrounded for so long that most speakers of Tamil pronounce it this way in LT as well as in ST, i.e. it is not an ST innovation. What is different in ST is the business of making இ *i* into [ɨ] or [ʉ] as well.

1.2.1.5 Words Ending in Sonorants, Liquids and Glides

In LT, words may not end in a consonant, but they may end in sonorants of various sorts, liquids and rhotics, and glides such as ய் *y*. In ST, words that in LT end in liquids such as ல் *l* and ள் *ḷ* usually double the liquid consonant if it is a monosyllabic word with a short vowel, or delete it in final position if it is polysyllabic. If it is monosyllabic but with a long vowel, epenthetic உ *u* is added. In some dialects, the liquid is deleted.[6] Many pronouns end in ள் *ḷ* and their final laterals are always deleted before pause, but reappear if a suffix is added.

- LT நில் *nil* 'stand' ⟶ ST நில்லு *nillu*
- LT ஆள் *aaḷ* 'man' ⟶ ST ஆளு *aaḷu*
- LT கள் *kaḷ* 'toddy' ⟶ ST கள்ளு *kaḷḷu*
- LT நாள் *naaḷ* 'day' ⟶ ST நாளு *naaḷu* or நா *naa* (in some dialects)
- LT நீங்கள் *niingaḷ* 'you (PL)' ⟶ ST நீங்க *niinga*
- LT வயல் *vayal* 'field' ⟶ ST வயலு *vayalu*
- LT வாசல் *vaasal* 'gate, door' ⟶ ST வாசலு *vaasalu*

The variability of deletion or non-deletion of final laterals is perhaps greater than any other consonant-final situation in Tamil; no other final consonants display this amount of variation. One other kind of change seen in some dialects is that ள் *ḷ* may simply be replaced by ல் *l* across the board. This model of neutralization is dispreferred in ST, so we will not give examples of it. It is, however, a pedagogical problem wherever Tamil literacy is taught, since some speakers simply have no contrast in their dialects.

[6] But many of these 'deleted' consonants then reappear if something is added, especially since ள் *ḷ* is often used in pronouns of various sorts and as a PNG marker on verbs; cf. § 1.3 below.

1.2.1.6 Rhotics, Final and Otherwise

The question of what is an r-like sound, and what is not, is a thorny question in Tamil. Tamil possesses, besides the laterals ல் *l* and ள் *ḷ*, some other sounds that are phonetically related, but because of variability and inconsistency in their pronunciation in some dialects, and because of some across-the-board changes in ST as compared to LT, this area is fraught with sociolinguistic complexity.[7]

In LT, there was originally a phonetic contrast between three r-like consonants:

- ர் *r*, a phonetically flapped or tapped r, more or less alveolar, phonetically [ɾ]. This sound could not occur in initial position in older forms of LT, but in ST occurs initially, medially, and finally (but usually finally is followed by epenthetic [ʉ] before pause.) This sound does not undergo gemination (doubling).

- ற் *ṟ* was originally an alveolar stop in Proto-Dravidian and in older forms of Tamil. It did not occur initially or finally (just like retroflex stops) and when geminated had the value of a voiceless alveolar stop: ற்ற் was phonetically [t̠t̠] or [t̠] with r-like offset: [t̠r̠]. Intervocalically, ற் was trilled: [r̃], and in some dialects, mainly southern (Kanniyakumari etc.) a real phonetic contrast between this sound and the previous one is maintained. However, in the speech of most Tamil speakers, a phonetic contrast is *not* maintained, even if speakers claim that they do so. This sound is orthographically maintained when writers depict spoken Tamil in plays and novels, since it is the marker, among other things, of the present tense. We therefore maintain it for spelling contrast in our transcriptions, e.g. the two 'r's of வர்றோம் *varroom* are not phonetically distinct, but we write them as ர் and ற் (in Tamil script) because Tamil linguistic culture prefers this. This sound is only found in native-Dravidian lexica.

- Another sound that is sociolinguistically complex is the retroflex frictionless continuant ழ் *r̤* which, under ideal conditions, is phonetically [ɹ].[8] In contemporary Tamil, many speakers replace this sound totally with the retroflex lateral ள் *ḷ* and a plain lateral [l] has also been the symbol used by most Europeans for the name of the language: 'Tamil' is தமிழ் *tamir̤*; the 'Chola' Kingdom is சோழ *coor̤a*, but there is also the item 'Coromandel' (from சோழமந்தலம் *coor̤amandalam*)

[7] I have tried to deal with this in my 1980 paper, 'The Tamil Liquids.'

[8] This was the symbol used by Firth (1934) in his appendix to Arden's grammar (Arden 1934:xvi).

for the coast south of Madras, with an /r/ instead of an /l/. Because of the 'mystique' surrounding this sound (Tamils seem to believe it is 'unique' in Tamil) it is learned only through literacy by many speakers, and even then, some never master it. Therefore, if foreigners can learn it, it gets them good *karma*, so we use ழ் *r̤* wherever it occurs in LT, even though it is rare in ST. Tamil second-language learners should note, however, that forms like கொழந்தெ *kor̤ande* 'child', வாழெ பழம் *vaar̤e par̤am* 'banana, plantain' are more likely to be pronounced [koḷande] and [vaːḷɛpəḷõ] than with corresponding ழ் *r̤*.[9]

The ழ் *r̤* sound is never geminated (another reason to consider it to be an r-sound) and does not undergo many of the morphophonemic rules that apply to ள் *ḷ*, e.g. it does not become replaced by nasals, or become a stop the way ள் *ḷ* does. Neither sound occurs in initial position, both because rhotics and liquids did not in LT, and because retroflex consonants never occur in initial position in native-Dravidian words. In some cases, intervocalic ழ் *r̤* may be deleted, with compensatory lengthening of the vowel: LT பொழுது *por̤udu* 'time' ⟶ ST போது *poodu*.

Our solution, therefore, is always to distinguish these three sounds, and the two l's, in all our transcriptions, even though many of them may be neutralized in many people's speech.

1.2.2 Nasal Consonants

LT script distinguishes six different nasal consonants, but ST only has three phonemically distinct nasal sounds.[10] LT also distinguishes a dental nasal ந் from an alveolar nasal ன், but even in LT these two are in complementary distribution: the ந் occurs initially and before த் *t*, while the alveolar nasal occurs finally and before ற் *ṟ*. Thus in our transcription, we only distinguish between *m*, *n* and *ṇ*; the palatal and velar nasals we simply write as *n* before the appropriate consonant, and we transliterate both ந் and ன் as *n*, since no Tamil speakers (despite claims otherwise) distinguish between these two sounds.

As noted above, if LT final ண் *ṇ* occurs in final position, in ST an epenthetic உ *u* is added to the word (and the consonant is doubled if the

[9] I have heard, however, a hawker selling bananas on a railway station platform in Trichy, with clear [ɹ] in all the appropriate places, i.e. [vaːɹɛpəɹõ].

[10] In LT as well, the nasal ங் [ŋ] only occurs before velars, i.e. க் *k*, and the palatal nasal ஞ் *ñ* generally only occurs before palatal ச் *c*. However, in a very few words, such as ஞாயிறு *ñaayiru* 'Sunday' and in some borrowed words like ஞானி *ñaani* 'sage' the initial palatal nasal does occur without any conditioning.

stem vowel is short), e.g. பெண் *peṉ* 'woman' ⟶ பொண்ணு *poṉṉu* 'ibid'.[11]

All other sequences of vowel plus nasal in final position undergo nasalization of the vowel as described previously.

1.2.3 Glides

Glides, particularly ய் *y* are also generally deleted in final position except in monosyllabic words, where they are instead doubled: LT செய் *cey* 'do, make' ⟶ செய்யி *seyyi*, ரூபாய் *ruubaay* 'rupee'⟶ [ruːbaː] (or [ruːwaː] 'ibid.').

1.2.4 Stop Consonants

In LT, as in Proto-Dravidian, it seems clear that there was a series of six stop consonants:

- Velar: க் *k*
- Palatal: ச் *c* or *s*
- Retroflex: ட் *ṭ*
- Alveolar: ற் *ṯ*
- Dental: த் *t*
- Labial: ப் *p*

In initial position (except for ட் and ற்) and when geminated, the above LT stops are phonetically voiceless (and unaspirated). When they occur after a nasal, all are voiced, and somewhat more lax. Intervocalically, they are laxed, and with the exception of க் and ச், voiced. This is shown in Table 1.1.

In ST, some things have changed, as shown in Table 1.2. Alveolar ற் when geminated, i.e. ற்ற் *ṯṯ*, has now merged with த்த் *tt*: பற்றி *paṯṯi* is [patti], etc. Its other (more r-like) phonetic realizations have merged phonetically with ர் *r*, except in southern dialects. Initial ச் which used to be unambiguously *c*, i.e. [ʧ], now varies widely; some speakers have [s] in initial position only, with the affricated pronunciation reserved for geminate [cc]. Other speakers have [c][12] before certain vowels and [s] before others, e.g. சின்ன *cinna* [cɪnnə] 'small' but சாவி *saavi* [saːvi] 'key.' Some speakers

[11] Note that the vowel also undergoes rounding because it occurs between a labial and a retroflex consonant.

[12] In all cases, the symbol [c] is an affricated stop [ʧ] similar to English 'ch' in 'cheese.'

Table 1.1: **Phonetics of LT Stop Consonants**

Stops	Initially	Medially and Geminated	Between Vowels	After Nasal
Velar க் *k*	[k]	[kk]	[h]	[g]
Palatal ச் *c*	[c]	[cc]	[s]	[j]
Retroflex ட் *ṭ*	...	[ṭṭ]	[ḍ]	[ḍ]
Alveolar ற் *ṯ*	...	[ṯṯ], [ṯr]	[r]	[r]
Dental த் *t*	[t]	[tt]	[ð]	[d̪]
Labial ப் *p*	[p]	[pp]	[b] ([v])	[b]

Table 1.2: **Phonetics of ST Stop Consonants**

Stops	Initially	Geminated Medially	Between Vowels	After Nasal
Velar க் *k*	[k]	[kk]	[h] or [...]	[g]
Palatal ச் *c*	[c] or [s]	[cc]	[s]	[j]
Retroflex ட் *ṭ*	...	[ṭṭ]	[ḍ]	[ḍ]
Alveolar ற் *ṯ*	...	[tt]	[r]	[r]
Dental த் *t*	[t]	[tt]	[ð]	[d̪]
Labial ப் *p*	[p]	[pp]	[b], [v] [w]	[b]

have only [c] except intervocalically; for many speakers, other sounds are also merged with ச் *c*, i.e. they have no contrasts such as ஷ் *ṣ* or ஜ் *j*.

Many speakers also have variation in their pronunciation of intervocalic ப் *b*—sometimes we get [b], sometimes we get [v] or even [w]. This seems to depend on the degree of indigenousness of certain borrowed words, as with [ruːwaː] 'rupee' above.

1.2.4.1 Deletion of Intervocalic வ் *v* and க் *k*

It must be noted that ST fairly systematically deletes intervocalic வ் *v* and க் *k* (phonetically [h]) in certain environments. The rules are very complicated, but for வ் *v* one can state that if it is not the expression of a future or causative marker of weak verbs, or the product of sandhi (cf. ∮1.3 below), வ் *v* and the vowel that follows it will probably be deleted after the second syllable of a word: போகவேணும் *poohaveeṇum* ⟶ [poːhəṇũ].[13]

In the case of intervocalic க் *k* (phonetically [h]) it is deleted regularly when it is the present-tense marker of a weak verb: போகிறாய் *poohiṟaay* ⟶ [poːrɛ] 'you (SG) go.' In other circumstances, e.g. போகலாம் *poohalaam* 'one may go', in slower speech [h] is present, in more rapid colloquial speech, it is absent: [poːlã]. Even across morpheme boundaries, e.g. with the postposition கிட்டெ *kiṭṭe* the க் *k* first laxes to [h] or [ʂ] and then may be deleted: அவங்ககிட்டெ *avangahiṭṭe* ⟶ [avəŋgɨṭṭɛ] 'with, near them.' The same may happen with the durative aspectual marker கிட்டிரு *kiṭṭiru*: சாப்பிட்டுகிட்டிருந்தா *saappiṭṭuhiṭṭirundaa* ⟶ [saːpṭʉṭrʉndaː] 'she was eating.'

1.2.4.2 Voiced Consonants

If Tamil had never borrowed any words from other languages, it could continue to use the above system, where voiced consonants are always in complementary distribution with voiceless consonants. Tamil, however, especially ST, has borrowed many words from Indo-Aryan languages, Arabic, Portuguese, Telugu, and from English that have voiced consonants in initial position. The Tamil writing system is currently unable to deal with this situation, but since many feel that Tamil should not allow borrowed words in its lexicon anyway, it can get away with this by keeping to a very puristic lexicon. Modern writers, journalists, and others, borrow freely from other languages, and ST, being subject to the rules of no academy, has many words with initial voiced consonants, as well as medially voiced (but not geminated) consonants. Thus the English words 'fence' and 'bench' can be (and have been) used in works of fiction, to the confusion of all readers, since all Tamil can do is spell them both பெஞ்ச which appears to be pronounced *penju*, which is neither 'fence' nor 'bench.' Some writers have called for a reform of orthography in order to allow for a way to write initial voiced consonants, but Tamil linguistic culture seems unwilling to have this happen.

For our purposes, we transliterate ST words with initial voiced consonants (indeed with any voiced consonants) in a manner as close to the phonetics as possible, so we also transliterate all instances of consonant plus nasal, which are automatically voiced (but not written as so in LT) in ST, with [b, d, g] etc.

1.2.5 Gemination

We have used the term 'gemination' to refer to the process whereby consonants can be doubled in Tamil. All the consonants referred to so far can

[13] For further details of this very complicated process, cf. Schiffman 1993.

be geminated except for the r-like sounds ர் *r* and ழ் *ṛ*. That is, all lateral sounds, nasal consonants, the glide ய் *y* and all stops, including alveolar ற் *r̲* can occur doubled, and many do get doubled as a result of some morphological or morphophonemic process. A sequence of two geminate consonants is actually twice as long as its single analog after short vowels; after long vowels, the sequence is not as long as after short vowels, but longer than a single consonant. We often write certain things as doubled (in order to preserve voicelessness, e.g.) when in actuality they are phonetically not doubled. The example given above, i.e.

> சாப்பிட்டுகிட்டிருந்தா *saappiṭṭuhiṭṭirundaa* ⟶ [sa:pṭʉṭrʉnda:]
> 'She was eating'

shows doubled consonants of various sorts in the Tamil and its transliteration, while the phonetic transcription does not show consonantal length after long vowels, or in clusters with other consonants.

1.2.6 Vowel Length

Similarly, not all phonemically long vowels in Tamil are actually twice the length of their short analogs. For one thing, all Tamil vowels in final position tend to be shortened; we write them as long in our transcription, but phonetically they may not be. As a speaker progresses through the pronunciation of a word, tonic vowels or vowels near the beginning of a sentence may be long, but towards the end of the word, short vowels get deleted and long vowels shortened. There are even some cases of deletion of long vowels, but only as part of the grammaticalization of certain morphemes, such as போல *poola* 'like' in certain constructions, or with the aspectual verb போடு *pooḍu*. Otherwise, long vowels are not deleted; they may be shortened by certain, albeit rare, morphophonemic processes, but that is all.

1.2.6.1 Transliteration of LT and ST

The Roman transliteration chosen represents a fairly phonetic attempt at rendering Tamil as it is spoken without getting into fine phonetic detail that is actually predictable from a general knowledge of Tamil. Unlike some Indian languages, Tamil does not have a single standard transliteration system. Authoritative sources such as the Madras University *English–Tamil Dictionary* (Chidambaranatha Chettiar 1965), the Madras University *Tamil Lexicon* and Burrow and Emeneau's *Dravidian Etymological Dictionary* use different transliterations, especially for some of the laterals and rhotics, where true confusion reigns. To make matters worse, popular transcriptions, such as those used in public signing, transliterations of personal names, etc. typically do not mark differences in vowel length, retroflexion, or other distinctions. This is unfortunate, but scholars and others have not been able or willing to agree on a standard transliteration, so we have chosen one that can be used by laypersons as well as scholars, and provide below a list showing the correspondences between some of these systems, where their differences are significant.

1. **Initial Stop Consonants** The stop consonants ப், த், ட், ச் and க் are usually represented in initial position as *p, t, ṭ, s* and *k*. Where words borrowed from Indo-Aryan, English, Arabic, Portuguese or some other language preserve voiced stops in initial position, we use the Roman letters *b, d, ḍ, j* (but sometimes also *s*) and *g*. Actually retroflex consonants almost never occur in initial position in Tamil words, so they will never occur in LT (with the exception of the word டிராவிட *ḍraaviḍa* 'Dravidian'), and in ST only in borrowed words, mostly from English.

2. **Medial Voiceless Geminate Stops** Medially, stops are voiceless in LT only if geminate, i.e. doubled, and we follow this convention as well, writing two consecutive consonants *pp, tt, ṭṭ, cc* and *kk* for what LT writes as ப்ப், த்த், ட்ட், ச்ச் and க்க். Geminate *cc* is to be understood as being phonetically twice as long as a single [ʧ], meaning essentially that the [t] is not released as quickly as for a single [ʧ], i.e. *pacce* 'fresh, green' is phonetically [pət:ʧɛ]. Geminate LT ற்ற் never occurs in ST as such, but is always realized as *tt*, e.g. பற்றி 'about' is *patti* in ST.[14] After short vowels, the phonetic value of geminate consonants is to be understood as longer in duration than a single voiceless consonant; after long vowels, geminate consonants are actually not as long as after a short vowel, but we represent them as double and long, anyway, in order to avoid the confusion that results when a single stop occurs intervocalically. That is, LT போடு 'put, place, serve' is *pooḍu* in ST, but போட்டு 'having put, placed, served' is *pooṭṭu* in our transcription, rather than **pooṭu*.

3. **Post-nasal Stops** The stop consonants ப், த், ற், ட், ச், க் following nasals are always voiced in both LT and ST. Except for -ற்-, which does not occur in such clusters in ST, they are represented in this transcription by the Roman letters *b, d* ([ð]), *ḍ, j* and *g*. Thus தம்பி 'younger brother' is *tambi*, அங்கே 'there' is *ange*, கெஞ்சு 'supplicate' is *kenju*, etc.

[14] The only exception to this is when LT words are 'borrowed' directly into ST, such as வெற்றி 'victory, win, goal' (used in sports journalism) which is pronounced in ST in the closest approximation to LT that can be mustered, i.e. *veṭri*.

4. **Medial Stop Consonants** Single stop consonants (i.e. not double or geminated) in medial position (i.e. between two vowels) in Tamil are typically laxed and fricativized. Thus the stop consonants ப், த், ற், ட், ச், க் in medial position are actually phonetically [v] (or even [β] but in loan words, sometimes [b], [ð], [r], [Ď], [s] and [h], respectively. That is, some of them are laxed and voiced, some are flapped (e.g. the retroflex stop), but some (the palatal and velar) are only laxed but not usually voiced (although the velar may in some speech be voiced as well, i.e. pronounced [ɣ]). In order to stick to a Roman transcription that does not require elaborate phonetic symbols that complicate our typography, we will use the voiced Roman letters *b* (or *v*), *d, r, ḍ* and the voiceless fricatives *s* and *h* for these lax and sometimes fricativized intervocalic Tamil stops. As noted above, Tamil, unlike some Indian languages, does not have a single standard transliteration system. Our choice was one that could be used by laypersons as well as scholars, hence the use of *h* for intervocalic -க்- rather than a morphophonemic //k// or a phonemic /g/. This does not follow a purely linguistic (e.g. phonemic) convention, or those used in most other grammars, but we have found through years of teaching Tamil that most dictionary representations of Tamil are not phonetic enough to permit non-Tamils to approximate usual spoken pronunciations.

   In all of our phonetic representations we give prefererence to those that preserve morphological clarity, so that even though it may be common for many speakers to convert LT intervocalic ட் to a flapped rhotic alveolar *r*, we still represent these as *ḍ*. Since the completive marker (LT விடு) may be realized in the speech of many people as non-retroflex, i.e. வந்துவிடுகிறேன் 'I am definitely coming' may come out in ST as [vəndirrẽː], we prefer the transcription *vandiḍreen*, as this shows more clearly that there is a completive aspect marker விடு present, even if it is realized phonologically only as *ḍ*. Otherwise it is hard to explain why the past of LT வந்துவிட்டேன் is always, in all dialects *vandiṭṭeen*. This will help avoid confusion with perfect forms also marked with இரு, contrasting with completive -விடு.

5. **Laterals and Rhotics** The Tamil sonorants ல், ள், ர் and ழ் are represented in our transliteration as *l, ḷ, r* and *ṟ* respectively. Tamil ற் is not treated as a sonorant in its underlying form, but as a stop. Neither in LT nor in ST can it occur in initial position; intervocalically it does occur in ST, where in most dialects it is indistinguishable from ர், so in this position it is simply transliterated by *r*. In ST, LT clusters such as ன்ற் are simplified in non-Brahman dialect to *ṉṉ* after short

vowels (e.g. LT என்று 'having said' becomes simply -*ṉṉu*); after long vowels in ST ன்ற் becomes simply *ṉ*, i.e. தோன்று 'seem, appear' is *tooṉu*.

In many spoken dialects of Tamil the sonorant ழ் is merged with ள், and never occurs in ordinary speech. Because this sound is socio-linguistically highly preferred, however, and foreigners who are able to pronounce it are praised for their efforts, we give *r̤* as the usual transliteration of ழ், even though many speakers, even educated ones, may be heard to use ள். That is, we give *mar̤e* for LT மழை 'rain', even if many speakers say *maḷe* or even *male*.

There are certain stem-final consonants in this group that tend to be not realized at all in ST, while others occur but with an epenthetic *u* vowel[15] added. Thus it is typical for the final ள் in LT pronouns அவள், அவர்கள், நீங்கள் ('she, they, you') to be deleted in final position in ST: *ava, avanga, niinga*. The same is true of ள் that occurs as the final segment in certain person-number-gender endings, as in இருக்கிறீர்கள் 'you are located' which is realized phonetically as *irukkriinga* if nothing follows it. If anything follows as a suffix, however, ள் is not deleted in ST: நீங்களா? 'you?' is realized in ST as *niingaḷaa*, essentially phonetically the same as the spelling pronunciation of LT. Final ள் of other words may be treated in different ways by different ST dialects. Some dialects delete ள் in நாள் 'day' to give *naa*, but most add an epenthetic உ *u*: நாளு *naaḷu*. We give preference to the dialects that do the latter, i.e. preserve morphological clarity.[16]

Monosyllabic words with short vowels ending in laterals (there are none that end in rhotics) such as பல் 'tooth', கள் 'toddy', சொல் 'say', etc. are realized in ST with doubled laterals and an added epenthetic *u* vowel: *pallu*, *kaḷḷu*, *sollu*, etc.

6. **Nasals** LT has graphemes for a labial nasal ம், a dental nasal ந், an alveolar nasal ன், a retroflex nasal ண், a palatal nasal ஞ் and a velar nasal ங். ST does not need this many phonemic or phonetic distinctions, requiring only *m, n* and *ṇ*.[17] Otherwise, monosyllabic

[15] For its pronunciation, see below.

[16] In this sense we take bits and pieces of different dialects as 'standard', since this is pedagogically sounder, even though there may be no speaker who actually replicates each and every pronunciation we prefer.

[17] But note the previously mentioned caveat for the palatal nasal in some positions. We therefore transliterate ம் as *m*, both ந் and ன் as *n* (with the exception that clusters ன்ற் usually become *ṉṉ*, as already noted), ண் as *ṇ*, while ஞ் and ங் which usually occur only before a homorganic nasal (i.e. the palatal and velar nasal, respectively) can be transcribed with *nj* and *ng* with the assumption that English speakers, at least,

words with short vowels ending in alveolar nasals, which are in fact mostly pronominal forms such as என் 'my', ஒன் 'your' convert the nasal segment into nasalization of the vowel: *ẽ, õ.*

7. **Glides** The Tamil glides வ and ய் are usually transliterated as *v* and *y*, respectively. In certain cases வ is closer phonetically to [w] or even to the bilabial [β], similar to Spanish 'v' in 'vaca', but we ignore this degree of phonetic detail. Often வ and ய் in LT forms will not have any phonetic representation at all in ST, since intervocalic வ in particular is deleted in weak positions, resulting in forms like ST *koṇḍaa* from LT கொண்டுவா. In such cases no representation of வ will appear in ST. Similarly, the presence of ய் in LT often conditions palatalization of adjacent consonants in ST, with subsequent assimilation or deletion of the ய் in ST. Thus, LT ஐந்து 'five' is *anju* in ST—the ய் causes palatalization of the dental ந்த், after which ய் disappears, leaving only ST *nj*. In final position also, many LT ய்'s are deleted, e.g. the adverbial ending -ஆய் is realized simply as *aa* in ST.

   In contrast, Tamil words beginning with the mid-vowels *e* and its long counterpart *ee* have an automatic [y] onset in Tamil (as in many South Dravidian languages). Thus என்ன 'what' is phonetically [yɛnnə]. Since this is automatic and predictable, we do not supply this [y] glide in our transcription, but transcribe என்ன always as *enna*. Similarly, the rounded vowels *o, oo, u* and *uu* are preceded in initial position with an automatic [w]-glide in Tamil. ஊர் 'town, city' is phonetically [wuːr(ʉ)], but again since these w-glides are predictable (in fact hardly even salient to a Tamil speaker), we do not provide them. In connected speech in non-sentence-initial position, these automatic glides are usually deleted: அவர் ஊர் என்ன? 'What is his town?' is in ST *avar-uur-enna* rather than *avaru wuuru yenna*.

8. **Oral Vowels** The Tamil vowel system consisting of five cardinal vowels அ, இ, உ, எ, ஒ and their long counterparts ஆ, ஈ, ஊ, ஏ, ஓ are represented in our transliteration as *a, i, u, e, o* and *aa, ii, uu, ee, oo*, respectively. The diphthong ஐ is usually simplified to *e* in ST; thus the accusative அவர்-ஐ 'him' is *avare* in ST. This is actually phonetically [ɛ], but we represent it as *e* for simplicity. In monosyllables, or in

will pronounce these with palatal and velar articulations automatically. ஞ occasionally occurs in prevocalic position in ST, in which case we do transliterate it as *ñ*, e.g ஞானி 'sage' *ñaani*.

Monosyllabic words with short vowels ending in ன் and retroflex ண் in LT, such as பொன் 'gold' பெண் 'girl' and கண், 'eye', etc. follow the pattern of doubled laterals with an added epenthetic *u*: *ponnu, poṇṇu* and *kaṇṇu* in ST. The form *poṇṇu* also undergoes vowel rounding; for an explanation see below.

the initial syllables of polysyllabic words, ஐ is not monophthongized, but the [i] element is lengthened, or followed by a glide [y]. Thus the verb வை 'put, keep' becomes *vayyi* in isolation (e.g. as a verb stem or imperative), but in more complex morphological constructions, e.g. followed by tense-markers, will change to [e]: வைத்தேன் 'I put, kept' will be *vacceen* or *vecceen*. Here the *i* element triggers palatalization of the த்த் to produce *cc*. The LT form பையன் *payyan* 'boy' is another form that retains a phonetic [ai], but only because of the [y] that follows it; we transliterate this as *payyan* rather than *paiyan*.

A special note must be made of the phonetic qualities of the short உ vowel when it occurs after the first syllable of a word, and in particular in final position. Its pronunciation in initial syllables is [ᴜ], but after the first syllable its phonetic quality is unrounded and somewhat fronted, i.e. more like IPA [ɯ] or [ʉ]. This is similar in quality to the short 'oo' vowel in 'book' as pronounced in southern American English, to the Russian *y* (jery) or to the final [u] in Japanese. Since it is again totally predictable when a Tamil உ will be pronounced in this way, we do not represent it as different from phonetically rounded [u]. This pronunciation is not different from the spelling pronunciation of LT *u*, so anyone with this knowledge will have no trouble predicting this.

This situation is complicated by the fact that in ST many short *i* vowels (phonetically [ɪ]) also merge with [ʉ]. For example, the vowel of the past-tense marker of Class III verbs spelled இன் as in வாங்கினேன் 'I bought, acquired, fetched' is pronounced like [ʉ] in ST: [va:ŋgʉnẽ:]. Some linguists who have worked on ST have regularly substituted [ʉ] in these positions, but since this pronunciation is predictable, and differs from the spelling of LT, we do not give either [u] or [ʉ] here, but transcribe it as *i*, leaving it to the knowledge of the speaker to provide the correct phonetic realization. The LT diphthong ஔ is rare even in LT, and does not occur in our data except in loan words, e.g. English 'pound', which we would represent as *paunḍu* or *pavunḍu*; சவுக்கியமா *saukkyamaa*? 'how are you?'

Another phonetic feature of the speech of many Tamils is the fronting of the short vowel அ *a* which we represent generally as [a] in transcription and transliteration. For many speakers, short அ *a* after the first syllable is fronted to [æ], [ə] or [ɛ], i.e. அந்த *anda* 'that' might be phonetically [andæ] or [andə]; similarly, many speakers pronounce நீங்க *niinga* 'you (PL)' as [ni:ŋgæ]; the same phenomenon may occur with infinitives, where final அ *a* may be fronted to [æ]: சாபிட *saappiḍa* ⟶ [sa:pɨḍæ] but we will not represent this level of phonetic detail in our normal transliteration of ST.

9. **Long Vowels** In final position in ST, LT long vowels are often shortened, so that what may be written with a long vowel may always occur short in ST. Thus அங்கே 'there' is always *ange* in ST, unless followed by another vowel, as in அங்கேயே 'there (emph)' *angeeyee*. Here the non-final ஏ remains long, but the final one is shortened. Often, to keep morphological processes clear, however, we represent long vowels in final position as long (in transcription), even though they are phonetically short. In rapid speech, moreover, long vowels anywhere in a word will be shorter than when the word is in isolation, and short vowels may be completely deleted.

10. **Nasal Vowels** ST possesses a set of nasal vowels [ã], [õ], [ẽ] and [ũ], some of which also have long counterparts [ã:], [õ:] and [ẽ:]. These nasal vowels are not found in LT, but arise from the nasalization of vowels followed by ன் or ம் in final position. Thus, [ã] arises from the sequence அன் in LT, e.g. அவன் 'he' becomes [avã]; in some dialects அவன் becomes [avẽ] instead, which accounts for some instances of [ẽ]. [õ] arises from the LT sequence -அம், so that LT மரம் 'tree' becomes [marõ]; [ũ] arises from the LT sequence -உம், e.g. நீங்களும் 'you, too' becomes [ni:ŋgaḷũ] in ST.

    Long nasal vowels [ã:], [õ:] and [ẽ:] may have several sources in LT. [ã:] may result from the nasalization of both LT -ஆன் and -ஆம், i.e. வந்தான் 'he came' becomes [vandã:], but இருக்கலாம் 'it may be, let it be' also has final [ã:], i.e. [irʉkkalã:]. Because of the shortening of long vowels in final position, these long nasal vowels also are shortened finally; but to preserve morphological clarity we usually represent them as long in our transcription. The long vowel [õ:] arises from the nasalization of the sequence ஓம், found typically as the marker of second person plural, as in வந்தோம் 'we came' [vandõ:]. Because of the shortening rule, however, it may be realized phonetically as [vandõ], but we usually avoid this representation, again for morphological clarity. The long vowel [ẽ:] usually arises from nasalization of the LT sequence -ஏன், found most typically in the person-number-gender ending for first person singular, as in வந்தேன் 'I came', i.e. [vandẽ:]. Again, by the shortening rule this usually becomes [vandẽ], but for clarity we avoid this representation. It does not become short in monosyllabic environments, so LT ஏன் 'why?' remains long: [yẽ:], contrasting with என் 'my', which is [yẽ].

    Monosyllabic words with long vowels ending in LT ன் usually do not nasalize, but instead an epenthetic உ *u* [ʉ] is added, e.g மான் 'stag', becomes *maanu*. LT words ending in ண் also do not produce nasalized vowels in ST, but if position-final, simply add *u*: e.g. தூண் 'pillar' becomes ST *tuuṇu* ([tu:ṇʉ]).

11. **Vowel Shifting** A number of other differences between vowels in LT and their realization in ST have to do with certain phonological changes in the Tamil vowel system since Tamil orthography was fixed.

    - **Lowering** LT words with short high vowels இ *i* and உ *u* in an initial syllable followed by *one* consonant and the vowel அ *a* or ஐ *ai* lower these vowels to எ *e* and ஒ *o* respectively in ST. Thus LT forms like இலை 'leaf' and குழந்தை 'child' become *ele* and *kor̤ande*, respectively, whereas forms like இல்லை 'no, not', where the vowel is followed by a double consonant, do not exhibit lowering. This change is totally regular, so that even some borrowed words, such as English 'glass', borrowed usually as கிளாஸ், may, in some dialects, become *keḷaas* or even *keḷasu*.
    - **Rounding** Another process that is less regular, and may therefore still be in progress as a sound change, is the rounding of short and long front vowels இ, ஈ, எ and ஏ (*i, ii, e* and *ee*) to their corresponding back vowels உ, ஊ, ஒ and ஓ (*u, uu, o* and *oo*.) This occurs usually when the initial consonant is a labial (*m, v, p*) and the following consonant is retroflex. Some forms that have undergone this change are socially quite acceptable, but others are considered to be somewhat substandard or casual (or even 'vulgar') so many speakers avoid this kind of rounding, or deny that they do it even when it is observed in their speech. Thus, the rounding of the vowel in LT பெண் to ST *poṇṇu* is quite normal, but the following are on a kind of sliding scale of acceptability: *porandadu* for LT பிறந்தது 'it was born' (this form undergoes lowering first); *puḍi* for LT பிடி 'like', *vuuḍu* for LT வீடு 'house'; *vooṇum* for LT வேண்டும் 'want, need, must', etc. Different speakers would rank these differently in acceptability, but the general scale of acceptability is as given. We try to avoid what are considered the most egregious of these, but in an attempt to remain colloquial, some may be present in our examples. Sometimes the conditioning factor does not even include a retroflex consonant, as in the example of பிற, where the following consonant is alveolar; in extreme cases no conditioning factor can be ascertained, and an initial labial alone is sufficient to cause rounding, as in LT மிதக்கும் *midakkum* 'it will float' becoming, in some dialects, *modakkum*. This is obviously an example of

a sound change in progress, and is therefore sociolinguistically marked.

- **Other Changes** There are a few other changes in vowel quality from LT to ST that cannot be described under the previous rubrics. These are mostly idiosyncratic, but may have to do with what is often called vowel harmony, i.e. vowels changing in order to agree with another vowel in height or rounding. Thus, for example, LT கொடு 'give' has a high vowel in its first syllable in ST, i.e. *kuḍu* rather than **koḍu*, which is the reading pronunciation of LT. There is no good explanation for this change, except that the two vowels agree in height; but there are many other counterexamples. Since this grammar is neither an etymological nor a historical grammar, its concern is not to explain such changes, but merely to catalogue them.

1.3 Sandhi

When sounds come together across word or morpheme boundaries, certain changes occur that are referred to as *sandhi*. LT has complicated sandhi rules that do not apply in LT, mostly because the LT rules were elaborated for poetic language, and they have never operated the same way in prose Tamil. We have already mentioned in various places above the deletion of final laterals, nasals and other sonorants, or the addition of epenthetic vowels at the end of words before pause.

The main sandhi processes that ST exhibits occur when words or morphemes ending in certain vowels are followed by morphemes beginning with certain vowels. Glides (ய் *y* and வ் *v*) are then inserted between these vowels in order to 'smooth the transition' from one vowel to another.[18] The choice of whether the glide inserted will be ய் *y* or வ் *v* in Tamil is determined by whether the vowel preceding the glide is a front vowel (such as இ *i*, ஈ *ii*, எ *e*, ஏ *ee* or ஐ *ai*) or a back vowel, such as உ *u*, ஊ *uu*, ஒ *o*, ஓ *oo*, அ *a* or ஆ *aa*. These are the theoretical possibilities; in actuality, some of these vowels (such as ஐ *ai*) do not occur in final position in ST. And in the case of உ *u*, unless it occurs in a small number of (usually borrowed) words, or is found as the last segment in a nickname, it is usually added word-finally (epenthetically) after other phonological rules have applied, so will not cause sandhi phenomena (which in this case would be the insertion of வ் *v*) to occur.

[18] In other languages of the world, when vowels conjoin, other things may happen, e.g. [a] + [i] may be replaced by [e:], as in Sanskrit.

1.3.1 Sandhi Following Front Vowels.

Examples of ordinary sandhi phenomena of this sort are as follows:

- Word- or morpheme-final இ *i*: நரி *nari* 'fox' + interrogative ஆ *aa* ⟶ நரியா *nariyaa* 'a fox?'
- Word- or morpheme-final ஈ *ii*: தீ *tii* 'fire' + interrogative ஆ *aa* ⟶ தீயா *tiiyaa* 'fire?'
- Word- or morpheme-final எ *e*: யானெ *yaane* 'elephant' + interrogative ஆ *aa* ⟶ யானெயா *yaaneyaa* 'an elephant?'
- Word- or morpheme-final ஏ *ee*: அங்கே *angee* 'there' + interrogative ஆ *aa* ⟶ அங்கேயா *angeeyaa* 'there?'
- Word- or morpheme-final ஐ *ai*: does not occur in ST.

1.3.2 Sandhi Following Back Vowels

Examples of ordinary sandhi phenomena of this sort are as follows:

- Word- or morpheme-final உ *u*: usually deleted, or added later after sandhi rules have applied. A few exceptions: குரு *guru* 'guru, teacher' + interrogative ஆ *aa* ⟶ குருவா *guruvaa* 'a guru?'
- Word- or morpheme-final ஊ *uu*: பூ *puu* 'flower' + interrogative ஆ *aa* ⟶ பூவா *puuvaa* 'a flower?'
- Word- or morpheme-final ஒ *oo*: does not occur in ST words, but might occur in a loan word.
- Word- or morpheme-final ஓ *oo*: இளங்கோ *iḷangoo* '(a name)' + interrogative ஆ *aa* ⟶ இளங்கோவா *iḷangoovaa* '(do you mean) Ilango?'
- Word- or morpheme-final அ *a*: இருக்க *irukka* 'to be' + emphatic ஏ *ee* ⟶ இருக்கவே(இருக்கு) *irukkavee (irukku)* 'it's there, all right!'
- Word- or morpheme-final ஆ *aa*: விழா *viẓaa* 'a festival' + interrogative ஆ *aa* ⟶ விழாவா *viẓaavaa* 'a festival?'
- Word- or morpheme-final ஔ *au*: does not occur in ST.

As already mentioned, glides that are inserted by sandhi may themselves be deleted in rapid speech, especially in polysyllabic words: இந்த்யாவுலெருந்து *indyaavulerundu* 'from India' may become ⟶ இந்த்யாலெருந்து *indyaalerundu*, which may then be further simplified to இந்த்யாலெந்து *indyaalendu* 'ibid.'

1.3.3 Deletion of Final Sonorants

We have already discussed above that words that in their underlying forms contain final laterals, nasals or other sonorants may lose these in final position. We give these forms with these consonants in parentheses, in order to indicate that they are only present when other suffixes follow them.

Typical examples of these 'parenthetical' consonants that are deleted when in word-final position, are the final retroflex laterals ள் *ḷ* of pronouns and their PNG markers: அவ(ள்)போறா(ள்) *ava pooraa* 'she goes.' These consonants are present if suffixes are added, e.g. அவளுக்கு *avaḷukku* 'to her' or அவ போறாளா? *ava pooraaḷaa*? 'Does she go?'

1.3.4 Sandhi and Noun Classes

There are nouns (cf. ∮2.1) that exhibit certain kinds of morphophonemic changes (*sandhi*) before case; some grammarians deal with this as a morphophonemic issue, and others deal with these stem-alternations as just that: alternate forms of the stem that must be present before case.

1.4 Appendix

Summary of Phonological "Rules" that have Applied in SST

1. Palatalization: *tt, nt* ⟶ [cc, nj] after high front vowels ([i, ai]) as in *paḍitteen* ⟶ [paḍicceen]. Found in all dialects, perfectly regular.
2. Doubling of sonorants in CVC where V is short: *kal* ⟶ *kallu* etc.
3. CVC where V is long, add *u*; (but not in all dialects: *naaḷu* ⟶ *naa*).
4. *ḷ* in plurals, pronouns, verbs, deleted in final position, otherwise present.
5. Nasalization of final [Vm, Vn̠] (but not [Vṇ]).
6. Lowering of [i, u] to [e, o] in sequence (C)...Ca, as in *iḍam* ⟶ *eḍam*, *uṭkkaaru* ⟶ *ukkaaru* ([ukkaːrʉ]).
7. Deletion of *l, r, ḷ* before stops, internally: *uṭkkaarndeen* ⟶ *ukkaandeen* etc.
8. General cluster reduction: *uṭkaaru* ⟶ *okkaaru*; *keeṭkireen* ⟶ *keekkreen*.

9. Monophthongization of *ai* to *e*: in accusatives, noun endings, internally. Exception: in monosyllables, *vai* ⟶ *vayyi* or in initial syllables of polysyllabic words.

10. Intervocalic *v* and *k* deletion. Complicated, but examples: *paarkkavillai* ⟶ *paakkalle* ([pa:kkəlɛ]; *poohaveeṇḍum* ⟶ *poohaṇum* ([po:həṇũ]); *poohir̲een* ⟶ *pooreen*; *koṇḍuvaa* ⟶ *koṇḍaa*, etc.

11. Intervocalic deletion of *r̤*, the retroflex frictionless continuant. This sound often is merged with [ḷ], but in some cases it is deleted instead, resulting in compensatory lengthening: LT பொழுது *por̤udu* 'time' ⟶ [po:dʉ]; LT எழுந்திருந்தார் 'he has arisen' *er̤undirundaar* ⟶ [e:ndrʉnda:rʉ].

12. Rounding: [i, e] ⟶ [u, o] between labial ...retroflex consonant: *poṇṇu, poṭṭi, vuuḍu, puḍi*, but also: *mida* ⟶ [moda] *pir̲andeen̲* ⟶ *porandeen*. Some of these may be more acceptable than others.

Optional or Stigmatized Developments

1. Already described: NC cluster reduction is variable, and somewhat stigmatized: வேண்டும் ⟶ *veeṇum* is okay, but வேண்டாம் ⟶ **veeṇaan* is not; கொண்டாந்தேன் *koṇḍaandeen* (கொண்டுவந்தேன் *koṇḍuvandeen*) is okay, but **koṇṇaandeen* is not.

2. Rounding of vowels before retroflex [ḷ] in Br. dialect: *niingo, avango*

3. Metathesis: Br. dialect: *enakku* ⟶ [ne:kʉ]; *unakku* ⟶ *onakku* ⟶ [no:kʉ] etc.

4. Other dialects: merge [l], [ḷ], [r̤]; some merge [n] and [ṇ]. Retroflexion is lost except in [ṭ] (vs. [t]).

5. Unrounding of final epenthetic *u*, (which would ordinarily, when nasalized, be [ũ]): Coimbatore: *veeṇum* ⟶ [ve:ṇʉ̃], etc.

Chapter 2

The Nominal System

2.1 Nouns and Noun Classes

Tamil nouns generally do not require classification into 'declensions' or form classes of any sort, because the morphology of the noun, which consists of the noun stem plus case suffixes, is quite regular. Even so, some nouns exhibit stem-alternates which show certain kinds of morphophonemic changes (*sandhi*) before case, however, and these are as follows.

2.1.1 Nouns Ending in அம் *-am*

Many nouns in Tamil end in அம் *-am*; these can be items such as மரம் *maram* 'tree', loans from Sanskrit like தூரம் *duuram* 'distance', and loans from English like ஸிஸ்டம் *sisṭam* 'system.' In fact any English word that phonetically ends in the sequence [əm] ('system, problem, museum', etc.) will be treated as belonging to this group. Sanskrit nouns that end in [-a] are borrowed in their accusative form ([-am]) into Tamil.

All such அம் *-am* ending nouns change this to அத்து *att(u)* before adding case: மரம் *maram* ⟶ மரத்து *marattu*. This form has often been referred to as the 'oblique' stem of the noun.

Note that the quantifier எல்லாம் *ellaam* 'all, everything' has an oblique form எல்லாத்து *ellaatt-* which appears before case. In LT this form actually comes from an oblique stem எல்லாவற்று *ellaavaṯṯu* so it more properly belongs with the nouns in the next section (2.1.2). Thus எல்லாத்துக்கும் *ellaattukkum* 'to everything', எல்லாத்தெயும் *ellaatteyum* 'everything (ACC)':

(1) அவனுக்கு எல்லாத்தெயும் குடுத்தேனே
avanukku ellaatteyum kuḍutteenee
him-to all-ACC-INCL gave-I-EMPH

'But I gave him everything!'

2.1.2 Nouns Ending in று *-ṟu*

A smaller number of nouns in Tamil end in று *-ṟu* (LT alveolar ṟ). All of these nouns change this to ற்று in LT and த்த் in ST *ttu* before case, i.e. they undergo *gemination*. Thus ஆறு *aaṟu* ⟶ ஆத்து *aattu*; 'pertaining to the river'; கெணறு *keṇaṟu* 'well' ⟶ கெணத்து *keṇattu* 'pertaining to the well.' Other examples are கயிறு *kayiṟu* 'rope', வயிறு *vayiṟu* 'stomach', சோறு *sooṟu* 'cooked rice', and a few more.

Note: the LT forms of these words undergo gemination from று to ற்று, but in ST the று *ṟu* forms are phonetically identical with ரு *ru*, while ற்று merges phonetically with த்து *ttu*.

2.1.3 Nouns Ending in டு *-ḍu*

A number of Tamil nouns that end in டு *-ḍu* undergo gemination (parallel to the situation with nouns in று *ṯu*) to ட்டு *ṭṭu*. The geminated sequences are voiceless; the intervocalic non-geminate டு *ḍu* is of course voiced and flapped.

Native Dravidian words and borrowed English words like ரோடு *rooḍu* alike undergo this process. (Some Tamil speakers feel that English loans should not be subjected to this process, but native speakers tend to do this anyway.)

Examples: பாடு *paaḍu* 'lot, part' ⟶ பாட்டு *paaṭṭu* '(of the) lot, part'; வீடு *viiḍu* ⟶ வீட்டு *viiṭṭu* 'of the house'; காடு *kaaḍu* ⟶ காட்டு *kaaṭṭu* 'of the forest, jungle.'

2.1.4 Syntactic Usage of Oblique Forms

These 'oblique' forms (stem alternates that occur before case endings) are often used adjectivally in Tamil (without case-marking), or to indicate possession:

- கொளத்து தண்ணி *koḷattu taṇṇi* 'tank, pond water'
- ஆத்தங்கரெ (LT ஆற்றங்கரை) *aattankare* 'river bank' ('bank of the river')

- வயித்து(LT வயிற்று) வலி *vayittu vali* 'stomach ache' ('ache of the stomach')

- வீட்டுக்காரன் *viiṭṭukaaran* 'husband; landlord' ('man of the house')

- காட்டு வழி *kaaṭṭu vaẓi* 'a forest road' ('road of the forest')

2.1.5 Oblique and Genitive

Since the oblique form of the noun may be used to indicate possession, it is often considered to be a case form (see below), i.e. equivalent to what is called 'genitive' in other case systems. But in fact the oblique form can have case markers added to it, or can stand alone. It thus presents a challenge to analysts of the Tamil case system.

In LT there were a number of possible additional genitive markers such as அன் *an* (used primarily with pronouns, and now used in ST only as a 'frozen' form in அதனாலெ *adanaale* 'therefore'); இன் *in* (not used in ST): and உடைய *uḍaiya*, obviously a postposition derived from the verb உடை *uḍai* 'possess.' உடைய *uḍaiya* could be attached to அன் *an* or இன் *in*, as in அதனுடைய *adanuḍaiya* 'its.'

In ST, உடைய *uḍaiya* has changed to ஓடெ *ooḍe*, and is used by many speakers, in addition to the 'bare' oblique stem.

- என் புஸ்தகம் *en pustaham* 'my book', along with என்னோடெ புஸ்தகம் *ennooḍe pustaham*'

- அவரு மனெவி *avaru manevi* 'his wife', along with அவரோடெ மனெவி *avarooḍe manevi*

2.2 Number

Tamil nouns are unmarked in the singular, but may be marked for plurality. Inanimate nouns are often not marked for plural:

- ரெண்டு புஸ்தகம் *reṇḍu pustaham* 'two books'

- அஞ்சு மேசெ *anju meese* 'five tables'

Typically, only animate nouns are marked for plural:

- ரெண்டு மனெவிங்க *reṇḍu manevinga* 'two wives'

- அஞ்சு கொழந்தெங்க *anju koẓandenga* 'five children'

2.2.1 Form of the Plural Marker

While LT is extremely regular in the formation of plurals[1] ST has great variability, and speakers disagree as to what is 'standard.'

The most common form of the plural in ST is ங்க(ள்) *nga(ḷ)*. The final retroflex lateral is not present in isolation, but when other suffixes are added, it appears:

- ரெண்டு மனெவிங்களா? *reṇḍu manevingaḷaa*? 'two wives?'
- அஞ்சு கொழந்தெங்களும் *anju koṟ̱andengaḷum* 'all five children'

This plural marker also appears in pronouns (cf. Table 4.3), also with final lateral: நீங்க(ள்) *niinga(ḷ)*. We will consider the final retroflex lateral to be part of the UNDERLYING FORM of the plural marker, which is deleted (not pronounced) before pause.

In some dialects, the ங்க(ள்) *nga(ḷ)* form is only used following nouns that end in a nasal, e.g. மரம் *maram* ⟶ மரங்க *maranga* 'trees.' Otherwise the plural marker is க(ள்) *ha(ḷ)*, e.g. மனெவிக *maneviha* 'wives.' In the speech of many, there are some 'irregular' plurals, involving changes of the noun stem before plural:

பையன் *payyan* 'boy' ⟶ பசங்க *pasanga* 'boys'

2.2.1.1 Use of எல்லாம் *ellaam* 'all, everything' for plural

Many Tamil speakers substitute எல்லாம் *ellaam* 'all, everything' as a postposed marker of plural, sometimes with other plural markers. English loan words are often used with their English plurals, or perhaps even with both English and Tamil plurals.

- புஸ்தங்களெல்லாம் எங்கெ இருக்கு *pustahangaḷellaam enge irukku*
  'Where are the books?'
- அந்த லேடிஸெல்லாம் பேசினாங்க *anda leeḍis-ellaam peesinaanga*
  'Those women spoke.'
- அந்த லேடிஸ ்ங்க போய்ட்டாங்க *anda leeḍisunga pooyṭṭaanga*
  'Those women left.'

[1]The LT plural marker is கள், which may be pronounced differently depending on whether it follows a vowel, a nasal or another stop: [haḷ], [gaḷ] or [kaḷ], respectively.

2.2.1.2 Plurality and Case

The case markers given below can be added to nouns marked for plural, in which case the final retroflex lateral ள் *ḷ* shows up. Nouns with final morphophonemic changes (∮∮2.1.1–2.1.3) do not exhibit these changes before the plural, but nouns ending in அம் *am* change this to அங் *ang* before plural.[2]

ஒங்க வீடுங்களெ பாத்தேன் *onga viiḍungaḷe paatteen*
'I saw your houses-ACC.'

2.3 The Case System

Tamil nouns consist of a noun stem (or root) plus a number of suffixes known as case suffixes in other languages. The traditional analysis of the Tamil case system delimits seven cases, as in Sanskrit, but in modern Tamil this delimitation does not function very well, and one must admit that many other suffixes, which in some analyses are known as postpositions, are not different in function from the traditional cases.

2.3.1 Dative Case

This case marker is used when a verb has a noun *toward which* motion is expressed; it is used to indicate possession (expressed in many other languages by a verb meaning 'have'), and is also used to indicate which thing or person is the *indirect object* or benefactor of some act. Finally it is used with certain stative and/or defective verbs (i.e. verbs which cannot be marked for PNG except third person neuter, cf. ∮3.15) to indicate who or what is the subject.

Thus, to indicate possession, Tamil uses a dative case and the verb இரு *iru* 'be (located)':

(2) எனக்கு பணம் இருக்கு
en-akku paṇam irukku
to-me money is
'I have money'

To indicate subject-hood of various stative verbs such as 'like' பிடி *piḍi*, 'know' தெரி *teri*, 'understand' புரி *puri*, 'be available' கெடெ *keḍe*, 'want'

[2] In ST this is not as serious in transliteration as it is in Tamil script, i.e. in script we must have மரங்க rather than *மரம்ங்க, but in transliteration we will just have *maranga* 'trees', phonetically [mərəŋgə̣].

வேணும் *veeṇum*, etc. the dative case is attached to the subject and the stative verb appears in the third person singular.

(3) ஒங்களுக்கு அவரெ தெரியுமா?
ongaḷukku avare teriyumaa?
to-you him known?
'Do you know him?'

This sentence may appear to be anomalous because of the lack of an overt subject, and the object marked accusative, but not only is it quite acceptable, any other case-marking would be ungrammatical.

(4) அவருக்கு தமிழ் தெரியாது
avarukku tamiṟ teriyaadu
to-him Tamil not-known
'He doesn't know Tamil.'

2.3.2 The Dative Case Marker

The dative case marker is உக்கு *ukku* except after front vowels, where it takes the shape (ய்)க்கி *(y)kki*. After pronominal stems whose oblique form consists of only (C)VC, the dative case has the form அக்கு *akku*:

1. மரம் *maram* 'tree' + *ukku* ⟶ மரத்துக்கு *marattukku* 'to the tree'
2. ஆறு *aaru* 'river' + *ukku* ⟶ ஆத்துக்கு (LT ஆற்றுக்கு) *aattukku* 'to the river'
3. வீடு *viiḍu* 'house' + *ukku* ⟶ வீட்டுக்கு *viiṭṭukku* 'to the house'
4. மதுரெ *madure* 'Madurai' + *ykki* ⟶ மதுரெய்க்கி *madureykki* 'to Madurai'
5. கோயில் *kooyil* 'temple'+ *ukku* ⟶ கோயிலுக்கு *kooyilukku* 'to the temple'
6. நரி *nari* 'fox' + *ykki* ⟶ நரிக்கி *narikki* 'to the fox'
7. நான் *naan* 'I' + *akku* ⟶ எனக்கு *enakku* 'to me'

As mentioned above, certain *postpositions* such as பக்கத்துலெ *pakkattule* 'near, in the vicinity of' govern the choice of the dative case (cf. ∮2.4.3). Syntactically, the dative is used to express possession, motion toward, benefaction to, and possession of states expressed by stative verbs (cf. ∮3.1.2).

2.3.3 Locative Case

The locative case is used to express 'location', 'lack of motion', 'containment in', and sometimes 'means of transportation', e.g. பஸ்லெ *bas-le* 'by bus.' The locative marker is *-le* with inanimate nouns and *-kiṭṭe* with animates. With animate nouns it means 'in the possession of, or in/on the person of.'

Note that in LT the locative case marker is இல், and many traditional grammarians prefer to think of *le(e)* as derived from இல் with an additional 'emphatic' *ee* ஏ added. In actuality, if emphasis is desired in modern Tamil another *ee* must be added (e.g. *viiṭṭleyee* 'right in the house'), so this cannot be taken be a true occurrence of emphatic *ee*. Since most semantically locative case markers, postpositions, points of the compass and deictic pronouns (*ange(e)* 'there' etc.) show this *ee* in modern ST, it should probably be taken as a marker of location, and not emphasis. (Note also that we represent ஏ *ee* as phonemically (underlyingly) long, which it is when not occurring in final position; in final position all long vowels tend to become short, so there may be variation here.)

Examples of inanimate nouns:

1. மரம் *maram* 'tree' + *-le* ⟶ மரத்துலெ *marattu-le* 'in the tree'
2. ஆறு *aaru* 'river' + *-le* ⟶ ஆத்துலெ *aattu-le* 'in the river'
3. வீடு *viiḍu* 'house' + *-le* ⟶ வீட்டுலெ *viiṭṭ(u)le* 'in the house'
4. கோயில் *kooyil* 'temple' + *-le* ⟶ கோயில்லெ *kooyil-le* 'in the temple'
5. மதுரை *madure* 'Madurai' + *-le* ⟶ மதுரைலெ *madure-y-le* 'in Madurai'

Examples of animate nouns with *kiṭṭe* கிட்டெ:

1. நரி *nari* 'fox' + *kiṭṭe* ⟶ நரிகிட்டெ *nari-kiṭṭe* 'in the possession of the fox'
2. நான் *naan* 'I' + *kiṭṭe* ⟶ என்கிட்டெ *en-kiṭṭe* 'I have (on my person)'

2.3.3.1 Syntax of கிட்டெ *kiṭṭe*

There are some complexities of syntax involved with the use of the animate locative marker கிட்டெ *kiṭṭe*. In some dialects, and/or in rapid speech, intervocalic கி *ki-* is deleted, and the resulting form is ட்டெ *-ṭṭe*, e.g. அவர்ட்டெ *avarṭṭe* 'with, on him'.

When the animate locative marker கிட்டெ *kiṭṭe* is attached to a noun in a sentence with certain kinds of stative verbs or the copula, there is a semantic contrast of the following sort:

1. கிட்டெ *kiṭṭe* 'animate locative': என்கிட்டெ பணம் இருக்கு *en-kiṭṭe paṇam irukku* 'I have money (on my person)'
2. with 'dative': எனக்கு பணம் இருக்கு *enakku paṇam irukku* 'I have money (I am a rich person)'

That is, use of *kiṭṭe* implies temporary possession or actual real-time possession, while use of the dative implies permanent, habitual or inalienable possession. The dative would be used to express the actuality of having siblings, a wife, children etc., and of being generally wealthy, rather than temporarily in the possession of money.

With verbs such as குடு *kuḍu* 'give' the contrast in the use of *kiṭṭe* versus the dative *-ukku* distinguishes between giving something *back* (restoring possession) to a person who originally owned it (*kiṭṭe*) versus transferring the ownership irrevocably, i.e. changing ownership (dative *ukku*).

(5) அவர்கிட்டெ முத்து மாலெயெ குடுத்தேன்
avar-kiṭṭe muttu maaleye kuḍutteen

'I gave the pearl necklace **back** to him.'

(6) அவருக்கு முத்து மாலெயெ குடுத்தேன்
avarukku muttu maaleye kuḍutteen

'I gave the pearl necklace to him (for good).'

With verbs meaning 'say' or 'ask', the use of *kiṭṭe* is more deferential, while the use of *-ukku* is less so, i.e. more direct, blunt, brusque, 'no uncertain terms.'

(7) டைரெக்டர் கிட்டெ என் காரியத்தெ சொன்னேன்
ḍairekṭar kiṭṭe en kaariyatte sonneen

'I laid my concern before the Director (i.e. I said it in a diplomatic and deferential way).'

(8) அவங்ககிட்டெ கொஞ்சம் சொல்லிவெக்கணுமே
avanga-kiṭṭe konjam sollivekkaṇumee

'You should explain things to them nicely but firmly.'

(9) போலீஸ்கிட்டெ எதெயாவது ஒளரிவெக்காதே
pooliiskiṭṭe edeyaavadu oḷari-vekkaadee
police-to something babble-FUTUTIL-NEG-IMP

'Don't go blabbing things to the police (to get yourself into even more hot water later).'

(10) கடெசிய்லெ அவனுக்கு எல்லாத்தெயும் சொல்லிட்டேனே
kaḍesiyle avanukku ellaatteyum solliṭṭeenee

'Finally I just told him everything flat out (and didn't mince words).'

2.3.4 Ablative Case

The ablative case is used to express motion away from an object or person.

2.3.4.1 Inanimate Nouns

(11) மதுரைய் + லெ + ருந்து
madurey + *le* + *rundu*
'Madurai' + LOC + 'ablative'
⟶ *madureylerundu* 'from Madurai'

(12) லய்ப்ரேரியிலெருந்து
laybreeriylerundu 'from the library'

2.3.4.2 Animate Nouns

With animate nouns the postposition கிட்டெ *kiṭṭe* 'near, on the person of' must be used as a locative base, with ருந்து *rundu* added to it.

(13) ராஜா + கிட்டெ + ருந்து
raajaa + *kiṭṭe* + *rundu*
'king' + LOC + 'ablative'
⟶ *raajaakkiṭṭeyrundu* 'from the king'

(14) என் + கிட்டெ + ருந்து
en + *kiṭṭe* + *rundu*
'me' + LOC + 'ablative'
⟶ *enkiṭṭeyrundu* 'from me'

2.3.4.3 Semantically Locative Expressions

Adverbs that are already semantically locative, such as the deictic particles (e.g அங்கெ *ange* 'there'), are never marked for locative, since they are already semantically locative, so the ablative, which is usually built on the locative form, is affixed directly to them. The same applies to adverbial expressions such as the points of the compass, positional markers involving height above (such as மேலெ *meele* 'above, on top of') or below, etc., which are also never locatively marked, add the ablative marker directly to their stems.

(15) அங்கெ + ருந்து
ange + *rundu*
'there' + 'ablative'
⟶ *angeyrundu* 'from there'

(16) மேலெ + ருந்து
meele + *rundu*
'above' + 'from'
⟶ *meeleyrundu* 'from above'

There is a morphophonemic ய் *-y-* following *-e* in most of these forms; in rapid speech it may not be phonetically obvious. In rapid speech or some dialects, *lerundu* may become *lerndu* or *lendu* ([lɛːndʉ]). In some cases, both *lerundu* and *kiṭṭerundu* can be used with animate nouns, with contrasting meanings, as is shown by the following example:[3]

(17) மந்திரிலெருந்து எல்லாரும் லஞ்சம் வாங்குறாங்க
mandirilerundu *ellaarum lanjam vaangraanga*
minister-LOC-from everyone bribe take
'Everyone takes bribes, from the Minister on down.'

(18) மந்திரிகிட்டெருந்து எல்லாரும் லஞ்சம் வாங்குறாங்க
mandirikiṭṭerundu *ellaarum lanjam vaangraanga*
minister's-person-from everyone bribe take
'Everyone takes bribes from the Minister.'

The LT equivalent of animate locative கிட்டெ *kiṭṭe* is a totally different form, இடம், not used in ST;

2.3.5 Associative/Instrumental Case

Because Tamil grammatical tradition was influenced from the beginning by Sanskrit grammatical theory, Tamil, even in its earliest grammar (*Tolkaappiyam*), borrowed the idea that Tamil had to have seven cases plus vocative. Because Sanskrit associative and instrumental cases are identical in form, Tamil has both forms under one rubric, even though the earliest grammarians were uncomfortable with this.

2.3.5.1 Associative Case

This case expresses social accompaniment, comparable to English 'with' or 'along with' in the sense 'I went with him' but not in the sense 'I cut it with a knife', where the latter use is *instrumental.*

The form of this case marker is ஓடெ *ooḍe* or ஓடு *ooḍu*. With animate nouns this always means 'associative' but with inanimate nouns *-ooḍe* can be instrumental, e.g. ரிக்‌ஷாவோடெ *rikṣaavooḍe* 'by rikshaw' instead of ரிக்‌ஷாவ்லெ *rikṣaavle 'ibid.'*, in other dialects.

[3] This example is from Ramanujan and Annamalai, 1967.

- சினேதர் *sneydar* 'friend' + ஓடெ *ooḍe* ⟶ சினேதரோடெ *sneydarooḍe* 'with (a) friend'
- எங்க *enga(ḷ)* 'our' + ஓடெ *ooḍe* ⟶ எங்களோடெ *engaḷooḍe* 'with us'
- நரி *nari* 'fox' + ஓடெ *ooḍe* ⟶ நரியோடெ *nari-y-ooḍe* 'with the fox'

2.3.5.2 Instrumental Case: Means by Which

Expressing the notion of 'means by which an action was done' corresponds least to any one set of prepositions or other constructions in English, and also varies widely dialectally in Tamil. Basically the form of the instrumental case marker is ஆலெ *-aale* (LT ஆல்) but some dialects use this only with pronouns:

- அதனாலெ *adan-aale* 'because of him'
- ஒங்களாலெ *ongaḷaale* 'because of you, by/through you; through your intervention'

Other dialects use ஓடெ *-ooḍe*, the associative case marker, with inanimate nouns to express instrumentality:

ரிக்ஷாவோடெ *rikṣaavooḍe* 'by rikshaw'

Most dialects use the locative லெ *-le* to express 'by means of' with modes of transportation:

- பஸ்லெ *basle* 'by bus'
- ரெயில்லெ *reyille* 'by train'

In some dialects no genuine instrumental case marker is found, and postpositions such as மூலம் *muulam* 'by means of' or ஒதவி *odavi* 'help' are used instead. Sometimes both are used:

டெப்டி ரெஜிஸ்ட்ரார் ஒதவி மூலம்
depṭi rejisṭraar odavi muulam
'under the auspices of (with the help of, with the intervention of) the deputy registrar'

In still other cases, verbal constructions involving a second verb meaning 'use, take, employ' substitute for a true instrumental case construction:

சோப் எடுத்து தொவெக்கலாம் *soop eḍuttu tovekkalaam*
'(one) may wash (it) with soap' ('taking soap, one may wash')

Research on causatives and instrumental constructions in various languages has shown this semantic area to be rather complex, so definitive statements about Tamil constructions of this sort must remain highly tentative. (Cf. ∮2.4 on postpositions for the equivalents of other English prepositions.) Note that ஆலெ *-aale* alternates with the dative when used with the modal verb முடியும் *muḍiyum* 'be able':

(19) என்னாலெ போகமுடியும்
enn-aale pooha-muḍiyum
by-me go-able

'I can go (I'm willing and able to go).'

(20) எனக்கு போகமுடியும்
en-akku pooha-muḍiyum
me-to go-able

'I can go (I'm able, but not necessarily willing).'

As we shall see later, there is often a difference of meaning: the instrumental implies that a person is not only physically able but also *willing* to make an effort, whereas the dative implies only physical capability, not necessarily willingness.

2.3.6 Accusative Case

The accusative case marks a noun as the 'object' or 'patient' of some action; it is the thing to which the action of the verb is applied or subjected. The marker for accusative is எ *e* (LT ஐ). Inanimate nouns are not normally marked for accusative unless the speaker wishes to indicate a SPECIFIC or DEFINITE thing; this is similar to the function of the definite article in English (which Tamil otherwise lacks). Animate nouns, however, are always marked accusative when they are the objects of verbs.

Examples of the accusative:

1. மரம் *maram* 'tree' + எ *-e* ⟶ மரத்தெ *maratte*
   (e.g.) மரத்தெ பாத்தேன் *maratte paatteen* 'I saw the tree.'

2. வீடு *viiḍu* 'house' + எ *-e* ⟶ வீட்டெ *viiṭṭe*
   (e.g.) வீட்டெ பாத்தேன் *viiṭṭe paatteen* 'I saw the house.'

3. அவரு *avaru* 'he' + *-e* ⟶ அவரெ *avare* 'him'
   (e.g.) அவரெ பாத்தேன் *avare paatteen* 'I saw him.'

4. ஆறு *aaru* 'river' + எ *-e* ⟶ ஆத்தெ *aattee*
   (e.g.) ஆத்தெ பாத்தேன் *aatte paatteen* 'I saw the river.'

Often mass nouns are not marked for the accusative because accusative marking makes these nouns *particular*. Thus, we get sentences like: தண்ணி *taṇṇi* 'water' + குடிச்சேன் *kuḍicceen* 'I drank' ⟶ தண்ணி குடிச்சேன் *taṇṇi kuḍicceen* 'I drank (some) water.' However, mass nouns may be used with the accusative marker to indicate particular or specific things: தண்ணியெ குடிச்சேன் *taṇṇiye kuḍicceen* would mean 'I drank THE water.'

(21) அவனெ அனுப்புச்சுடு
avane anuppuccuḍu
him send-CAUS-COMPL-IMP
'Send him away; get rid of him.'

(22) அதெ சாப்பிட்டுட்டேன்
ade saappiṭṭuṭṭeen
it-ACC eat-COMPL-PAST-PNG
'I ate it all up.'

(23) எல்லாத்தெயும் பாத்தேன்
ellaatteyum paatteen
all-ACC-INCL saw-PNG
'I saw the whole thing.'

Note that in dative-stative constructions (§3.15.1) animate objects are marked for accusative, the subject is marked dative, and no nominative-marked noun may appear in the sentence. (Despite the apparent ungrammaticality of such a construction, this is not ungrammatical.)

(24) அவனெ எனக்கு தெரியும்
avane enakku teriyum
him me-to known
'I know him'

2.4 Postpositions

For certain notions expressed in English by prepositions, Tamil case endings are not sufficient. Instead, additional 'postpositions' are affixed after the case marker. For all practical purposes, these are not suffixes, but separate free forms.

> கோயில் *kooyil* 'temple' + உக்கு *-ukku* 'dative case marker' + பக்கத்துலெ *pakkattle* 'near' ⟶ கோயிலுக்கு பக்கத்துலெ *kooyilukku pakkattle* 'near the temple'

Different postpositions take different case markers and do not seem to be very predictable (some even take more than one case marker, with different meanings; some even follow the nominative). The reason for this may be that many postpositions seem to be derived historically from verbs, so that the case marker which occurs with them is governed by some semantic or syntactic properties of the original verb. Others are derived from nouns, and have an 'adjectival' relationship with the rest of the clause (cf. ∮2.1.4).

2.4.1 Postpositions Occurring with the Nominative

2.4.1.1 சேந்து *seendu* 'together'

சேந்து *seendu* is derived from the past participle of the verb சேரு *seeru* meaning 'join (INTR)' or 'come together.' It is used when the main verb of the sentence is intransitive. (For usage with transitive verbs, cf. சேத்து *seettu* 'together' ∮2.4.4.1.)

அவங்க	ரெண்டு	பேரும்	சேந்து	வந்தாங்க
avanga	*reṇḍu*	*peerum*	*seendu*	*vandaanga*
they	two	persons	together	came

'The two of them arrived simultaneously.'

2.4.1.2 மூலம் *muulam* 'with; by means of; through (the agency of); under the auspices of'

மூலம் *muulam* is a noun meaning 'means, method, auspices' and is often used as a postposition, with the nominative.

டெப்யுட்டி	ரெஜிஸ்ட்ரார்	ஒதவி	மூலம்
ḍepyuṭi	*rejisṭraar*	*odavi*	*muulam*

'under the auspices of (with the help of) the deputy registrar'

2.4.1.3 வரெக்கும் *varekkum*, வரெ *vare*, வரெய்லெ *vareyle* 'up to, until'

Following nominative case:

ஏழு மணி வரெக்கும் *eeṟu maṇi varekkum* 'up to, until 7:00'

Note that since வரெ *vare* and its case-marked variants (வரெக்கும் *varekkum*, வரெய்லெ *vareyle*) are nouns, they may be preceded by the AJP form (cf. ∮6.3) of verbs to express time when an action occurs:

- சம்பளம் வாங்குற வரெக்கும் ***sambaḷam vaangra varekkum*** 'until (one) draws (one's) pay'

- அவரு வர்ற வரெக்கும் *avaru varra varekkum* 'until he comes; up to the point when he comes'

2.4.2 Postpositions Occurring with the Oblique (Genitive)

Note that nouns that do not have an oblique form distinct from the nominative form look like they have the postpositions in this section attached to the nominative, since the nominative and the genitive are not distinct.

2.4.2.1 கூடெ *kuuḍe* 'along with'

This postposition has the same meaning and operates syntactically the same way as 'sociative' -ஓடெ *-ooḍe.*

- என் கூடெ *en kuuḍe* 'with me'

- அத்தான் கூடெ *attaan kuuḍe* 'with brother-in-law'

Note that கூடெ *kuuḍe* or கூட *kuuḍa* also means 'also, too' as in அவரு கூடெ (அவர்-உம்) போறாரு *avaru kuuḍe (avar-um) pooraaru* 'He's going, too. Thus it can also be synonymous with the clitic உம் *-um* in the sense of 'also, too.'

2.4.2.2 மேலெ *meele* 'above, on top of, after'

This postposition is used with both location and with time expressions.

1. With genitive/oblique: on top of the upper surface of, in contact with the upper surface of.

   - மரத்து மேலெ ***marattu meele*** 'on top of the tree'
   - மேசெ மேலெ ***meese meele*** 'on the table'

2. With dative, cf. §2.4.3.4.

2.4.2.3 பக்கம் *pakkam* 'near, in the vicinity of, by'

- என் பக்கம் *en pakkam* 'near me, in my vicinity'

- நம்ம ஜன்னல் பக்கம் *namma jannal pakkam* 'near our window'

- மெட்ராஸ் பக்கம் *meḍraas pakkam* 'near Madras, in the Madras area, 'Madras-side'

2.4.2.4 தொணெய்லெ *toṇeyle* 'in the company of, with'

எங்க தொணெய்லெ *enga toṇeyle* 'with us'

2.4.2.5 உச்சிய்லெ *ucciyle* 'top, at, on the top of'

மரத்து உச்சிய்லெ *marattu ucciyle* 'at, on the top of the tree'

2.4.2.6 கீழெ *kiiṟe* 'below, under'

1. With genitive/oblique: underneath and in contact with the underside of a thing.

   - வீட்டு கீழெ *viiṭṭu`kiiṟe* 'under the house'

2. With dative: cf.§2.4.3.4.

   (In some dialects கீழெ *kiiṟe* is pronounced கீளெ *kiiḷe*)

2.4.2.7 -ண்டெ, அண்டெ *-ṇḍe, aṇḍe* 'near'

This item is found primarily in Brahman dialect.

- அவரண்டெ *avar-aṇḍe* 'near him'
- சொவரண்டெ *sovar-aṇḍe* 'near the wall'

2.4.3 Postpositions Occurring with the Dative

2.4.3.1 ஆக *aaha* 'for the sake of, on behalf of'

- ஒங்களுக்காக *ongaḷukkaaha* 'for you, for your benefit'
- சர்காருக்காக *sarkaarukkaaka* 'for the government'

2.4.3.2 அடிய்லெ *aḍiyle* 'at the base, foot of'

- மரத்துக்கு அடிய்லெ *marattukku aḍiyle* 'at the foot, base of the tree'

2.4.3.3 எதிரெ *edire* 'opposite, across from; contrary to, facing, against'

வீட்டுக்கு எதிரெ *viiṭṭukku edire* 'across from, opposite the house'

In some dialects, எதிரெ *edire* combines with தான்+போலெ *taan + poole* 'as if (just)' to form எதிர்தாப்லெ *edittaaple* 'just opposite, facing, right across.'[4] In some dialects, the final அ *a* of போல *poola* may be phonetically more fronted, i.e. [æ] or even [ɛ]. We represent it therefore as ப்லெ *ple* but ப்ல *pla* can also occur.[5]

(25) எதிர்தாப்லெ இருக்குற கட்டடம் என்ன?
edi(r)taaple irukkra kaṭṭaḍam enna?
as-if-opposite being building what?
'What's that building across from us?'

2.4.3.4 மேலெ *meele* 'above, on top of, after'

This item may be used both with location (LXP) and with time expressions (TXP).

- With dative: located above but not touching: மரத்துக்கு மேலெ *marattukku meele* 'above the tree'
- After (with time expressions) ஆறு மணிக்கி மேலெ *aaru maṇikki meele* 'after 6:00'
- With oblique: cf. ∮2.4.2.2 for location above, with contact.

2.4.3.5 பக்கத்துலெ *pakkattule* 'near, in the vicinity of'

வீட்டுக்கு பக்கத்துலெ *viiṭṭukku pakkattule* 'near the house'

2.4.3.6 உள்ளெ *uḷḷe* 'by, within; into the inside of'

1. Time expressions (TXP)
   - ஆறு மணிக்குள்ளெ *aaru maṇikkuḷḷe*
     'by 6:00, within the period ending at 6:00'
   - அதுக்குள்ளெ *adukkuḷḷe* 'by then, already then'
   - இதுக்குள்ளெ *idukkuḷḷe* 'by this time, by now, already'
2. Locative expressions (LXP)

[4] The LT form of எதிர்தாப்ப்லெ *edi(r)taaple* would be எதிர்-தான்-போல *etir taan poola* but the historical derivation of the ST form from the LT is not without problems.

[5] This follows the general rule that the அ *a* of infinitives (or words that are derived from infinitives) is often fronted to [æ], while other pre-pausal அ *a* vowels, such as those marking adjectives, may remain phonetically lower and more central.

- கோயிலுக்குள்ளெ *kooyilukkuḷḷe* 'into the interior (inner sanctum) of the temple'
- வீட்டுக்குள்ளெ போகக்கூடாதுங்க *viiṭṭukkuḷḷe pooha-kuuḍaadunga* 'Please don't go into the interior of the house.'

2.4.3.7 பதிலா *badilaa* 'instead of'

இதுக்கு பதிலா *idukku badilaa* 'instead of this'

2.4.3.8 பின்னாலெ *pinnaale* 'after'

இதுக்கு பின்னாலெ *idukku pinnaale* 'after this'

2.4.3.9 முன்னாலெ *munnaale* 'before'

சாப்பிடுறதுக்கு முன்னாலெ *saappiḍradukku munnaale* 'before eating'

2.4.4 Postpositions Occurring with the Accusative

Note that in LT, when case-marked nouns ending in a vowel, such as the accusative, are followed by words (usually verbs or postpositions) that begin with hard consonants, those consonants are doubled. Thus அவனைப் பார்த்தேன் 'I saw him', அவனைப் பார்த்து சிரித்தேன் 'I laughed at him', etc. This doubling rule is followed by some writers when writing ST, but we will not use it in this grammar, since the LT rule is essentially a spelling rule, and no such rules exist for ST.

2.4.4.1 சேத்து *seettu* 'together'

Historically, சேத்து *seettu* is the past participle of the transitive verb சேரு *seeru* 'join, cause to come together, bring together.' சேத்து *seettu* occurs only with transitive verbs.

- புஸ்தகங்களெ சேத்து குடுத்தேன் *pustahangaḷe seettu kuḍutteen* 'I gave the books together.'
- ரெண்டு கடிதங்களெ சேத்து அனுப்பினேன் *reṇḍu kaḍidangaḷe seettu anuppineen* 'I sent the two letters together.'
- For சேந்து *seendu* 'together' with intransitive verbs, cf. §2.4.1.1.

2.4.4.2 பத்தி *patti* 'about, concerning the topic of, regarding'

'About' here does not mean 'approximately' or 'around', for which சுமாரு *sumaaru* or சுமாரா *sumaaraa* is more appropriate.

- அதெ பத்தி கவலெ படாதெ *ade patti gavale paḍaade*
  'Don't worry about that.'

- இதெ பத்தியும் பேசினாரா? *ide pattiyum peesinaaraa*
  'Did he talk about this, too?'

- அவருக்கு பணம் இல்லெங்குறதெ பத்தி மறந்திட்டேன் *avarukku paṇam ille-ngrade patti maranditteen* 'I forgot about the fact that he doesn't have any money.'

2.4.4.3 பாத்து *paattu* 'at, to, towards'

பாத்து *paattu* is derived from the past participle of the verb பாரு *paar* 'see' and literally means 'having seen', but used with certain verbs, notably verbs such as சிரி, *siri*, 'laugh', கேளு *keeḷu* 'ask', கொலெ *kole* 'bark' and other 'psychological' verbs involving the senses, locution, and perception, it means 'direct the attention toward', i.e. 'laugh, bark, etc. AT someone.'

- அவனெ பாத்து கேட்டாளா *avane paattu keeṭṭaaḷaa?*
  'Did she ask him?'

- நாயி காக்காயெ பாத்து கொலெச்சுது *naayi kaakkaaye paattu koleccudu*
  'The dog barked AT the crow.'

- குருடன் திருடனெ பாத்து சிரிச்சான் *kuruḍan tiruḍane paattu ciriccaan*
  'The blind man laughed at the thief' (rather than 'The blind man looked at the thief and laughed.')[6]

2.4.4.4 தவிர *tavira* 'besides, except (for)'

- என்னெ தவிர *enne tavira* 'besides me'

- அரசாங்கத்து ஒதவியெ தவிர *arasaangattu odaviye tavira*
  'besides the government assistance'

[6] It is clear that பாத்து *paattu* does not mean 'see' literally in such examples since the subject of the verb can even be குருடன் *kuruḍan* 'blind man' which semantically cannot occur with பாரு *paaru* 'see.'

2.5 NP-ஒட NP-ஆ: 'within a particular time or context'

2.5.1 NP-ஒட *ooḍa* NP-ஆ *aa*

The construction NP-*ooḍa* NP-*aa* is one that limits something to a time or a place. If the NP is a 'time expression', the meaning indicates within a particular time, as in:

- ராத்திரியோட ராத்திரியா *raattriyooḍa raattriyaa* 'within one night, before the night was over, overnight'
- ராத்திரியோட ராத்திரியா வீட்டெ காலி பண்ணிட்டு போய்ட்டாங்க *raattriyooḍa raattriyaa viiṭṭe kaali paṇṇiṭṭu pooyṭṭaanga* 'They vacated the house overnight (they flew the coop in the middle of the night).'

2.5.2 NP-*ooḍa* NP-*aa* with Non-Time Expressions

However, with non-time expressions the meaning 'along with X' or 'accompanying X' or 'mixed in with X' is expressed.

- கூட்டத்தோட கூட்டமா மறெஞ்சிட்டான் *kuuṭṭattooḍa kuuṭṭamaa marenjiṭṭaan* 'he disappeared into the crowd'
- சாமானோட சாமானா *saamaanooḍa saamaanaa* 'along with (interspersed with) the baggage'
- கஷ்டத்தோட கஷ்டமா *kaṣṭattooḍa kaṣṭamaa* 'along with these troubles'

2.5.2.1 Mass Nouns

Note that only mass nouns can be used in this non-temporal type of construction. When the noun denotes a single unit, accompaniment is expressed with -*ooḍa* only, as in புஸ்தகத்தோட *pustahattooḍa* 'with the book, along with the book'

Chapter 3

The Tamil Verb Phrase

3.1 The Verb Stem

In a simple sentence, Tamil verbs are usually found in one of two forms—FINITE or NON-FINITE. Finite verbs are complete as they stand; non-finite forms require some additional suffix, another clause, or another syntactic construction to make the sentence they occur in complete and grammatical. Finite verbs usually end a sentence; non-finite verbs never do.

The simplest form of the verb is called the stem, and verbs are listed in most dictionaries in the stem form. It is identical to the simple imperative in almost all cases.

3.2 Imperatives and Infinitives

3.2.1 The Imperative

Tamil verbs exhibit a number of forms which express commands or exhortations. These are the imperative singular non-polite, the imperative singular polite and the imperative plural polite. There is also the 'hortative' form which is actually the modal 'may', but which can also be interpreted as a first person plural imperative 'let's (do something).' Verbs are ordinarily listed in the dictionary in the stem form, which is (with two exceptions) identical to the imperative singular non-polite form. Suffixes are then added directly to this stem. This is the *formally least complex* of all verb forms. The singular polite forms, though given in LT grammars, are rare in most modern dialects, but may be used between high status equals, or in cases of social uncertainty. This is illustrated in Table 3.1.

Table 3.1: Sample Imperative Forms, Three Verbs

	SG *Non-polite*	SG *polite*	*Plural/polite*
stem	[zero]	-உம் *um* -ரும் *rum*	ங்க(ள்) *nga(l)*
வா *vaa* ஒக்காரு் *okkaar* படி *paḍi*	வா *vaa* 'come' ஒக்காரு *okkaaru* 'sit' படி *paḍi* 'read'	வாரும் *vaarum* ஒக்காரும் *okkaarum* படியும் *paḍiyum*	வாங்க *vaanga* ஒக்காருங்க *okkaarunga* படியுங்க *paḍiyunga*

3.2.2 Negative Imperative

The Negative Imperative, expressing 'do not do such-and-such', is formed by adding the suffix -ஆதெ *aade* or -ஆதெங்க *-aadenga* (POL) to the infinitive (see ∮3.7.5 below) of the verb.

- வராதெ *varaade* 'don't come'
- போகாதெங்க *poohaadenga* 'please don't go'
- கவலெ படாதெ *kavale paḍaade* 'don't worry'
- இங்கெ தூங்காதெங்க *inge tuungaadenga* 'please don't sleep here'

Occasionally, the prohibitive கூடாது *kuuḍaadu* 'one must not, should not' (the negative of the modals லாம் *laam* and வேணும் *veeṇum*) is used to express the same notion as the negative imperative:

துப்பக் கூடாது! *tuppa kuuḍaadu*! 'Do not spit!'

3.2.3 Imperative plus ஏன் *een* 'why'

To soften the force of an imperative, or to make it more deferential, ஏன் *een* 'why' can be affixed to the imperative. The meaning is 'why don't you (VERB)' or 'why not (VERB)' or 'how would it be if you (VERB).' When the imperative is negative, the English might be 'Don't bother/trouble (yourself) to (VERB).' When ஏன் *een* is added to a polite imperative, the final ள் *ḷ* is present.

(26) மறுபடியும் பாரேன்
marubaḍiyum paareen
again look-why
'Why don't you have another look?'

(27) அவனுக்கு பணத்தெ தாயேன்
avanukku paṇatte taayeen
him-to money-ACC give-why
'How about you give him the money?'

(28) நாளெக்கி வராதெங்களேன்
naaḷekki varaadengaḷeen
tomorrow come-NEG-IMP-why
'Don't bother to come tomorrow'

3.3 Forms of Address

In Tamil there are a number of suffixes found in a sentence which indicate the amount of respect the speaker accords the addressee (or some other person). In South Asian society the choice is determined by the relative social status of the interlocutors. Westerners are generally accorded high status, and addressed with high-status respect suffixes.

3.3.1 Use of Singular Polite உம் *um*

This form is rarely used, except in some dialects, perhaps for ambiguous social relationships, such as with tradesmen of low status, fairly good friends of equal status, and in general where one would not want to be either particularly respectful *or* disrespectful. Westerners may find it more comfortable to use this form where Tamilians would use the non-polite form, but it is rare. Formally, this category is realized as a suffix -உம் *um* added to the verb stem (SG non-pol form). Examples: போடும் *pooḍum* 'give, serve'; வாங்கிக்கோரும் *vaangikkoorum* 'take along.' If the verb stem ends in a vowel, as in the previous form, a morphophonemic -ர்- *r* is inserted between the vowel and the -உம் *um* suffix.

3.3.2 Plural (Honorific) Polite (உ)ங்க(ள்) *(u)nga(ḷ)*

3.3.2.1 Polite (Honorific) Plural

This form is used when addressing people of equal or higher status, older relatives (father, mother, older siblings), and (traditionally) by women to their husband. Westerners will probably almost always be safe using this form, except to children or servants. The form of this suffix is -(உ)ங்க(ள்) *(u)nga(ḷ)*. This is added to the verb stem or to any other sentence-final word. Examples: போங்க *poonga* 'please go'; செய்யுங்க *seyyunga* 'please do'; வாங்க *vaanga* 'please come.'

3.3.3 Honorific உங்க(ள்) *(u)nga(ḷ)*

3.3.3.1 Other Uses

In sentence-final position the honorific suffix உங்க(ள்) *(u)nga(ḷ)* is often added to non-verbs: இல்லெங்க *illenga* 'no, Sir/Ma'am'; ஆமாங்க *aamaanga* 'yes, Ma'am/Sir; பத்து மணியுங்க *pattu maṇiyunga* 'It's 10:00, Sir/Ma'am.' (This is particularly true of the western dialects (Coimbatore, Salem). The morphophonemic -உ- *u* may be deleted after a vowel. The morphophonemic ள் *ḷ* is present if a question marker ஆ? *aa?* or other clitic beginning with a vowel is present: அஞ்சு மணியுங்களா? *anju maṇiyungaḷaa*? '(Do you mean/is it) 5 o'clock, Ma'am/Sir?'

3.3.4 Singular Non-Polite

3.3.4.1 Singular Informal Non-Polite

The form is the same as that listed as the verb stem in most dictionaries. Examples: குடு *kuḍu* 'give', பாரு *paaru* 'see', வாங்கிக்கொ *vaangikko* 'take along (for oneself).' This form is used with one's younger relatives, small children, servants, good friends and one's wife.[1] Used with other people it conveys disrespect.

3.3.5 Hortative லாம் *laam* 'let's (VERB); 'shall we (VERB)?'

3.3.5.1 Hortative

The suffix லாம் *laam*[2] is added to the INFINITIVE (cf. ∮3.7.5 below) of the verb. Examples: போகலாம் *poohạlaam* 'let's go', பாக்கலாம் *paakkalaam* 'let's see.' This form is homophonous with the modal லாம் *laam* 'one may (do something).' The semantic difference becomes obvious when an answer is given—the affirmative answer to the hortative is சரி *sari* 'all right, okay', while the affirmative answer to the modal is ஆமாம் *aamaam* 'yes.'

Q: போகலாமா? *poohalaamaa*? 'Shall we go?'

A: சரி *sari* 'Okay, let's.'

Q: போகலாமா? *poohalaamaa*? 'May (I) go?'

[1] Typically, traditional women do not use this with their husbands; the formal form is more usual.

[2] I treat this suffix as if it were one unit; historically it is probably derived from the verbal noun forms that end in அல் *al* plus ஆகும் *aakum* 'it will become', i.e. போகல் + ஆகும் *pookal* + *aakum* 'going will become.' Since ஆகும் *aakum* is now reduced to ஆம் *aam* and the verbal noun forms in அல் are rare in ST, I prefer the unitary analysis.

A: ஆமாம் போகலாம் *aamaam, poohalaam* 'Yes, you may.'

In the hortative, the addressee is understood as included in the exhortation. Therefore, if used without deleted pronoun, the *inclusive* first person plural நாம *naama* must be chosen. If used with the exclusive நாங்க *naanga* it cannot mean 'let's' but only 'one may.' Thus:

Q: நாம போகலாமா? *naama poohalaamaa*? 'Shall we (including you) go?'

A: சரி *sari* 'Okay, let's.'

Q: நாங்க போகலாமா? *naanga poohalaamaa*? 'Is it all right for us (not including you) to go, may we go?'

A: ஆமாம் *aamaam* 'Yes, you may.'

3.3.6 Other Address Forms

The forms discussed below are used differently from situation to situation, family to family, dialect area to dialect area. Examples are given to provide some insight into the general use of these suffixes, rather than to legislate usage. Essentially they are kinship terms but may be used with non-kin or 'fictive kin', i.e. Tamils (and Indians in general) prefer social relationships that are kin-like, since the expectations having to do with kin relationships are known. Indians therefore often try to fit everyone into a kind of kinship system, addressing non-kin as if they were (fictive) kin. When foreigners are included in this system, they also have to deal with the *expectations* pertaining to kin, i.e. sharing property, money, food, etc., accepting advice about one's life, marriage prospects, sexual behaviour, etc.

3.3.6.1 (அ)டா *(a)ḍaa* and (அ)டீ *(a)ḍii* (non-polite)

டா *ḍaa* is usually used in addressing small male children and close male friends that are younger than the speaker. When the word to which it is affixed ends in a vowel, the அ *a* is deleted. For addressing female children and close female friends -டீ *ḍii* may be used.

- போடா *pooḍaa* 'run along, get lost, kid!'
- சும்மா இருடீ *summaa iruḍii* 'be quiet, girl'

3.3.6.2 (அ)டா *(a)ḍaa* with Female Child

-டா *daa* may also be used to address a female child, usually affectionately. Less commonly, டீ may be used with a very small male child, one that has not yet reached 'the age of reason', i.e. the point of toilet training or when other expectations about purity and pollution are made of the child's behaviour. Use of this form assumes great familiarity with the child; usually only parents or relatives use this form of address.

3.3.6.3 Use of (அ)டா *(a)ḍaa* and (அ)டீ *(a)ḍii* with Non-Kin

These forms are generally used when addressing non-kin of much lower social status than the speaker, often pejoratively, and/or in anger, with impatience.

- போடா! *pooḍaa*! 'get lost, kid!'

3.3.6.4 (அ)ப்பா *appaa* 'father, older man' and (அ)ம்மா *ammaa* 'mother, older woman (POL)'

(அ)ப்பா *(a)ppaa* and (அ)ம்மா *(a)mmaa* can be used when addressing persons younger than the speaker or persons older than the speaker, but perhaps of lower professional or social status, or between friends and equals.

- இங்கெ வாப்பா *inge vaappaa* 'Come here, man'
- இங்கெ வாங்கப்பா *inge vaangappaa* 'please come here, Father'
- இங்கெ வாங்கம்மா *inge vaangammaa* 'please come here, Mother'
- இங்கெ வாம்மா *inge vaammaa* 'Come here, girl (AFFECT).'

3.3.6.5 Imperative Honorifics

Both (அ)ப்பா *(a)ppaa* and (அ)ம்மா *(a)mmaa* may be also used in the imperative when addressing mother and father; when used in this way, these forms are honorific.

3.3.6.6 (அ)ய்யா *(a)yyaa* and (அ)ம்மா *(a)mmaa*

3.3.6.7 (அ)ய்யா *(a)yyaa* (masculine) and (அ)ம்மா *(a)mmaa* (feminine)

These forms differ from those in ∮3.4.6.4 since they may be added to both the polite and non-polite imperatives. They are usually used to address elders or another person considered to be the speaker's equal. When used with forms other than imperative, the polite distinctions are not apparent.

இங்கெ வாய்யா *inge vaa-yaa* 'come here, man'

3.3.6.8 அண்ணாச்சி *aṇṇaacci*; அண்ணா *aṇṇaa*; அக்கா *akkaa*; தம்பி *tampi*; தங்கச்சி *tangacci*

The address forms, அண்ணாச்சி, *aṇṇaacci*, அண்ணா *aṇṇaa*; (அ)க்கா *akkaa*; தம்பி *tambi* and தங்கச்சி *tangacci* are essentially kinship terms: elder brother, elder sister, younger brother and younger sister, respectively. When used with non-kin, they combine politeness and familiarity, for example, when exaggerated politeness (ங்க *-ngka*), etc. would be inappropriate because of age similarities (as with அண்ணா *aṇṇaa* and அக்கா *akkaa*, or when a low status older speaker addresses a higher status younger speaker (தம்பி *tambi*).[3]

3.4 Finite Verbs

One of the commonest types of finite verbs is the verb marked for tense and for person, number and gender (PNG). Verbs which are marked for PNG are *always* marked for tense, although some tense-marked verbs are not marked for PNG.[4] Such PNG-less, tense-marked verbs are called 'non-finite verbs.'

Verbs marked for tense and PNG have the structure shown in Table 3.2, that is, they consist of the verb *stem* (usually identical with the non-polite *imperative* stem), plus a *tense marker* and finally a PNG marker.

As is obvious from the examples in Table 3.2, not all verbs have the same present tense marker. In fact, Tamil verbs must be divided into several classes, depending on which tense-markers they require.[5]

Depending on one's linguistic bias, Tamil verbs can be arranged into as few as three or as many as thirteen classes, according to the consonantal

[3] In the play ஸிங்கிள் ட (Schiffman 1971: *Reader for Advanced Spoken Tamil*, Part I: Radio Plays), the 'tea-master' Sundaram addresses the robbers with அண்ணாச்சி for 'solidarity with politeness' while in the play ஆறு மணிக்குள், the various delivery men address கண்ணன் *Kannan* with தம்பி *tambi* because they are older but of lower social status.

[4] In Old Tamil, verbs may consist of a stem plus PNG markers, and the absence of a tense marker implies negation; but this is not a productive process in LT or in ST. A few relic forms, such as காணோம் *kaaṇoom* 'I don't see (anything)' (lit. 'we do not see') remain in the language as idiomatic phrases.

[5] Because of Tamil spelling conventions, certain consonant clusters are usually avoided by adding epenthetic உ *u* between consonants; one such convention is that the LT present tense marker க்கிற் is usually written க்குற் whenever ST *is* written (in novels etc.) even though phonetically it is [kkr], and our transliteration is *kkr*.

Table 3.2: Structure of Finite Verbs

Stem	Tense Marker	PNG	Gloss
இரு *iru* 'be located'	க்குற் *kur* 'present'	ஏன் *een* '1st SG'	
இருக்குறேன் *irukkreen*			'I am located'
வர் *var* 'come'	உற் *r* 'present'	ஆரு *aaru* '3 hon'	
வர்றாரு *varraaru*			'He comes'

Table 3.3: Strong Verbs

	Stem	Gloss	Infinitive	Present	Past	Future
1.	எடு *eḍu*	'take'	எடுக்க *eḍukka*	எடுக்குற்- *eḍukkr-*	எடுத்த்- *eḍutt-*	எடுப்ப்- *eḍupp-*
2.	நட *naḍa*	'walk'	நடக்க *naḍakka*	நடகுற்- *naḍakkr-*	நடந்த்- *naḍand-*	நடப்ப்- *naḍapp-*
3.	கட *kaḍa*	'cross'	கடக்க *kaḍakka*	கடக்குற்- *kaḍakkr-*	கடந்த்- *kaḍand-*	கடப்ப்- *kaḍapp-*
4.	கல *kala*	'mix'	கலக்க *kalakka*	கலக்குற்- *kalakkr-*	கலந்த்- *kaland-*	கலப்ப்- *kalapp-*
5.	மற *mara*	'forget'	மறக்க *marakka*	மறக்குற்- *marakkr-*	மறந்த்- *marand-*	மறப்ப்- *marapp-*

alternations which occur when tense markers are added to the stem. It has been a traditional analysis to set up seven classes of the Tamil verb (known as the 'Graul' classification, and used in Arden 1942, Fabricius' various dictionaries, etc.) and to handle verbs that do not fit into the seven classes by applying certain rules to them. Verbs are listed in Table 3.3 and Table 3.4 by stems (identical in most cases to the imperative) followed by the English gloss, then the infinitive, the present, the past and the future.

3.4.1 'Strong Verbs' with Tense Markers க்குற்/த்த/ப்ப

Verbs with final இ *i*, எ *e* and ய் *y* in the stem, change த்த் *tt* to ச்ச் *cc* and ந்த் *nd* to ந்ச் *nj* automatically (Graul's Class VI).

Table 3.4: Weak Verbs, Graul's Class III, with Tense Markers உற்/இன்/வ

Stem	Gloss	Infinitive	Present	Past	Future
சொல்லு *sollu*	'say'	சொல்ல *solla*	சொல்(லு)றேன் *sol(lu)reen*	சொன்னேன் *sonneen*	சொல்லுவே *solluveen*
பேசு *peesu*	'speak'	பேச *peesa*	பேசுறேன் *peesureen*	பேசினேன் *peesineen*	பேசுவேன் *peesuveen*
போ *poo*	'go'	போக *pooha*	போறேன் *pooreen*	போனேன் *pooneen*	போவேன் *pooveen*
வாங்கு *vaangu*	'buy, get, 'fetch'	வாங்க *vaanga*	வாங்குறேன் *vaangureen*	வாங்குனேன் *vaanguneen*	வாங்குவே *vaanguve*

3.4.2 'Weak' Verbs, with Tense Markers உற்/இன்/வ

The so-called weak verbs are Graul's Classes I, II and III, which have tense markers உற் *r* for the present, த் *d*, ந்த் *nd* or இன் *in* for the past, and வ *v* for the future. The இன் *in* past may be phonetically [ən] or [ʉn]. (Graul's Class II has the same tense markers in the present and future, but in the past, the marker is ந்த் (in LT) and ந்த் *nd* and ஞ்ச் *nj* in spoken.) Examples of Class III verbs are shown in Table 3.4.[6]

The verb சொல்லு *sollu* is exceptional in that the ல் *l* assimilates in the past to ன்ன் *nn*: சொல்லினேன் ⟶ சொன்னேன் *sonneen*. The verbs கொண்டுபோ *kondupoo* 'take (s.t.) and கூட்டிகிட்டுப்போ *kuuttikittupoo* 'take (s.o.)' are conjugated exactly like போ *poo* 'go.' They have a different past *neuter* form (cf. ∮3.7.3) போச்சு *pooccu* instead of the expected *போனது **poonadu*. ஆகு *aahu* is also similar, with past neuter ஆச்சு *aaccu*. Note also that neuter future forms are different for *all* verbs: they are formed by adding உம் *um* to the infinitive (after deleting the அ *a*.)

3.4.3 Graul's Class II: Weak Present/Future, ந்த் Past

As mentioned earlier, the Graul classification II has weak present and future markers, but ந்த் *nd* and ஞ்ச் *nj* in the past. There are a number of different kinds of verbs in this class.

[6] Graul's Class I is almost non-existent in ST; many of the verbs of that class (which is very small already in LT) change class, e.g. to II in ST, or are not used in ST as lexical verbs; a few remain, such as அழு *aẓu* 'weep, cry' so this class can not be subsumed under any other.

1. Verbs whose imperative forms have long vowels, but have alternant stem forms with short vowels when tense is marked. Essentially there are only two members of this subclass:

   - வா *vaa* 'come': Weak present/future, past: வந்தேன் *vandeen*
   - தா *taa* 'give': Weak present/future, past: தந்தேன் *tandeen*[7]

2. Verbs formed on the base of வா *vaa* 'come':

   - கொண்டுவா *koṇḍuvaa* 'bring s.t.': conjugated like வா.

     கொண்டா *koṇḍaa* (variant of கொண்டுவா *koṇḍuvaa* 'bring s.t.'): conjugated like வா but vowel remains long throughout: கொண்டாறேன் *koṇḍaareen*, etc.

   - கூட்டிகிட்டுவா *kuuṭṭikiṭṭuvaa* 'bring a person'

3. Intransitive verbs that have transitive analogs are numerous in this class. Many of these verbs end in vowels other than உ *u*, e.g. LT ஐ, ST எ *e*, இ *i*; their transitive analogs are members of Class VI.

   - வளரு *vaḷaru* 'grow (INTR)': வளர்ந்தது *vaḷa(r)ndadu* 'it grew'
   - கலெ *kale* 'be separate, be excluded, dispersed': கலெஞ்சது *kalenjadu* 'it was dispersed'

4. Verbs that end in LT ஐ *ai* and இ *i* (and ST எ *e(y)*), causing palatalization in the past marker; in our classification these are IIIb:

   - ஒடெ *oḍe* 'break (of its own accord)': ஒடெஞ்சது *oḍenjadu*
   - தெரி *teri* 'be known': தெரிஞ்சது *terinjadu* 'it was known'

5. Verbs with final rhotics (*r* sounds), which are deleted or otherwise changed before the past marker:

   - ஒக்காரு *okkaaru* 'sit': ஒக்காந்தான் *okkaandaan* 'he sat'
   - ஆழு *aaṟu* 'be deep': ஆழ்ந்தது *aa(ṟ)ndadu* or *aaḷndadu* 'it was deep'

[7] In some dialects, this verb is only used with first and second person subjects.

Table 3.5: Strong Verbs, Graul's Class IV

	Stem	Gloss	Infinitive	Present
1.	சாப்பிடு *saappiḍu*	'eat'	சாப்பிட *saappiḍa*	சாப்பிடுறேன் *saappiḍureen*
2.	போடு *pooḍu*	'place, put,' 'serve (food)'	போட *pooḍa*	போடுறேன் *pooḍreen*
3.	போட்டுக்கோ *pooṭṭukko*	'put on, wear'	போட்டுக்க *pooṭṭukka*	போட்டுக்குறேன் *pooṭṭukkreen*

	Stem	Gloss	Past	Future
1.	சாப்பிடு *saappiḍu*	'eat'	சாப்பிட்டேன் *saappiṭṭeen*	சாப்பிடுவேன் *saappiḍuveen*
2.	போடு *pooḍu*	'place, put,' 'serve (food)'	போட்டேன் *pooṭṭeen*	போடுவேன் *pooḍuveen*
3.	போட்டுக்கோ *pooṭṭukko*	'put on, wear'	போட்டுக்கிட்டேன் *pooṭṭukkiṭṭeen*	போட்டுக்குவேன் *pooṭṭukkuveen*

- விழு *vir̤u* 'fall': விழுந்தது *vir̤undadu* or *viḷndadu* 'it fell'

6. Verbs belonging to Class I in LT, but showing nasal palatalization in the past in ST:

   - செய் *seyyi* 'do, make': செஞ்சது *senjadu* 'it made'
   - பெய் *peyyi* 'rain': பெஞ்சது *penjadu* 'it rained'

3.4.4 Verbs with Weak Present/Future but Past with Doubled Retroflex Consonant

This class (cf. Table 3.5) is intermediate between the weak and strong verbs; in Graul's classification it is Class IV. Stems usually have ட் *ḍ* as their last consonant, but not all verbs with ட் belong to this class, e.g. பாடு *paaḍu* 'sing' belongs to Class III.

In some dialects, the infinitive of போட்டுக்கோ *pooṭṭukko* put on, wear' is a back formation from the past: போட்டுக்கிட *pooṭṭukkiḍa*.[8]

[8]The LT verb கொள் *koḷ* is involved in the formation of this compound, but has lost

3.4.5 Verbs of the Problematical Class V

The Class V of the Graul classification, shown in Table 3.6, is a problematical one, containing a number of verbs that are weak in the present but strong in the future, or 'stronger' in the past than the weak classes but not quite as 'strong' as Classes VI and VII.[9]

Class V verbs usually contain sonorants (laterals, nasals, rhotics) in stem-final position, and both in LTTamil and in ST unpredictable things happen to these sonorants. In ST some of these verbs are not in use, or are used only with an aspectual auxiliary. For example கல் *kallu* 'learn', with LT past கற்ற்- *kaṟṟ-* usually occurs in ST only with aspectual இரு *iru* or aspectual கொள் *koḷḷu*, e.g. *kattiru* or *kattu-kkoo*, as in தமிழ் எங்கெ கத்திருக்கீங்க *tamiẓ engee kattirukkiinga?* 'Where (in the world) did you learn Tamil?'[10]

Other LT Class V verbs are not used at all, or only in certain idioms. The LT verb காண் 'see' is not common in ST as a main verb, only in certain collocations or idioms such as கனா காண் *kanaa kaaṇu* 'have (i.e. see) a dream', or in the archaic frozen negative form காணோம் *kaaṇoom* '(I) don't see (a thing, etc.).' Other class V verbs are shifted to Class III, e.g. தின் 'eat' which has the LT Tamil past தின்றேன் 'I ate' is realized as *tinnineen* (with usual shortening of the cluster *nnin* to *nn*) and the LT future தின் பேன் would be *tinnuveen*. But not all speakers do this, and some retention of this class, even at a minimal level, must be recognized. For example, the quotative verb என் *en*, phonologically reduced as it is, usually to just [-n-], is in standard ST more or less a predictably Class V verb, with past in ண்ணு *ṇṇ-*, present ங்குற் *ngr-* and future ம்ப் *mb-*, although the future may also occur as ன்னுவ *nnuv-*, e.g. அப்படிங்குறான் *appaḍi-ngraan* 'that's what he says' or அப்படிம்பான் *appaḍi-mbaan* 'that's what he'll say.' The pervasive use of this verb as a quotative marker and embedding marker in Tamil guarantees that it will appear very often in conversation and spoken

its morphophonemic value. The LT verb கொள் is not normally used in ST, except with the meaning 'contain', i.e. இந்தச் சாடி எவ்வளவு கொள்ளும் *inda jaaḍi evvaḷavu koḷḷum* 'How much will this jar contain?' கொள் is also used in the compounds கொண்டுப்போ *koṇḍupoo* 'take (s.t.) and கூட்டிகிட்டுப்போ *kuuṭṭikiṭṭupoo* 'take (s.o.)' and கொண்டுவா *koṇḍuvaa* 'bring s.t.' and கூட்டிகிட்டுவா *kuuṭṭikiṭṭuvaa* 'bring a person'; and கொள் is also an aspect marker (cf. ∮3.12.16).

[9] The notion of 'strong' and 'weak' as a classifying system for verbs is borrowed from the tradition used in Germanic languages, where verbs are so classified; here 'strong' seems to mean possessing doubled (stop) consonants and 'weak' seems to mean possessing single consonants as tense markers.

[10] Note that this is not a very complementary statement; in fact the illocutionary force is 'You don't know Tamil.' If someone really wants to know where a foreigner learned Tamil, s/he would ask தமிழ் எங்கெ கத்துக்கிட்டீங்க? *tamiẓ engee kattukiṭṭiinga?* using aspectual கொள் *koḷḷu*.

Table 3.6: Graul's Class V, LT and ST

Subclass	Verb Stem	Present	Past	Future
1	நில் 'stand' *nillu*	நிற்கிறேன் *nikkreen*	நின்றேன் *ninṇeen*	நிற்பேன் *nippeen*
2	உண் 'eat' *uṇṇu*	உண்கிறேன் *uṇṇureen*	உண்டேன் *uṇḍeen*	உண்பேன் *uṇṇuveen*
3	என் 'quote' *-(e)n(u)*	என்கிறேன் *(e)ngreen*	என்றேன் *(e)ṇṇeen*	என்பேன் *(e)nnuveen* *(e)mbeen*
4	கேள் 'ask' *keeḷu*	கேட்கிறேன் *keekkureen*	கேட்டேன் *keeṭṭeen*	கேட்பேன் *keeppeen*
5	காண் 'see' *kaaṇu*	காண்கிறேன் *kaaṇureen*	கண்டேன் *kaṇḍeen*	காணுவேன் *kaaṇuveen*

texts, so despite the fact that என் may be almost the only verb that retains features of Class V morphology, its functional load is high in the language.

3.4.5.1 The Verb: Person-Number-Gender (PNG) Agreement

Most Tamil finite verbs are marked for 'agreement' in person, number and gender (PNG) with their subjects. ('Finite' verbs are verbs which can stand alone in a sentence without needing another verb, auxiliary verb or whatever, to make the sentence complete and grammatical.) This means that a suffix, called a PNG marker, is added to the verb; it follows the tense marker and is the same for all tenses, except for the *neuter present and future*, which does not have the same form as the neuter PNG marker in the past, for example. Furthermore, some verbs have unpredictable neuter PNG forms in the past, as well. Non-neuter PNG markers, however, are regular.

Tables 3.7 to 3.15 give complete paradigms, in all persons, of the verbs வா *vaa* 'come', போ *poo* 'go', பாரு *paaru* 'see', இரு *iru* 'be located', சாப்பிடு *saappiḍu* 'eat', வாங்கு *vaangu* 'buy, fetch, get, take', வந்திடு *vandiḍu* 'come for sure', படி *paḍi* 'study.' Note a number of anomalies: the neuter future is based on the infinitive, rather than on the future marker; the neuter plural is not distinguished (unlike in LT); the feminine polite form is the same as the plural non-polite; and the first person plural pronoun(s) are distinguished for 'exclusive' and 'inclusive.'

Table 3.7: Paradigm of வா *vaa* 'come', all PNG

PNG	**Present**	**Past**	**Future**
1 SG	நான் வர்றேன் *naan varreen*	நான் வந்தேன் *naan vandeen*	நான் வருவேன் *naan varuveen*
2 SG	நீ வர்றே *nii varree*	நீ வந்தே *nii vandee*	நீ வருவே *nii varuvee*
3 SG M	அவன் வர்றான் *avan varraan*	அவன் வந்தான் *avan vandaan*	அவன் வருவான் *avan varuvaan*
3 SG F	அவ(ள்) வர்றா *ava varraa*	அவ (ள்) வந்தா(ள்) *ava vandaa*	அவ(ள்) வருவா(ள்) *ava varuvaa*
3 SG N	அது வர்றது *adu varradu*	அது வந்தது *adu vandadu*	அது வரும் *adu varum*
1 PL EXCL	நாங்க வர்றோம் *naanga varroom*	நாங்க வந்தோம் *naanga vandoom*	நாங்க வருவோம் *naanga varuvoom*
1 PL INCL	நாம வர்றோம் *naama varroom*	நாம வந்தோம் *naama vandoom*	நாம வருவோம் *naama varuvoom*
2 PL(POL)	நீங்க வர்றீங்க *niinga varriinga*	நீங்க வந்தீங்க *niinga vandiinga*	நீங்க வருவீங்க *niinga varuviinga*
3 PL (POL)	அவரு வர்றாரு *avaru varraaru*	அவரு வந்தாரு *avaru vandaaru*	அவரு வருவாரு *avaru varuvaaru*
3 PL NON-POL F POL	அவங்க வர்றாங்க *avanga varraanga*	அவங்க வந்தாங்க *avanga vandaanga*	அவங்க வருவாங்க *avanga varuvaanga*

3.4.5.2 வா *vaa* 'come'

வா *vaa* 'come' infinitive: வர *vara* 'to come'; AVP: வந்து *vandu* 'having come.' The complete paradigm of this verb is shown in Table 3.7.

3.4.5.3 போ *poo* 'go'

poo 'go' infinitive: போக *pooha*; AVP: போயி *pooyi* 'having gone.' The complete paradigm of this verb is shown in Table 3.8.

3.5 Transitivity and Verb Classes

As noted earlier, non-Tamils cannot reliably form grammatically correct forms of the Tamil verb without knowledge of the verb class and transitivity

Table 3.8: Paradigm of போ *poo* 'go', all PNG

PNG	**Present**	**Past**	**Future**
1 SG	நான் போறேன் *naan pooreen*	போனேன் *pooneen*	போவே *pooveen*
2 SG	நீ போறே *nii pooree*	போனே *poonee*	போவே *poovee*
3 SG M	அவன் போறான் *avan pooraan*	போனான் *poonaan*	போவான் *poovaan*
3 SG F	அவ போறா *ava pooraa*	போனா *poonaa*	போவா *poovaa*
3 SG N	அது போறது *adu pooradu*	(போனது) போச்சு *(poonadu) pooccu*	போகும் *poohum*
1 PL EXCL	நாங்க போறோம் *naanga pooroom*	போனோம் *poonoom*	போவோம் *poovoom*
1 PL INCL	நாம போறோம் *naama pooroom*	போனோம் *poonoom*	போவோம் *poovoom*
2 PL(POL)	நீங்க போறீங்க *niinga pooriinga*	போனீங்க *pooniinga*	போவீங்க *pooviinga*
3 PL(POL) PL(POL)	அவரு போறாரு *avaru pooraaru*	போனாரு *poonaaru*	போவாரு *poovaaru*
3 PL NON-POL	அவங்க போறாங்க *avanga pooraanga*	போனாங்க *poonaanga*	போவாங்க *poovaanga*
F POL	அவங்க போறாங்க *avanga pooraanga*	போனாங்க *poonaanga*	போவாங்க *poovaanga*

specification of a given verb.[11]

3.5.1 Overview: Classification of the Tamil Verb

Tamil verbs have been classified in a number of different ways, depending on the shape of the morphemes used to mark tense. The **Tamil Lexicon** uses a schema involving thirteen separate classes; other scholars have proposed smaller numbers of classes but each involve subclasses and there are always exceptional forms that do not fit neatly into any kind of scheme. We use a modification of the seven-class scheme given in Arden (1942:148-9) and Fabricius (1972:vi–vii), which is known in the literature as 'Dr. Graul's classification'.

This classificatory scheme does not work perfectly for ST, however, so we have proposed additional subclassifications for certain of Graul's Classes, notably verbs in Classes II and VI, where stem-final front vowels trigger palatalization of the past tense markers ந்த் and த்த் to *nj* and *cc*, respectively. Verbs of Classes II and VI whose stems do not meet these conditions are not specially marked, but those that do are marked IIb and VIb, respectively. Thus the verb தெரி *teri*, II INTR, with stem-final இ *i* triggering palatalization of the past marker ந்த் to *nj* in spoken is classified as IIb, and சமை (in ST *same*, VI TR, which has a palatalized past tense marker *cc* in ST, is classified as VIb.

In addition, in Classes II, III and V there are a number of irregular verbs that do not follow the regular rules in one or another tense form, so we have marked certain verbs as members of subclass IIc, or IIIb, or Vc, to try to fit them into the class they most closely resemble. Most irregularities or complexities of the Tamil verb are to be found in the past tense; were it not for these past tense problems, most verbs could be classified simply as "strong" or "weak", depending on whether they have doubled consonants in the present (க்கிற்-) and future (ப்ப்) tense marker, or single consonants (கிற்) and (வ/ப). This strong–weak scheme is used by some scholars and in some pedagogical materials for Tamil as a general description of the verb, but it is not adequate to predict the details of the past tense. It is useful if the discussion centres on the formation of infinitives or of neuter futures, and the strong–weak distinction also correlates in some ways with transitivity and intransitivity. But this correlation is not perfectly regular and can only serve as a mnemonic device when the exact classification is

[11] There are a few patterns that can be guessed at: any verb that ends in அ *a*, such as நட *nada*, is a member of Graul's Class VII; most verbs with the structure CVCVCCV, VCVVNC-u, (வாங்கு *vaangu*, தொடக்கு *todakku*, திரும்பு *tirumbu*, etc.) can probably be placed in Graul's Class III. But many others may belong to more than one class, with intransitive and transitive possibilities.

not known.

In ST, subclassifying Classes II, III, V, and VI into palatalizing, non-palatalizing, and otherwise irregular helps to take care of most areas where ST forms are different from LT, but it does not take care of all. In some cases, ST verbs are members of totally distinct classes from their LT counterparts, and this is particularly true of members of LT Classes I and V—LT Class I is a very small class, i.e. has very few members, and given that some of these LT verbs are never used in ST, while other members shift to another class, Class I as a spoken class is an almost empty set. There are, however, a few members that retain and duplicate the morphology of the LT set, so it must be retained. The LT verb செய், I TR 'do, make' changes to Class II in ST: its past is *senj-* rather than the LT செய்த்- *seyd-* (the verb பெய் 'rain' also shifts to II in ST). But verbs like அழு 'weep' and உழு 'plow' remain in Class I in spoken, with pasts in *d* analogous to LT single த் pasts: அழுதேன் *aṟudeen* 'I wept.'

3.5.1.1 Graul's Verb Classes

As the verb classifications are dependent on the form of the tense markers used with different stems, we give in Table 3.9 a chart showing the shape of these tense markers in the different classes (both LT and ST), followed by a table (3.10) showing illustrations of typical members of the various classes, in LT and ST. (Exceptionally for these tables (but cf. also Table 3.6), only the LT forms are in Tamil script, while the ST forms are in transliteration only.)

3.5.2 Transitivity

Most grammars of Tamil have discussed the transitivity status of Tamil verbs as being essentially binary, i.e. either transitive or intransitive, i.e. as if this distinction were exactly parallel to that of English or some other western language. Actually any cursory examination of the Tamil verb will reveal that the semantic distinction so clearly marked in the morphology, i.e. the distinction between pairs like ஓடு *ooḍu* and ஓட்டு *ooṭṭu*, which is usually glossed as 'run' vs. 'cause to run' or 'run of one's own volition' vs. 'run something' is not as simple when all the verbs of the language have been taken into account.[12] Some researchers on Tamil, such as Paramasivam 1979, have rejected the dichotomy between transitivity and intransitivity

[12] This is not just the case with Tamil, but with many other languages of the world, as has been shown very clearly by the research of Hopper and Thompson (1980), for example.

Table 3.9: Graul's Verb Classification System with LT and ST Tense Markers

Class	Present	Past	Future
LT 1	-கிற்-	-த்-	-வ-
ST 1	[-r-]	[-d-]	[-v-]
LT 2	-கிற்-	-ந்த்-	-வ-
ST 2	[-r-]	[-nd-]	[-v-]
ST 2b	[-r-]	[-nj-]	[-v-]
LT 3	-கிற்-	-இன்-	-வ-
ST 3	[-r-]	[-in-]	[-v-]
ST 3b	[-r-]	[-n-]	[-v-]
ST 3c	[-r-]	[-nn-]	[-v-]
LT 4	-கிற்-	-ட்ட்-	-வ-
ST 4	[-r-]	[−ṭṭ-]	[-v-]
LT 5	-கிற்-	-ன்ற்-	-ப்-
ST 5	[-gr-]	[-ṇṇ-]	[-b-]
LT 5b	-கிற்-	-ற்ற்-	-ப்-
ST 5b	[-kr-]	[-tt-]	[-pp-]
LT 5c	-கிற்-	-ட்ட்-	-ப்-
ST 5c	[-kkr-]	[-ṭṭ-]	[-pp-]
LT 6	-க்கிற்-	-த்த்-	-ப்ப்-
ST 6	[-kkr-]	[-tt-]	[-pp-]
ST 6b	[-kkr-]	[-cc-]	[-pp-]
LT 7	-க்கிற்-	-ந்த்-	-ப்ப்-
ST 7	[-kkr-]	[-nd-]	[-pp-]

Table 3.10: Tamil Verb Classes, LT and ST

Class	Verb stem	Present	Past	Future
I	அழு 'weep' [ar̤u]	அழுகிறேன் [ar̤ureen]	அழுதேன் [ar̤udeen]	அழுவேன் [ar̤uveen]
II	உட்கார் 'sit' [okkaaru]	உட்காருகிறேன் [okkaarreen]	உட்கார்ந்தேன் [okkaandeen]	உட்காருவேன் [okkaaruveen]
IIb	உடை 'break' [oḍe] (INTR)	உடைகிறது [oḍeyradu]	உடைந்தது [oḍenjadu]	உடையும் [oḍeyum]
IIc	வா 'come' [vaa]	வருகிறேன் [varreen]	வந்தது [vandadu]	வருவேன் [varuveen]
III	வாங்கு 'buy' [vaangu]	வாங்குகிறேன் [vaangureen]	வாங்கினேன் [vaangineen]	வாங்குவேன் [vaanguveen]
IIIb	போ 'go' [poo]	போகிறேன் [pooreen]	போனேன் [pooneen]	போவேன் [pooveen]
IIIc	சொல் 'say' [sollu]	சொல்லுகிறேன் [sol(lu)reen]	சொன்னேன் [sonneen]	சொல்லுவேன் [solluveen]
IV	போடு 'put' [pooḍu]	போடுகிறேன் [pooḍureen]	போட்டேன் [pooṭṭeen]	போடுவேன் [pooḍuveen]
V	உண் 'eat' [uṇṇu]	உண்கிறேன் [uṇṇureen]	உண்டேன் [uṇḍeen]	உண்பேன் [uṇṇuveen]
	என் 'quote' [-(e)n(u)]	என்கிறேன் [(e)ngreen]	என்றேன் [(e)ṇṇeen]	என்பேன் [(e)nnuveen] [(e)mbeen]
Vb	கேள் 'ask' [keeḷu]	கேட்கிறேன் [keekkureen]	கேட்டேன் [keeṭṭeen]	கேட்பேன் [keeppeen]
Vc	காண் 'see' [kaaṇu]	காண்கிறேன் [kaaṇureen]	கண்டேன் [kaṇḍeen]	காணுவேன் [kaaṇuveen]
VI	பார் 'see' [paaru]	பார்க்கிறேன் [paakkreen]	பார்த்தேன் [paatteen]	பார்ப்பேன் [paappeen]
VIb	சமை 'cook' [same]	சமைக்கிறேன் [samekkreen]	சமைத்தேன் [samecceen]	சமைப்பேன் [sameppeen]
VII	நட 'walk' [naḍa]	நடக்கிறேன் [naḍakkreen]	நடந்தேன் [naḍandeen]	நடப்பேன் [naḍapeen]

as inadequate for Tamil, and have opted for a distinction known as 'affective' vs. 'effective', which Paramasivam feels more adequately captures the distinction between the two.

3.5.2.1 Dative Subjects

Another issue that enters into the discussion of this area is that of verbs that take 'dative subjects'. These are stative verbs whose semantic subject is marked with the dative case, and the verb itself marked with a neuter person-number-gender marker. The object (or target of the action) is marked accusative if animate; otherwise it is unmarked, i.e. nominative. In Tamil these verbs are all *stative,* i.e. they describe psychological *states,* rather than actions. Such Tamil verbs as பிடி *piḍi* 'like', தெரி *teri* 'know', வேண்டும் *veeṇum* 'want, need', போதும் *poodum* 'suffice' கிடை *keḍe* 'be available' which all describe states, take the subject in the dative and if the object (or target, i.e. that which is known, liked, wanted, etc.) is animate, it is marked accusative. For example, எனக்கு அவரைத் தெரியும் *enakku avare teriyum* 'I know him' has the subject in the dative and the object in the accusative, with no nominative case–marking possible.

On a scale of transitivity, such verbs are obviously very low, and in normal usage either the dative-marked subject or the object, or both, may be missing, i.e. a well-formed sentence can consist simply of தெரியுமா *teriyumaa* 'Do you know?' or வேண்டாம் *veeṇḍaam* '(I) don't want (it).' In our analysis, these are called 'dative–stative' verbs which means that they are stative verbs that are always marked for third person with dative subject. These verbs are either low on the transitivity scale or in some cases definitely *in*transitive, as with போதும் *poodum* 'suffice' and கிடை *keḍe* 'be available'. Some Tamil verbs can be used dative-statively, but also with first and second person subjects, so when this happens, this is marked.

Our solution to this problem is to issue caveats but not to attempt a wholesale reclassification or scaling of transitivity for the Tamil verbs. We continue to use the (probably archaic) bipolar scale of transitivity, with the two உ.டை's shown in Tables 3.17 and 3.18 given the traditional 'intransitive/transitive' labels, often with information about restrictions on person and number of 'subject'. Were it not for the fact that Tamil usually marks the distinction between intransitive and transitive morphological differences in the tense-marking of the two types, it would not be obvious to most non-Tamils that distinctions must be kept separate. English, for example, has only a small set of verbs that are paired in this way, one being transitive and the other intransitive. Even these (sit/set, lie/lay, fall/fell, rise/raise, and perhaps some others) are not grammatically salient for many speakers. In Tamil either the stem itself is different (such as the (C)VC/(C)VCC-

Table 3.11: Examples of Strong Verbs (Graul's Class VI and VII)

	Stem	Gloss	Infinitive	Present	Past	Future
1.	இரு *iru*	'be located'	இருக்க *irukka*	இருக்குற- *irukkr-*	இருந்து- *irund-*	இருப்ப- *irupp-*
2.	படு *paḍu*	'lie'	படுக்க *paḍukka*	படுக்குற- *paḍukkr-*	படுத்த- *paḍutt-*	படுப்ப- *paḍupp-*
3.	குடு *kuḍu*	'give'	குடுக்க *kuḍukka*	குடுக்குற- *kuḍukkr-*	குடுத்த- *kuḍutt-*	குடுப்ப- *kuḍupp-*
4.	வையி *vayyi*	'put, keep'	வெக்க *vekka*	வெக்குற- *vekkr-*	வெச்ச- *vecc-*	வெப்ப- *vepp-*
5.	படி *paḍi*	'study, read'	படிக்க *paḍikka*	படிக்குற- *paḍikkr-*	படிச்ச- *paḍicc-*	படிப்ப- *paḍipp-*
6.	சமெ *same*	'cook'	சமெக்க *samekka*	சமெக்குற- *samekkr-*	சமெச்ச- *samecc-*	சமெப்ப- *samepp-*

type exemplified by ஓடு/ஓட்டு *ooḍu/ooṭṭu)*, 'run' vs. 'drive') or there is an alternation (C)VNC-/(C)VCC- (as with திரும்பு/திருப்பு *tirumpu/tiruppu* 'return'), or the differences are marked in the tense markers, usually with weak types for intransitive and strong types for transitive.

3.6 Sample Paradigms of Common Verbs

3.6.1 Examples of Strong Verbs (Graul's Class VII)

3.6.1.1 பாரு *paaru* 'see': INF: பாக்க *paakka* AVP: பாத்து *paattu* 'having seen'

The complete paradigm of this verb is shown in Table 3.12. Note that any verb compounded with பாரு *paaru* 'see' as the final element will be conjugated in the same way, such as வேலெ பாரு *veele paaru* 'work'; மேல் பாரு *meelpaaru* 'supervise.'

3.6.1.2 இரு *iru* 'be located' INF: இருக்க *irukka* AVP: இருந்து *irundu* 'having been'

The present tense markers of இரு *iru* 'be located' are given in Table 3.13 with க்குற *kkr*; this is a possible standard pronunciation, but in actuality most speakers have a different form of the present tense marker with இரு

Table 3.12: Paradigms of பாரு *paaru*, 'see', all Tenses and PNG

PNG	**Present**	**Past**	**Future**
1 SG	பாக்குறேன் *paakkreen*	பாத்தேன் *paatteen*	பாப்பேன் *paappeen*
2 SG	பாக்குறே *paakkuree*	பாத்தே *paattee*	பாப்பே *paappee*
3 SG M	பாக்குறான் *paakkuraan*	பாத்தான் *paattaan*	பாப்பான் *paappaan*
3 SG F	பாக்குறா *paakkraa*	பாத்தா *paattaa*	பாப்பா *paappaa*
3 SG N	பாக்குறது *paakkradu*	பாத்தது *paattadu*	பாக்கும் *paakkum*
1 PL	பாக்குறோம் *paakkuroom*	பாத்தோம் *paattoom*	பாப்போம் *paappoom*
2 PL & POL	பாக்குறீங்க *paakkriinga*	பாத்தீங்க *paattiinga*	பாப்பீங்க *paappiinga*
3 PL (POL)	பாக்குறாங்க *paakkraanga*	பாத்தாங்க *paattaanga*	பாப்பாங்க *paappaanga*
3 PL NON-POL &F POL	பாக்குறாங்க *paakkraanga*	பாத்தாங்க *paattaanga*	பாப்பாங்க *paappaanga*

Table 3.13: Paradigms of இரு *iru* 'be located', all Tenses and PNG

PNG	**Present**	**Past**	**Future**
1 SG	இருக்குறேன் *irukk(r)een*	இருந்தேன் *irundeen*	இருப்பேன் *iruppeen*
2 SG	இருக்குறே *irukk(r)ee*	இருந்தே *irundee*	இருப்பே *iruppee*
3 SG M	இருக்குறான் *irukk(r)aan*	இருந்தான் *irundaan*	இருப்பான் *iruppaan*
3 SG F	இருக்குறா *irukk(r)aa*	இருந்தா *irundaa*	இருப்பா *iruppaa*
3 SG N	இருக்கு (இருக்கது) *irukku* (*irukkudu*)	இருந்தது *irundadu*	இருக்கும் *irukkum*
1 PL	இருக்குறோம் *irukk(r)oom*	இருந்தோம் *irundoom*	இருப்போம் *iruppoom*
2 PL & POL	இருக்குறீங்க *irukk(r)iinga*	இருந்தீங்க *irundiinga*	இருப்பீங்க *iruppiinga*
3 PL (& HON)	இருக்குறாரு *irukk(r)aaru*	இருந்தாரு *irundaaru*	இருப்பாரு *iruppaaru*
3 PL (NON-POL)	இருக்குறாங்க *irukk(r)aanga*	இருந்தாங்க *irundaanga*	இருப்பாங்க *iruppaanga*
F POL	இருக்குறாங்க *irukk(r)aanga*	இருந்தாங்க *irundaanga*	இருப்பாங்க *iruppaanga*

Table 3.14: Paradigms of சாப்பிடு, all Tenses and PNG

PNG	Present	Past	Future
1 SG	சாப்பிடுறேன் *saappiḍreen*	சாப்பிட்டேன் *saappiṭṭeen*	சாப்பிடுவேன் *saappiḍuveen*
2 SG	சாப்பிடுறே *saappiḍree*	சாப்பிட்டே *saappiṭṭee*	சாப்பிடுவே *saappiḍuvee*
3 SG M	சாப்பிடுறான் *saappiḍraan*	சாப்பிட்டான் *saappiṭṭaan*	சாப்பிடுவான் *saappiḍuvaan*
3 SG F	சாப்பிடுறா *saappiḍraa*	சாப்பிட்டா *saappiṭṭaa*	சாப்பிடுவா *saappiḍuvaa*
3 SG N	சாப்பிடுறது *saappiḍradu*	சாப்பிட்டது *saappiṭṭadu*	சாப்பிடும் *saappiḍum*
1 PL	சாப்பிடுறோம் *saappiḍroom*	சாப்பிட்டோம் *saappiṭṭoom*	சாப்பிடுவோம் *saappiḍuvoom*
2 PL & Pol.	சாப்பிடுறீங்க *saappiḍriinga*	சாப்பிட்டீங்க *saappiṭṭiinga*	சாப்பிடுவீங்க *saappiḍuviinga*
3 PL (& HON)	சாப்பிடுறாரு *saappiḍraaru*	சாப்பிட்டாரு *saappiṭṭaaru*	சாப்பிடுவாரு *saappiḍuvaaru*
3 PL (NON-POL)	சாப்பிடுறாங்க *saappiḍraanga*	சாப்பிட்டாங்க *saappiṭṭaanga*	சாப்பிடுவாங்க *saappiḍuvaanga*
F POL	சாப்பிடுறாங்க *saappiḍraanga*	சாப்பிட்டாங்க *saappiṭṭaanga*	சாப்பிடுவாங்க *saappiḍuvaanga*

iru, i.e. simply க்க் *kk* without any ற் *r*. We therefore list both, by marking the *r* as optional, i.e. we give the tense marker as *kk(r)-*. The neuter form is also 'irregular' with this verb.

Note that any verbs formed of a compound with இரு *iru* are conjugated in the same way, e.g. எழுந்திரு *er̤undiru* 'arise, get up.' (But note that எழுந்திரு may be simplified to ஏந்திரு *eendiru* by deletion of ழ் *r̤*.)

3.6.1.3 சாப்பிடு *saappiḍu* 'eat' INF: சாப்பிட *saappiḍa* AVP: சாப்பிட்டு *saappiṭṭu* 'having eaten'

The complete paradigm of this verb is shown in Table 3.14.[13]

[13] Note that for neuter subjects, usually a different verb, தின்னு *tinnu*, is used with inanimates.

Table 3.15: Paradigms of வாங்கு *vaangu* 'buy, fetch, get', all Tenses and PNG

PNG	Present	Past	Future
1 SG	வாங்குறேன் *vaangureen*	வாங்கினேன் *vaangineen*	வாங்குவேன் *vaanguuveen*
2 SG	வாங்குறே *vaanguree*	வாங்கினே *vaanginee*	வாங்குவே *vaanguvee*
3 SG M	வாங்குறான் *vaanguraan*	வாங்கினான் *vaanginaan*	வாங்குவான் *vaanguvaan*
3 SG F	வாங்குறா *vaanguraa*	வாங்கினா *vaanginaa*	வாங்குவா *vaanguvaa*
3 SG N	வாங்குறது *vaanguradu*	வாங்கினது *vaanginadu*	வாங்கும் *vaangum*
1 PL	வாங்குறோம் *vaanguroom*	வாங்கினோம் *vaanginoom*	வாங்குவோம் *vaanguvoom*
2 PL & Pol.	வாங்குறீங்க *vaanguriinga*	வாங்கினீங்க *vaanginiinga*	வாங்குவீங்க *vaanguviinga*
3 PL (& HON)	வாங்குறாரு *vaanguraaru*	வாங்கினாரு *vaanginaaru*	வாங்குவாரு *vaanguvaaru*
3 PL (NON-POL)	வாங்குறாங்க *vaanguraanga*	வாங்கினாங்க *vaanginaanga*	வாங்குவாங்க *vaanguvaanga*
F POL	வாங்குறாங்க *vaanguraanga*	வாங்கினாங்க *vaanginaanga*	வாங்குவாங்க *vaanguvaanga*

3.6.1.4 வாங்கு *vaangu* 'buy.' INF: வாங்க *vaanga*; AVP: வாங்கி *vaangi* 'having bought'

The complete paradigm of this verb is shown in Table 3.15. With verbs of this class, the past இன் *in* may be pronounced உன் [ʉn], i.e. வாங்கினேன் *vaangineen* may be phonetically closer to *vaanguneen*, or there may be a very reduced vowel in this position.

3.6.1.5 வந்திடு *vandiḍu* 'definitely come' INF: வந்திட *vandiḍa;* AVP: வந்திட்டு *vandiṭṭu* 'having definitely come'

This verb is conjugated like சாப்பிடு *saappiḍu*, as in Table 3.14. Note that in some dialects, the present and future forms sometimes have -ṟ instead of ட், e.g. they have forms such as வந்திர்றேன் *vandirreen* 'I am coming for sure' and வந்திருவேன் *vandiruveen* 'I'll definitely come.

Table 3.16: Paradigms of படி *paḍi*, all Tenses and PNG

PNG	**Present**	**Past**	**Future**
1 SG	படிக்குறேன் *paḍikkreen*	படிச்சேன் *paḍicceen*	படிப்பேன் *paḍippeen*
2 SG	படிக்குறே *paḍikkuree*	படிச்சே *paḍiccee*	படிப்பே *paḍippee*
3 SG M	படிக்குறான் *paḍikkuraan*	படிச்சான் *paḍiccaan*	படிப்பான் *paḍippaan*
3 SG F	படிக்குறா *paḍikkraa*	படிச்சா *paḍiccaa*	படிப்பா *paḍippaa*
3 SG N	படிக்குறது *paḍikkradu*	படிச்சது *paḍiccadu*	படிக்கும் *paḍikkum*
1 PL	படிக்குறோம் *paḍikkuroom*	படிச்சோம் *paḍiccoom*	படிப்போம் *paḍippoom*
2 PL (& POL)	படிக்குறீங்க *paḍikkriinga*	படிச்சீங்க *paḍicciinga*	படிப்பீங்க *paḍippiinga*
3 PL & HON	படிக்குறாங்க *paḍikkraanga*	படிச்சாங்க *paḍiccaanga*	படிப்பாங்க *paḍippaanga*
3 PL (NON-POL)	படிக்குறாங்க *paḍikkraanga*	படிச்சாங்க *paḍiccaanga*	படிப்பாங்க *paḍippaanga*

But *all* dialects have the past with ட்ட், *ṭṭ* as in Table 3.14.

3.6.1.6 படி *paḍi* 'study' INF: படிக்க *paḍikka* AVP: படிச்சு *paḍiccu* 'having studied'

The complete paradigm of this verb is shown in Table 3.16.

Note that all verbs with stems that end in ள, இ or ய் of the strong type (with க்குற் *kkr* present and ப்ப் *pp* future) will have the past in ச்ச். Otherwise, they are just like verbs with த்த் *tt* pasts.

There is also a verb ஒடெ *oḍe* that is intransitive, and belongs to Class IIb (the complete paradigm of which is shown in Table 3.18). Intransitive verbs of this sort take only neuter subjects, i.e. ஒடெய்றது *oḍeyradu* 'it breaks (of its own accord, volition'. Such verbs thus only display the present, past and future neuter singular.

Table 3.17: Paradigms of Transitive ஒடெ *oḍe* 'break (s.t.)'

PNG	**Present**	**Past**	**Future**
1 SG	ஒடெக்குறேன் *oḍekkreen*	ஒடெச்சேன் *oḍecceen*	ஒடெப்பேன் *oḍeppeen*
2 SG	ஒடெக்குறே *oḍekkree*	ஒடெச்சே *oḍeccee*	ஒடெப்பே *oḍeppee*
3 SG M	ஒடெக்குறான் *oḍekkraan*	ஒடெச்சான் *oḍeccaan*	ஒடெப்பான் *oḍeppaan*
3 SG F	ஒடெக்குறா *oḍekkraa*	ஒடெச்சா *oḍeccaa*	ஒடெப்பா *oḍeppaa*
3 SG N	ஒடெக்குறது *oḍekkradu*	ஒடெச்சது *oḍeccadu*	ஒடெக்கும் *oḍekkum*
1 PL	ஒடெக்குறோம் *oḍekkroom*	ஒடெச்சோம் *oḍeccoom*	ஒடெப்போம் *oḍeppoom*
2 PL & Pol.	ஒடெக்குறீங்க *oḍekkriinga*	ஒடெச்சீங்க *oḍecciinga*	ஒடெப்பீங்க *oḍeppiinga*
3 PL (& HON)	ஒடெக்குறாங்க *oḍekkraanga*	ஒடெச்சாங்க *oḍeccaanga*	ஒடெப்பாங்க *oḍeppaanga*
F POL	ஒடெக்குறாங்க *oḍekkraanga*	ஒடெச்சாங்க *oḍeccaanga*	ஒடெப்பாங்க *oḍeppaanga*

Table 3.18: Neuter Paradigm of ஒடெ *oḍe* 'break (INTR)'

PNG	**Present**	**Past**	**Future**
3 SG N	ஒடெய்றது *oḍeyradu*	ஒடெஞ்சது *oḍenjadu*	ஒடெயும் *oḍeyum*

3.6.2 Neuter Past

Some verbs also have an irregular neuter past, i.e. a PNG marker or verb stem different from that of other verbs is used for the neuter past of these verbs.

The verbs போ *poo* 'go' and ஆகு *aahu* 'become' have the past neuter forms போச்சு and ஆச்சு, respectively. The expected forms *போனது *poonadu* and *ஆனது *aanadu* do not occur.

In some dialects, the neuter past marker ச்சு *ccu* or ச்சி is used with verbs other than போ *poo* and ஆகு *aahu*, i.e. one also encounters forms like ஆய்டுச்சி *aayḍucci* or ஆய்ருச்சி *aayrucci*, போய்டுச்சி *pooyḍucci* or போய்ருச்சி *pooyrucci*, etc. For some speakers, the ச்சி form is used only with the verbs போ *poo* and ஆகு *aahu*, either plain or when aspectually marked, i.e. as in these examples where the completive aspect marker (வி)டு *viḍu* is present.

With verbs that are aspectually marked with (வி)டு *(v)iḍu*, some speakers eliminate any overt PNG marker of the neuter past, that is, neither ச்சி *cci* nor அது *adu* is present; thus instead of வந்திட்டுது *vandiṭṭudu* or வந்திடுச்சி *vandiḍucci* 'it definitely came' one hears simply வந்திட்டு *vandiṭṭu* for 'it definitely came.'

3.6.3 Use of ச்சி *cci* with Class III Verbs

For still other speakers, however, the ச்சு/ச்சி past neuter is used with many other verbs as well, so that one encounters forms like சொல்லிச்சி *sollicci* 'it said' instead of the expected சொன்னது *sonnadu*, வந்திச்சி *vanducci* instead of வந்தது *vandadu* 'it came', etc. We will consider the use of ச்சு/ச்சி to be 'standard' only with போ *poo* and ஆகு *aaku*, although its use with other verbs is not wrong. It is helpful, however, to remember that in LT, the LT equivalent of ச்சு occurs usually only with போ *poo* and ஆகு *aahu*, and all other verbs have the 'regular' neuter past. A minor exception to this statement is that the use of ச்சு as a neuter past is *optional* with the so-called Class III verbs (those in ∮3.5.2) in LT, but not required. Thus, LT Class III verbs like வாங்கு *vaangu* may have neuter past வாங்கிற்று. Thus, the spoken equivalent வாங்கிச்சி *vaangicci* is not as unusual as is the occurrence of ச்சி *cci* with, e.g. இரு *iru* 'be' as in இருந்திச்சி *irunducci* (LT இருந்தது). The use of this latter is strongly identified with the dialects of the Kaveri delta area (Trichy and Tanjore areas), and is also a marker of Malaysian and Singaporean Tamil, whose ancestors emigrated in large numbers from those parts of Tamilnāḍu.

3.6.4 Neuter Future

The neuter future is exceptional also in that the regular future tense makers ப்ப், ப் or வ *pp-*, *p-*, *v-* do not occur. Instead, the neuter future is formed by the addition of the suffix உம் to the *infinitive* of the verb, with அ *a* deleted.

3.6.5 The Infinitive

The infinitive is a form of the verb that is not complete, i.e. it cannot occur alone in a sentence, but must be accompanied by some other verb, such as an auxiliary (modal) verb (cf. ∮3.9). In many languages of the world, the infinitive is the form listed in the dictionary as the basic form, but this is not the case for Tamil; the imperative serves this purpose, as the most unmarked, general form.

3.6.6 Infinitives of Strong Verbs

The suffix க்க is affixed to strong verb stems to form the infinitive. If the root of the strong verb ends in ரு, லு, ல்லு or ளு *-ru*, *-lu*, *-llu* or *-ḷu*, these endings are dropped before க்க.

- நட *naḍa*: நடக்க *naḍakka* 'to walk'
- கேளு *keeḷu*: கேக்க *keekka* 'to ask, hear'
- நில்லு *nillu*: நிக்க *nikka* 'to stand'

3.6.7 Infinitives of Other Verbs

Most other (weak) verbs use அ *a* as the infinitive morpheme; this ending is added directly to the verb stem. The final vowel of the root is always deleted.

- சொல்லு *sollu*: சொல்ல *solla* 'to tell'
- சாப்பிடு *saappiḍu*: சாப்பிட *saappiḍa* 'to eat'
- செய்யி *seyyi*: செய்ய *seyya* 'to do' (Note deletion of யி *yi* before addition of அ.)

3.6.8 Exceptions

The infinitives of the following verbs are unpredictable:

- போ *poo*: போக *pooha* 'to go'

- கொண்டா *koṇḍaa*: கொண்டார *koṇḍaara* 'to bring'
- வா *vaa*: வர *vara* 'to come'
- தா *taa*: தர *tara* 'to serve, give, bring'

3.7 Transitivity, Causation and Verb Classes

In Tamil there is a syntactic (and semantic) distinction between verbs which corresponds in most languages to what is called intransitive/transitive, or causative/non-causative. This has to do with whether an action has an object (either animate or inanimate) or whether it takes place without affecting some other person or thing.

Some native speakers of Tamil intuitively feel that the distinction in their language is not one of *cause and effect* but one of *volition* (Paramacivam 1979). That is, the important thing is whether an action is performed with the free will of the agent, as contrasted with his/her will being controverted or somehow impeded in its function, or controlled by something exterior to the person.

3.7.1 Phonological Correlates of Transitive/Intransitive Distinction

Whatever this distinction is in Tamil, it is not only a semantic/syntactic one, but also in some cases a phonological one, i.e. a transitive verb is distinguishable from an intransitive one, in some cases, by its phonological characteristics.

In English we also have pairs like 'rise' and 'raise' ('cause to rise'), 'sit' and 'set' ('cause to sit'), 'fall' and 'fell' ('cause to fall'), 'lie' and 'lay' ('cause to lie'), 'drink' and 'drench' ('cause to drink'), but aside from this small list, there are few others. Many English verbs can be either transitive or intransitive, e.g. 'hang' ('be suspended') and 'hang' ('suspend' something), though, like Tamil, some distinctions show up in the past tense, with 'hanged' meaning 'execute (a person) by hanging' ('He was hanged by the neck until dead) while 'hung' means 'suspend (an inanimate object)' ('I hung the pictures on the walls').

In Tamil there are many more sets like these English pairs, and it appears that historically this distinction may have been pervasive and all-inclusive, at least from the evidence in Proto-(South) Dravidian. However, in the development of the language some of the phonological characteristics have become lost or obliterated. Some, nevertheless, do remain and still function.

3.7.2 Strong/Weak vs. Transitive/Intransitive

The most obvious phonological characteristic that distinguishes transitive from intransitive verbs is that which has been called the distinction between strong verbs (those with present tense marker க்குற் *kkr*, past marker த்த்/ச்ச் *tt/cc*, and future marker ப்ப் *pp*) and weak verbs (present tense marker உற் *ur*, past இன் *in*, etc., and future வ *v-*. Strong verbs are *usually* transitive/causative and weak verbs are *usually* intransitive/non-causative.

Examples of strong transitive verbs are numerous, and need not be listed, as is also the case for weak intransitive verbs.

3.7.3 Exceptions

The exceptions to the statement (in ∮3.7), however, are more problematical:

- *Strong intransitive:*

  இரு *iru* 'be': இருக்குறேன் *irukkreen*, இருந்தேன் *irundeen*, இருப்பேன் *iruppeen*

  நட *naḍa* 'walk': நடக்குறேன் *naḍakkreen*, நடந்தேன் *naḍandeen*, நடப்பேன் *naḍappeen*

- *Weak transitive:*

  செய்யி *seyyi* 'do': செய்றேன் *seyreen*, செஞ்சேன் *senjeen*, செய்வேன் *seyveen*

  போடு *pooḍu* 'put': போடுறேன் *pooḍreen*, போட்டேன் *pooṭṭeen*, போடுவேன் *pooḍuveen*

3.7.4 Other Patterns Distinguishing Transitive and Intransitive

Aside from the usual situation described in ∮3.8.2, there are some other phonological characteristics of verbs which follow various sorts of patterns.

3.7.5 Stems with NC Versus CC

Other pairs are distinguished by a contrast between stems with a nasal consonant plus homorganic stop in the intransitive versus no nasal but double consonant stop in the transitive/causative.

- திரும்பு *tirumbu* (INTR): 'return, come back'
- திருப்பு *tiruppu* (TR) 'return (s.t.), bring back'

Sometimes there are verbs where the semantic relationship is obscured historically, as in:

தூங்கு *tuungu* 'sleep' vs. தூக்கு *tuukku* 'lift'

The semantic relationship here may have originally been தூங்கு *tuungu* 'hang, be suspended' (e.g. in a hammock) vs. தூக்கு *tuukku* 'hang, suspend something' (e.g. hang up a hammock).

3.7.6 Causative Pairs with Doubled Stem-Final Consonant

Some intransitive verbs have transitive analogs formed by doubling the final consonant of the intransitive member:

- ஓடு *oodu* (INTR) 'run'

  ஓட்டு *oottu* 'cause to run; drive'
- ஊது *uudu* (INTR) 'blow'

  ஊத்து *uuttu* 'pour, cause to flow'
- ஊறு *uuru* 'ooze, flow'

  ஊத்து (LT ஊற்று) 'pour, squeeze'
- ஆகு *aahu* 'become'

  ஆக்கு *aakku* 'cause to become, make (s.t. become s.t.)'

Such pairs are usually both Class III verbs.

3.7.7 Causative Marking with an Added Suffix வி or ப்பி

- தெரி *teri* 'know'

  தெரிவி *terivi* 'cause to know, make known, teach, inform'
- அனுப்பு *anuppu* 'send'

  அனுப்புவி *anuppuvi* 'cause to send, dispatch'

Weak verbs (with futures in வ *v*) form the causative this way. Strong verbs, with future markers in ப்ப் *pp*, have a causative formative ப்பி *ppi*. Both then become members of Class VI.

- படி *padi* 'study'
- படிப்பி *padippi* 'cause to study, teach'

For some speakers, these kinds of derived causatives are appropriate only for a LT style of Tamil; others use them in ST, too.

3.7.8 Derived Causatives

In modern ST a newer causative stem formation process is becoming more common. Under this process a new stem is derived from the past stem of another verb, e.g.

- நடத்து *naḍattu* 'cause to run, go; manage' (from நட *naḍa*)
- படுத்து *paḍuttu* 'cause to feel' (from படு *paḍu* 'feel, experience')

Note that although the past stem of படு *paḍu* 'feel' is பட்ட் *paṭṭ* rather than படுத்த் *paḍutt-*, the causative is formed on the past stem of படு *paḍu* 'lie', a Class VI verb, but used as the causative of படு *paḍu* 'feel' also.

3.8 Modal Auxiliaries

The English so-called modal auxiliaries 'may, can, must, might, should, ought, could', etc., have their Tamil equivalents in auxiliary verbs that are attached to the infinitive of the verb. If that verb happens to be aspectually marked (cf. ∮3.10) the modal is attached to the infinitive of the aspect marker. The negative forms of the modals differ from the positive forms, often strikingly, but behave syntactically the same. The Tamil modal verbs are invariant for PNG, but some exhibit a basic distinction between habitual and non-habitual action, and some can be distinguished for tense, especially in the negative. Pragmatic considerations enter in, because the speech act may result in the giving (or denying) of permission, or prohibition of certain actions.

The Table in 3.19 oversimplifies things to a great extent, because negation with modality tends to be skewed, i.e. the SCOPE of the negation can vary: one can be negating the need to do something, or emphasizing the need *not* to do something. This results in different negative forms for the same positive modal verb. Modal verbs also often involve a semantic component of HABITUALITY so there can be a contrast between simple one-time negation, and habitual negation.

Tamil tends to omit pronouns (cf. ∮4.2) when it is clear to speaker and hearer who the actors are, for example, when verbs are clearly marked for person-number-gender. But in sentences where pronouns have been deleted, and the verbs are themselves negated, there can be other (perhaps serious) pragmatic considerations. Modal verbs are good candidates for these pragmatic ambiguities, since they are not marked for person-number-gender; if the situation is compounded by pronoun deletion, speakers and hearers may not communicate clearly. For example, அட்டும் *aṭṭum* is normally used with

Table 3.19: Tamil Modal Verbs

English	*Tamil*	*Negative*	*Other negatives*
can; be able	முடி *muḍi*	முடியல்லே *muḍiyalle*	முடியாது *muḍiyaadu*
may; let's	லாம் *laam*		கூடாது 'should not' *kuuḍaadu*
must, should, ought	(வே)ணும் *(vee)ṇum*	வேண்டியதுல்லே *(vee)ṇḍiyadulle*	வேண்டாம் 'need not' *veeṇḍaam*
let; may	அட்டும் *aṭṭum*	கூடாது *kuuḍaadu*	வேண்டாம் *veeṇḍaam*

third persons in mind, e.g. அவன் வரட்டும் *avan varaṭṭum* 'let him come', இருக்கட்டும் *irukkaṭṭum* 'let it be' in declarative sentences. But in interrogatives, the implicature is that the speaker is *asking* to be given permission, not asking whether someone else has (or is granted) permission:

Q: வரட்டுமா? *varaṭṭumaa?* 'May I go (i.e. go and come), may I take leave?'

A: வாங்க *vaanga* 'please go (and come).'

Q: அவன் வரட்டுமா? *avan varaṭṭumaa?* 'May he come?'

A: ஓ வரட்டுமே *oo, varaṭṭumee* 'Oh, certainly he may'

In Table 3.20 are more examples of the complexities of the use of modals. Note that since modals are never marked for PNG, the same forms are used regardless of the person-number-gender of the subject. Note also that the modal வேணும் *veeṇum* has the form ணும் *ṇum* after a verb, but the full form வேணும் *veeṇum* when it stands alone. This deletion of வே *vee-* does not occur with வேண்டாம் *veeṇḍaam*.[14]

3.8.1 Homonymy with Lexical Verbs

It may be noticed that some of the modals in ∮3.9.1 as well as some of the aspect markers in ∮3.12 ff. seem to resemble certain 'lexical' or 'main' verbs.

[14] The deletion of intervocalic வ *v* is complicated, and while some regular principles of its application may be noted, there are some irregularities that are difficult to explain. I have dealt with this extensively in Schiffman 1993.

Table 3.20: Complexities of Tamil Modal Verbs

English	*Tamil*	*Negative*	*Negative Habitual*
'be able'	வரமுடியும் *varamuḍiyum* 'X can come'	வரமுடியல்லெ *varamuḍiyalle* 'X couldn't come'	வரமுடியாது *varamuḍiyaadu* 'X is never able to come'
'may' ('be permitted')	போகலாம் *poohalaam* '(s.o.) may go'	போகவேண்டாம் *poohaveeṇḍaam* '(s.o.) doesn't have to go'	போகக்கூடாது *poohakuuḍaadu* 'shouldn't go'
'let's go' (hortative)	போகலாம் *poohalaam* 'let's go'	போகவேண்டாம் *poohaveeṇḍaam* 'let's not go'	போகக்கூடாது *poohakuuḍaadu* 'don't let's go'
'(s.o.) must eat' should, ought need to, have to	சாப்பிடணும் *saappiḍaṇum* 'want to eat'	சாப்பிடவேண்டியதுல்லெ *saappiḍaveeṇḍiyadulle* 'didn't want to eat'	சாப்பிடவேண்டாம் *saappiḍaveeṇḍaam* 'isn't supposed to eat'
'let (s.o.) go'	போகட்டும் *poohaaṭṭum* 'let (s.o.) go'	போகக்கூடாது *poohakuuḍaadu* 'don't let (s.o.) go'	போகவேண்டாம் *poohaveeṇḍaam* 'doesn't need to go'

An example above is முடி *muḍi* (II INTR) 'be finished.' It is best to consider these modals and aspect markers to be totally different and separate from the lexical verbs they resemble, as their meanings and their use are quite different. Historically, the may be derived from or metaphorically related to lexical verbs, but in the modern language, equating them causes more problems than it solves.

3.8.2 Use of Aspect Marker ஆகு *aahu* with Modal ணும் *ṇum*

The aspect marker ஆகு *aahu* (cf. ∮3.12.8) is often used to indicate that the action of the main verb to which it is attached is the 'expected result.' Thus, a sentence like போஸ்ட் வந்தாச்சு *poosṭ vandaaccu* means 'the mail has come, as was expected', or 'the mail finally came.'

When the modal ணும் *ṇum* 'must' is affixed to a verb marked with the aspect marker ஆகு *aahu*, the construction means 'X MUST happen because Y expects it' and thus indicates that a great deal of certainty or definiteness is involved. This is perhaps equivalent to the English adverb 'absolutely' rather than 'definitely', i.e. 'You absolutely have to come' (for many speakers) is more definite than 'You definitely have to come.' Compare:

- நீங்க வரணும் *niinga varaṇum* 'You must come'
- நீங்க வந்திடணும் *niinga vandiḍaṇum* 'You definitely must come'
- நீங்க வந்தாகணும் *niinga vandaahaṇum* 'You ABSOLUTELY MUST come'

Since ஆகு *aahu* is an aspect marker, it is added to the PAST stem (the AVP) of the verb.

3.9 Verbal Aspect

Tamil has a number of verbs, sometimes referred to as 'aspectual verbs'[15] that are added to a main or lexical verb to provide semantic distinctions such as duration, completion, habituality, regularity, continuity, simultaneity, definiteness, expectation of result, remainder of result, current relevance, benefaction, antipathy, and certain other notions.

Researchers have generally found these aspectual verbs difficult to describe in a categorical way, and not until Annamalai 1981 has any attempt

[15] They have been referred to by various names: aspectual verbs, aspect markers, aspectual auxiliaries, verbal extensions, post-verbs, intensive verbs, etc.

been made to treat aspect in Tamil (or for that matter, any Dravidian language) as a *variable* component of the grammar. This makes it difficult to give hard and fast statements about aspect in Tamil; we must recognize both the variability of usage, and that aspect is a category that is in the process of *grammaticalization*, that is, certain verbs are still in the process of becoming grammaticalized in Tamil.

Tamil aspect is a category that is on the road to grammaticalization. Some aspectual verbs are already fully aspectualized, others are partly aspectualized, but some are just getting started. Furthermore aspect is a variable category within the grammar of a given speaker, but is also variable across dialects and idiolects, and between LT and ST.[16]

3.9.1 Aspect and Commentary

Tamil aspectual verbs provide commentary about the **manner** in which an action occurred, especially how it began or ended, whether it was intentional or unintentional, whether it had an effect on the speaker or on someone else, whether it continued, was interrupted, is habitual, and so on. Some of these notions are what have been considered ASPECTUAL[17] in other languages (having to do with the completion or non-completion, the continuity or duration, the manner of inception or completion) but some have little or no relation semantically to classical notions of aspect. These 'extended' uses of aspectual verbs sometimes therefore involve value judgments by the speaker about the actions of others, i.e. they indicate what the speaker's **attitude** about the verbal action in question is; their aspectual 'meaning' is a *metaphorical extension* of their literal meaning.

3.9.2 Where Do Aspectual Verbs Come From?

Most aspectual verbs are derived historically and metaphorically[18] from some lexical verb that is still in use in Tamil but has its own lexical meaning. The 'meaning' of aspectual verbs is arrived at by a metaphoric extension of the literal meaning of the original lexical verb, which then becomes

[16] Most examples given here are from ST rather than LT, but many are quoted from their LT versions given elsewhere.

[17] This term comes from Russian *vid* which means 'point of view'; in Tamil the term நோக்கு *nookku* or வினை நோக்கு *vin̠ai nookku* is quite apt here.

[18] One can either treat the notion of being 'derived' from something else as historical or as a process of derivational morphology, using the rhetorical device of the *metaphor*. Typically, native and missionary grammarians have dealt with aspectual verbs as if they were special or *idiosyncratic* usages of lexical verbs, rather than being semantically and synchronically different. Arden, for example, refers to them as *intensifying* the meaning of the lexical verb (Arden 1942:282-3).

primarily grammatical or syntactic in its 'meaning', and can then usually only be related to the lexical meaning of the verb from which it is derived by considering what kinds of metaphoric extensions of meanings might have been involved.

3.9.3 Syntax of Aspectual Verbs

Syntactically, aspectual verbs are added to the adverbial participle (AVP)[19] of the lexical ('main') verb. Aspectual verbs then are marked for tense and PNG, since the AVP preceding them cannot be so marked. Morphologically they then act identically to the lexical verb from which they are derived, i.e. take the tense markers etc. of the class of lexical verb they are identical to.

3.10 Aspect and Markedness

Since in Tamil aspect is an optional rather than an obligatory category, aspect must be seen as a polarity of marked versus unmarked. The lack of occurrence of an aspectual verb indicates that the aspectual notion that is not present is unmarked, or neutral, rather than absent. That is, a sentence that contains a completive marker, such as விடு *(v)iḍu*, certainly marks completive aspect, but its absence is not a 'zero' marker for non-completion, the way absence of a plural marker in English is a 'zero' marker of singularity. Absence of a completive aspectual verb does not indicate that there was no completion, but simply that it is unmarked, and therefore vague, for completion.[20]

[19] This is a form of the verb that is essentially its past stem minus person-number-gender (PNG) markers; it expresses in ordinary syntax the notion that some verbal action preceded another verbal action, that expressed by the next verb in the sentence. A sentence may have only one finite verb; all other verbs must be non-finite, such as the adverbial participle (AVP), the infinitive, or some other. The AVP is essentially the past stem of the verb, and has various morphological and syntactic functions. We give examples of the AVP forms when we list paradigms of verbs; the function of the AVP is explained in Chapter 6, Syntax (∮6.8.3)

[20] Tamil (and other Dravidian languages) differ from, e.g. English in this respect, since it seems to be the case that English speakers share the presupposition that an action is completed unless otherwise stated, whereas Tamil speakers seem to share the presupposition that an action is not completed unless stated as definitely complete. Thus a sentence like 'I went to the library yesterday' seems odd if followed by 'but I never got there.' Rather, the first sentence would have to be replaced by something like 'I *started out* for the library yesterday' if it is to be followed by 'but I never got there.' In Tamil, in contrast, the analogous sentence நான் நேத்து லய்பிரெரிக்கி போனேன் *naan neettu laybrerikki pooneen* is not strange if followed by ஆனா போய் சேரல்லெ *aanaa, pooy seeralle* ('I never arrived') since போனேன் *pooneen* 'I went' is unmarked for

3.11 Primarily Aspectual Verbs

The aspectual verbs that are primarily aspectual (and minimally attitudinal or metaphorical) are விடு *(v)iḍu* 'completive', கிட்டிரு *kiṭṭiru* 'durative', வையி *vayyi* 'future utility', ஆகு *aahu* 'finality, expected result', வா *vaa* 'iterative', போ *poo* 'change of state', இரு *iru*[1] 'perfect', இரு *iru*[2] 'result remains', and இரு *iru*[3] 'epistemic.'[21]

The aspectual verbs that are primarily attitudinal (but nonetheless aspectual) are தள்ளு *taḷḷu* 'distributive', 'exdeictic',[22] தொலெ *tole* 'riddance', போடு *pooḍu* 'malicious intent', and some others that vary from dialect to dialect.[23] Finally, there is கோ *koo* 'self-benefactive', that displays more versatility than almost any other AM except possibly இரு *iru* 'be; perfect; epistemic; suppositional.' It displays both aspectual and attitudinal semantics, and is perhaps the most radically different in phonology from its lexical analog of all the AM's.

3.11.1 Inventory of Aspect Markers

An inventory of aspectual verbs is given in Table 3.21.

3.11.2 Morphophonemics of Aspectual Verbs

In fact, one of the signs that lexical material is being grammaticalized is that the phonology of the item begins to act differently from its lexical analogs. This is particularly true of கோ *koo* and விடு *viḍu*.

3.11.3 Primarily Aspectual Verbs

3.11.4 விடு *(v)iḍu* 'completive'

This aspectual verb adds a notion that an action was, is, or will be complete or definite. It is similar to aspectual verbs in other languages (Russian,

completion—it declares simply that motion away from the addressee occurred. However, if போனேன் *pooneen* were changed to add aspectual விடு *(v)iḍu*, i.e. போய்ட்டேன் *pooyṭṭeen* then adding ஆனா போய் சேரல்லெ *aanaa, pooy seeralle* is odd.

[21] I have dealt with the details of the three இருs *iru*'s in my 1969 dissertation.

[22] That is, away from the speaker.

[23] The attitudinal aspectual verbs are not a closed set, and different dialects may use different verbs as markers of aspectual and metaphoric nuance. The non-attitudinal aspectual verbs are a closed set and show less variation from dialect to dialect. But there are some differences between LT and ST, even in this set. Annamalai 1981 also lists கொடு *koḍu* 'benefactive.' I am indebted to Annamalai for his many cogent examples of Tamil aspectual verbs.

Table 3.21: Inventory of Aspectual Verbs, with Examples

AM	Meaning	Example	Gloss
இடு *iḍu*	'Definitely, for sure'	வந்த்-இடு-ங்க *vand-iḍu-nga*	'be sure to come'
(LT விடு)	COMPLETIVE	போயிடலாம் *pooyiḍalaam*	'one may go **along**'
		பாத்துட்டேன் *paattuṭṭeen*	'I **definitely** saw'
இரு[1] *iru*	PERFECT tense CURRENT RELEVANCE	வந்திருக்குறேன் *vandirukkreen* போயிருந்தப்ப *pooyirundappa*	'I **have** come (and am still here)' 'when (x) went and **stayed**'
இரு[2] *iru*	STATIVE	பாத்திருக்கணும் *paattirukkaṇum*	'(x) must **have** seen
இரு[3] *iru*	SUPPOSITIONAL	மழெ பெஞ்சிருக்கு *mar̤e penjirukku*	'it **seems** to **have** rained'
கிட்டிரு *kiṭṭiru*	DURATIVE	பேசிகிட்டிருக்கோம் *peesikiṭṭirukkoom*	'we have **been** **speaking**'
		வந்துகிட்டிருப்பேன் *vandukiṭṭiruppeen*	'I will **be** com**ing**'
கோ *koo*	REFLEXIVE SELF-BENEFACTIVE	வாங்கிக்கோங்க *vaangikoonga*	'buy **for yourself**'
	SIMULTANEOUS	போட்டுகிட்டு *pooṭṭukiṭṭu*	'**while** wearing'
ஆச்சு *aaccu*	FINALITY EXPECTED RESULT	வந்தாச்சு *vandaaccu*	'it **finally** came'
போடு *pooḍu*	COMPLETIVE	எழுதிபோட்டான் *er̤udipooṭṭaan*	'he wrote it **off**'
	MALICIOUS INTENT	கொண்ணு போட்டாங்க *koṇṇupooṭṭaanga*	'they killed (s.o.) **in cold blood**'
தள்ளு *taḷḷu*	COMPLETIVE DISTRIBUTIVE	(x) குடுத்து தள்ளாரு *kuḍuttu taḷnaaru*	'he gave (s.t.) **away**'
தொலெ *tole*	COMPLETIVE IMPATIENCE, DISGUST	போய் தொலெ! *pooy tole!*	'go **get lost**!'
வையி *vayyi*	FUTURE UTILITY ('in reserve')	குடிச்சி வெப்போம் *kuḍicciveppoom*	'we'll **tank up** on (s.t.)'
போ *poo*	COMPLETIVE CHANGE OF STATE	ஒடெஞ்சிபோகும் *oḍenjipoohum*	'it'll **get** broken'

Hindi, etc.) that impart the notion of 'PERFECTIVE' (not PERFECT). Its lexical correlate is விடு *viḍu* 'leave, let.'[24]

Examples:

(29) அவன் போயிட்டான்
avan pooyṭṭaan
he went-COMPL-PNG

'He went away; he's definitely gone.'

(30) நான் வந்திடுறேன்
naan vand-iḍreen
I come-COMPL-PRES-PNG

'I am definitely coming; I'll come for sure.'

(31) அவனெ அனுப்புச்சுடு
avane anuppuccuḍu
him send-CAUS-COMPL-IMP

'Send him away; get rid of him.'

(32) அதெ சாப்பிட்டுட்டேன்
ade saappiṭṭuṭṭeen
it-acc eat-COMPL-PAST-PNG

'I ate it all up.'

3.11.5 வையி *vayyi* 'future utility, put away, put somewhere for safekeeping'

The aspectual verb வையி *vayyi*[25] has a lexical analog வையி *vayyi* 'take, put s.t. somewhere for safekeeping.' It is usually used with transitive main verbs only (since the main verb வையி *vayyi* is definitely transitive), but may occur with some intransitive verbs, such as சிரி *siri* 'laugh' (see example below). Other aspectual verbs (e.g. விடு *(v)iḍu*) may follow வையி *vayyi* , but when present வையி *vayyi* always follows immediately after the AVP of the main verb. The aspectual notion conveyed by *vayyi* is the notion that some action is performed because it will have future consequences, use or benefit; it is often translatable as 'in reserve' or 'up', e.g. 'stock up (on)', 'read up (on) something, 'study up on something', 'lay in (or up) a

[24] Note the phonological differences between விடு *(v)iḍu* 'completive' and விடு *viḍu* 'leave, let': the completive AM has a deletable வ *v*, while the initial வ *v* of the lexical verb is never deleted. The question of whether the completive AM actually requires an initial *v* in its underlying form (which is then deleted), and the whole issue of intervocalic *v*-deletion is one I have tried to deal with elsewhere (Schiffman 1993).

[25] Annamalai (1981) calls this the 'verb of anticipated consequence.'

stock of (something)', and implies that an action is done with an eye to future consequences, or preemptively. In the examples below, the glossed portion within parentheses is not literally present in the Tamil sentence, but is given as one or more of the semantic consequences that the use of வையி *vayyi* implies.

(33) தண்ணியெ குடிச்சு வெப்போம்
      taṇṇiye   kuḍiccu veppoom
      water-ACC drink   FUTUTIL-FUT-1PL

      'We will tank up on water (We will drink our fill of water so as to avoid future thirst).'

(34) தலெவர்   கூட்டத்தெ   தள்ளிவெச்சார்
      talevar   kuuṭṭatte˘   taḷḷi-veccaar
      head-person assemblage-ACC push-FUTUTIL-PAST-3 SG-EPIC

      'The chairman postponed the meeting.'

(35) அம்மா பிள்ளெங்களுக்கு தோசெ சுட்டுவெச்சா
      ammaa piḷḷengaḷukku   doose   suṭṭu-veccaa
      mother children-DAT   pancake heat-FUTUTIL-PAST-3 SG-FM

      'The mother cooked up some dosas (to have ready) for the children.'

(36) கல்யாண விட்டுலெ   தும்மி கிம்மி   வெச்சிடாதெ
      kalyaaṇa viiṭṭle   tummi kimmi   veccidaadee
      marriage house-LOC sneeze ECHOREDUP FUTUTIL-NEG-IMP

      'Don't do anything stupid like sneeze or anything during the wedding ceremony (and bring bad omens).'

(37) போலீஸ்கிட்டெ எதெயாவது   ஒளரிவெக்காதெ
      pooliiskiṭṭe edeyaavadu   oḷari-vekkaadee
      police-to   something-or-other babble-FUTUTIL-NEG-IMP

      'Don't go blabbing to the police (and make more trouble).'

(38) நான் நாயெ   கட்டிவெக்கல்லெ
      naan naaye   kaṭṭi-vekkalle
      I   dog-ACC bind-FUTUTIL-NEG

      'I neglected to tie up the dog (and prevent a nuisance, etc.).'

(39) சுந்தரம்   தன் மகளுக்கு   நல்ல எடத்துலெ கல்யாணம்
      sundaram tan mahaḷukku   nalla edaṭṭle   kalyaaṇam
      Sundaram his daughter-DAT nice place-LOC marriage
      செஞ்சுவெச்சார்
      senju-veccaar
      did-FUTUTIL

'Sundaram got his daughter married off well (i.e. nicely set up for the future).'

(40)   டைரெக்டர் ஒரு ஜோக் சொன்னார் நான் சும்மா சிரிச்சு
    dairekṭar *oru jook* *sonnaar;* *naan summaa siriccu*
    Director   a   joke   said;   I   just   laugh
  வெச்சேன்
    vecceen
    FUTUTIL-PAST-1 SG

'The Director told a joke, and I laughed (dutifully, just in case.)'

3.11.6 வையி *vayyi* 'future utility.' and Tense Marking

The AM வையி *vayyi* can occur with other aspect markers, but வையி *vayyi* always immediately follows the main verb, with other AM's following வையி *vayyi*. It is used only with TRANSITIVE verbs. The idea underlying the use of வையி *vayyi* is that the action of the main verb is performed with the intent of its having some 'future benefit' or 'future utility.' Ordinary tense forms may be affixed to வையி *vayyi* so that வையி *vayyi* does not replace tense markers, i.e. வையி *vayyi* is not a substitute for future tense, for example. வையி *vayyi* as an AM is translated in English in many different ways, but one common way is verb + 'up', e.g. stock up, buy up, lay up, do in advance, in reserve, etc.

That is, we can get the following contrasts:

(41) ஐஸ் வாட்டரெ குடிச்சி வெப்போம்
    ais   *vaatṭare kuḍicci veppoom*

    'We will drink ice water for future use.'

(42) ஐஸ் வாட்டரெ குடிச்சி வெச்சோம்
    ais   *vaatṭare kuḍicci veccoom*

    'We drank (tanked up on) ice water.'

(43) ஐஸ் வாட்டரெ குடிச்சி வெக்குறோம்
    ais   *vaatṭare kuḍicci vekkroom*

    'We drink (tank up on) ice water.'

3.11.7 இரு *iru*

இரு *iru*, which is identical in morphology to the copula, gives a number of aspectual nuances to a sentence. One is the nuance that we have in English with the 'perfect' tense, i.e. that something has happened, but the result of the action continues, or is still relevant. நான் வந்திருக்குறேன் *vandirukkreen* 'I have come (and I'm still here).' It must not be confused with (வ)இடு *vidu* although it is easy to do so in dialects where it is realized phonetically in the non-past, at least, as இரு *iru*. However, the tense markers of the two are quite different.[26] Tamil uses இரு *iru* often for verbal actions directed away from the speaker, since the results of such actions are not so obvious to the speaker. If a person says

(44) நான் வந்திருக்குறேன்
naan vandirukkreen
'I have come (and I'm still here).'

it is obvious that the person is present; what the speaker is emphasizing is perhaps the relevance of his/her arrival to the present. But if a person says

(45) நான் இந்தியாவுக்கு போயிருக்குறேன்
naan indyaavukku pooyirukkreen
'I have (gone) been to India.'

what is being emphasized is not that the person is still there (in India) but that at some point in the past the result of the action remained for some time, that is, s/he not only started to go to India, but actually got there.

Another nuance is 'stative' or 'epistemic', i.e. 'it must be the case that such and such', e.g.

(46) அவன் இந்தியாவலெ போய் சேந்திருக்கணும்
avan indyaavle pooy seendirukkaṇum
'He must have arrived in India (he must be there by now; it must be the case that he is there now).'[27]

A third use of இரு *iru* is 'suppositional' as in மழெ பெஞ்சிருக்கு *maṟe penjirukku* 'it seems that it rained' (lit. it will have rained).

3.11.8 ஆகு *aahu* 'expected result; finality'

This aspectual verb has the lexical analog ஆகு *aahu* 'become'. It is usually found only in the neuter past, i.e. ஆச்சு *aaccu*. Suffixed to a main verb it

[26](வ)இடு *(v)iḍu* has the tense marker இடுற் *iḍur* or இர்ற் *irr* for present; இட்ட் *iṭṭ* for past, and இடுவ் *iḍuv* or இருவ் *iruv* for future. இரு *iru* has the tense markers க்குற் *kkr* for present, ந்த் *nd* for past, and ப்ப் *pp* for future.

[27]This is similar to sentences like English 'he must like peanut butter' which does not mean 'he is required to like peanut butter, but 'It must be the case that he likes peanut butter, because he eats it a lot etc.'

expresses the notion that the action was expected, or occurred after a long wait, or as a regularly expected occurrence.

(47) போஸ்ட் வந்தாச்சு
poost̤ vand-aaccu
mail came-XPRESLT

'The mail has come (as it usually does by this time of day).'

(48) இந்த கணக்குகளெல்லாம் பாத்தாச்சு
inda kaṇakkukaḷ-ellaam paatt-aaccu
this bills-all seen-XPRESLT

'These bills have all been checked (as they were supposed to be).'

(49) சாப்பிட்டாச்சா?
saappiṭṭ-aaccaa?
eat-XPRESLT-Q

'Have you eaten? (as you ought to have, given the time of day)'

3.11.9 ஆகு *aahu* 'expected result'

The AM ஆகு *aahu* is completive, but also adds a nuance of finality, i.e. that the result was expected, or is customary.

(50) தபால் வந்தாச்சு
tabaal vand-aaccu

'The mail came (as usual)' or 'The mail finally came.'

(51) இந்த கணக்கு எல்லாம் பாத்தாச்சு
inda kaṇakku ellaam paattaaccu
'These bills have all been checked'

Because of the non-agreement of the apparent subject with ஆச்சு *aaccu*, sentences with this AM often translate best in English by passive constructions, where the 'agent' of the action is not specified. This is apparent in the example immediately above; the literal translation might be 'the seeing of these bills is finally completed' but the looser, better translation is the 'passive' one shown above. Since Tamil has no real passive, however, the passive translations in English must be attributed to the 'agent-less' nature of the Tamil sentence.

3.11.10 போடு *pooḍu* 'malicious intent'

This verb has an analogous lexical verb போடு *pooḍu* which means 'put, drop; plunk down; serve (food)' or 'put on (clothes)'. There is a semantic notion of some lack of care with this verb, so if deliberate careful placing or setting is intended, வையி *vayyi* is used instead. This verb is appropriate as used for serving food, since in order to avoid contact (and ritual pollution), food is often 'dropped' on the plate, rather than placed carefully. The AM போடு *poodu* varies semantically more than some AM's; for many the notion conveyed is that of bad faith, bad motives or even malicious intent.[28] For others the main notion implied by the use of போடு *poodu* is that speakers think of other speakers' motives as involving careless disregard for the likes and desires of others, malice aforethought, etc. When bad motives are being attributed, the most felicitious English translations for these AM's are with expletives or pejorative adjectives, etc. Phonologically, the AM போடு *poodu* may be reduced to ப்டு *ptu* by a by-no-means regular rule that deletes long vowels in morphemes that are involved in the grammaticalization process.[29]

(52) *neettu varakkuudaadunnu sonneenee aanaa neettu paattu vanduptaanga*
yesterday come-NEG-NECESS-QT said-EMPH but yesterday FOCUS came-MALICE-TENSE-PNG
'I told them not to come yesterday, but they deliberately came **anyway** (the jerks!)'

(53) திருடங்க என் நாயெ கொண்ணுப்போட்டாங்க
tirudanga en naaye konnupttaanga
thieves my dog-ACC kill-MALICE-TENSE-PNG
'(Those dirty rotten) thieves (deliberately and in cold blood) went and killed my dog.'

(54) கொழந்தெ தாளெ கிழிச்சு போட்டது
korande taale kiriccu poottadu
child paper-ACC tear MALICE-TENSE-PNG
'The child (carelessly) tore the paper.'

(55) அவன் அஜாக்கிரதெயா கதவெ திறந்து போட்டுட்டு
avan ajaakkradeyaa kadave terandu poottuttu
he carelessly door-ACC opened MALICE
போயிருக்கான்
pooyirukkaan
go-PERF-PNG
'He has gone out, inconsiderately leaving the door ajar.'

[28] Annamalai (1985) calls this AM the verb of *casualness;* for him the main notion is that speakers attribute motives of 'lack of care, inconsiderateness' etc. to others when using this AM.

[29] This also happens with போல *poola* as noted earlier.

3.11.11 வா *vaa* 'iterative; connected continuity'

The aspectual verb வா *vaa* has a lexical analog வா *vaa* which of course means 'come.' The notion conveyed by aspectual *vaa* is that an occurrence is or was of long-standing duration, but more as a series of connected events (or waves of occurrences) rather than as uninterrupted continuity. (The latter is expressed by கிட்டிரு *kiṭṭiru*.) வா *vaa* may often express a kind of 'narrative' or 'historical' (or perhaps even 'mythological') past, describing an action that was common practice in a past time. (Since it is rarely used in ST, the example below is in LT rather than ST.)[30]

(56) அந்த காலத்தில் இந்தியாவில் அனேக அரசர்கள் ஆண்டு
anta kaalattil intiyaavil an̲eeka aracarkaḷ aaṇṭu
those times-in India-in many kings rule
வந்தார்கள்
vantaarkaḷ
ITER-PAST-3 PL

'In those times, many kings were ruling in India.'

3.11.12 போ *poo* 'change of state'

The aspectual verb போ *poo* resembles the lexical verb போ *poo* 'go' in its morphology. It is used to express the notion that a change of state has definitely taken place (or will definitely occur). As such it is aspectually completive but the main verbs to which it is attached always themselves have some semantic notion of change; the addition of போ *poo* shows that the change is complete. Usually the net result is also judged to be unfortunate or undesirable.

(57) அவன் செத்து போனான்
avan settu poonaan
he died CHGOFST

'He died. (He is definitely dead, alas.)'

(58) அது கெட்டு போச்சு
adu keṭṭu pooccu
it spoiled CHGOFST

'It got spoiled.'

[30] This aspectual verb is often erroneously translated as English 'used to', e.g. 'Many kings used to rule at that time,' whereas 'used to' probably ought to be reserved for translating *habitual* actions, which வா *vaa* does not express.

(59) துணியெல்லாம் காஞ்சு போகும்
      tuṇiyellaam   kaanju   pookum
      clothes-all   dry   CHGOFST-NTR-FUT

      'The clothes will all get dry.'

போ *poo* as an aspect marker 'change of state' is often used with verbs
that themselves indicate a 'change of state', such as கெடு *keḍu* 'spoil' and
ஆறு *aaru* 'cool.' The use of போ *poo* for change of state usually implies that
the change of state in question was undesirable, or unforeseen.

- முத்தி போ *mutti poo* 'go to seed'

- பெருகி போ *peruhi poo* 'get big(ger)'

- ஆறி போ *aari poo* 'cool off'

- முழுகி போ *muṛuhi poo* 'sink; get ruined'

- காஞ்சு போ *kaanju poo* 'dry up, wither, fade'

- கெட்டு போ *keṭṭu poo* 'get spoiled, rotten'

- ஏற்பட்டு போ *eerpaṭṭu poo* 'get so that, develop'

- ஒடெஞ்சி போ *oḍenji poo* 'get broken'

- செத்து போ *settu poo* 'die'

- அழுகி போ *aṛuhi poo* 'rot, get overripe'

3.11.13 Primarily Attitudinal Aspectual Verbs

The aspectual verbs that express, in addition to various aspectual notions,
notions about the speaker's **attitude** toward actions or other speakers, are,
as mentioned, தள்ளு *taḷḷu* 'distributive', தொலெ *tole* 'riddance', போடு *pooḍu*
'malicious intent', and others that we will mention only in passing.

3.11.14 தள்ளு *taḷḷu* 'distributive', 'riddance', 'exdeixis'

The main verb that this AM is derived from is தள்ளு *taḷḷu* 'push, shove.' In
addition to its basic aspectual notion implying completion, தள்ளு *taḷḷu* also
gives the notion that an action 'got rid of' something; this may range from
the satisfaction of having cleaned up some sort of mess to that of giving all
one's wealth to the poor. There is also the notion that the recipients of this
distribution are unspecified. That is, a sentence like ராமன் புஸ்தகங்களெ

கொடுத்து தள்ளினான் *raaman pustahangaḷe koḍuttu taḷnaan* 'Raman gave away his books' will not have a dative-marked recipient. Verbs marked with தள்ளு *taḷḷu*, though in themselves completive, may have completive விடு *(v)iḍu* attached, for good measure, especially in the past tense.

(60) புஸ்தகம் புஸ்தகமா படிச்சு தள்ளுறியே
pustaham pustahamaa paḍiccu taḷriyee!
book book-ADV reading RIDDANCE-PNG

'You're reading book after book (and tossing them aside)!'

(61) நான் அந்த கடிதத்தெ படிச்சு தள்ளிட்டேன்
naan anda kaḍidatte paḍiccu taḷḷiṭṭeen
I that letter-ACC read EXDEIC

'I read that letter (and got the task out of the way, over with).'

(62) அவன் அடுத்த விட்டுகாரன் வாங்கின கடனெ எழுதி தள்ளனான்
avan aḍutta viiṭṭukkaaran vaangna kaḍane erudi taḷnaan
he next house-person taken loan-ACC wrote EXDEIC

'He wrote off (as a bad debt) the loan (taken, i.e.) owed (him) by his next-door neighbour.'

(63) ராஜா தன் பணத்தெ குடுத்து தள்ளிட்டான்
raajaa tan paṇatte kuḍuttu taḷḷiṭṭaan.
king his money-ACC give EXDEIC-TNS-PNG
'The king gave **away** all his money.'

3.11.15 தொலெ *tole* 'impatience, disgust'

This verb is related to the lexical verbs தொலெ *tole* 2 intr 'come to an end, die, be ruined' and தொலெ *tole* 6b tr, 'finish, exhaust, destroy, kill, rout.' There is a nominalization of this verb தொல்லெ *tolle* , which means 'trouble, care, vexation, perplexity.' The use of the AM தொலெ *tole* expresses the speaker's impatience or even disGust with another person's actions, and in some cases, even their general personal attributes. In English this would also often be translated by some expletive, or pejorative adjective ('the dumb kid', 'the rotten bastard').[31] Even though this AM expresses impatience and disGust and must be used with caution, it does not necessarily express lack of respect, since it may be used by wives to husbands, with politeness markers. When so used, the antipathy is toward the event rather than the person.

[31] The intransitive தொலெ *tole* is usually used with intransitive verbs, and probably originally the transitive was used only with transitive main verbs. But now transitive தொலெ *tole* may occur with intransitive main verbs as well; there is variability according to dialect.

(64) எழவு தீஸஸெ இன்னும் முடிச்சுதொலெக்கல்லெயா?
eṛavu tiisase innum muḍiccu-tolekkalleyaa?
worthless thesis-ACC still finish-IMPAT-NEG-Q

'Haven't you finished that troublesome thesis yet (slowpoke)?'

(65) போய்தொலெ, எங்கெயாவது போய்தொலெ
pooy-tole, engeyaavadu pooy-tole
go-IMPAT-IMP, somewhere go-IMPAT-IMP

'Oh all right go on, go, go somewhere, (what the hell).'

(66) அதெ சாப்பிட்டுட்டு போய்தொலெங்க!
ade saappiṭṭuṭṭu pooy-tolenga!
it-ACC eat-COMPL go-IMPAT-POL-IMP

'(please) eat it and go! (or there'll be even more botheration)'

(67) காரு தொந்தரவு கொடுத்துகிட்டிருந்தது; அதெ வித்து
kaaru tondaravu koḍuttu-kiṭṭirundadu; ade vittu
car trouble give-DURATIVE; it-ACC sell
தொலெச்சுட்டேன்
toleccuṭṭeen.
IMPAT-COMPL-PAST-PNG

'My car was giving me trouble; I sold the (dumb) thing off (and was finished with it).'

(68) அவன் சொந்தக்காரனா வேற இருந்து தொலெக்குறான்
avan sondakkaaranaa veera irundu tolekkraan
he kinsman-ADV moreover be IMPAT-PRES-PNG

'He happens to be a relative of mine (so I have obligations).'

(69) எல்லாரும் பீர் குடிக்க ணும் ண்ணாங்க; நானும் குடிச்சு
ellaarum biir kuḍikka ṇum -ṇṇaanga; naanum kuḍiccu
everyone beer drink must they-said. I-also drink
தொலெச்சேன்.
tolecceen
IMPAT-PAST-PNG

'Everyone was (expected to be) drinking beer (which I don't like), (but) I drank some too (to get it over and done with).'

(70) அவன் நம்ம விஷயத்தெ டைரக்டர்கிட்டெ
avan namma viṣayatte ḍairakṭarkiṭṭe
he our matter-ACC director-to
சொல்லிதொலெச்சிட்டான்
solli-tolecciṭṭaan
say-IMPAT-COMPL

'(Mr. Bigmouth) has blabbed (let the cat out of the bag) about our (little) matter to the Director (and now we're in for it).'

(71) அதெ ஏன் முன்னாலெயே சொல்லி தொலெக்க கூடாது?
ade een munnaaleyee solli tolekka kuuḍaadu ?

'Why couldn't you say that beforehand, damn it?'

3.11.16 The Aspectual Verb கோ *koo*

One of the most complex of the Tamil aspectual verbs is கோ *koo*, derived from the lexical verb கொள் *koḷ-* which means 'hold, contain.' In LT lexical கொள் *koḷ* is quite rare, occurring usually only with neuter subjects, i.e. sentences in which some**thing** holds or contains some**thing**, not some**one**. Lexical கொள் *koo* does occur as an AVP with verbs of motion போ *poo* 'go' and வா *vaa* 'come', and the combination கொண்டுபோ *koṇḍupoo* and கொண்டுவா *koṇḍuvaa* mean 'take (s.t.)' (i.e. 'hold and go') and 'bring (s.t.)' (i.e. 'hold and come') respectively. Since lexical கொள் *koḷ* is a Class I verb, with present கொள்றேன் *koḷreen*,[32] past கிட்டேன் *kiṭṭeen*, and future கொவேன் *koveen*, these are also the forms for aspectual கோ *koo*. Its AVP is கிட்டு *kiṭṭu*. The phonology of the spoken form of this AM is much more different from its LT counterpart than could be predicted by regular historical or morphophonemic rules, and moreover varies tremendously from dialect to dialect; in some dialects there is a present form கிடுறேன் *kiḍreen* and infinitive கிட *kiḍa* that are back-formations from the past கிட்டு *kiṭṭu*.[33]

3.11.17 Aspectual Distinctions

The aspectual verb கோ *koo* can provide a number of aspectual distinctions to a sentence. Traditionally (Arden 1942:282ff.) LT கொள் *koḷ* is referred to as a 'reflexive' verb, but this is hardly the best analysis of its meaning. Some of the notions provided by aspectual கோ *koo* are:

1. Self-affective or self-benefactive action.[34]

2. Simultaneous action: one action occurring together with another action; sometimes these actions are wholly coterminous, but at other

[32] The short /o/ in many forms of this morpheme is actually phonetically [ə], i.e. கொறேன் *koreen* is [kərẽ], etc.

[33] The extreme variability of the phonology of this AM bespeaks a radical departure of some sort that is one of the symptoms of the process of grammaticalization.

[34] E. Annamalai refers to this verb as 'ego-benefactive'. Many of the examples of aspect (which he refers to as verbal extension), are taken from his 1985 book on the subject, but converted from LT to ST.

times it merely states that some portion of the time of the two actions overlapped.

3. Completive aspect: indicates that an action is, has been, or will be definite and complete(d).

4. Inchoative vs. Punctual. கோ *koo* is used with a number of stative verbs to indicate that a state has begun or been entered into.

5. Purposeful vs. accidental. The action was purposeful and volitional; or, (paradoxically) the action was accidental. This can only be judged by what would be considered culturally appropriate under the given circumstances.

6. Lexicalization. Sometimes கோ *koo* has only marginal lexical or aspectual value of its own, and is attached to verb stems which no longer occur alone as bare stems. It is thus only a verbalizing suffix.

3.11.18 Self-affective or Self-benefactive Action

Self-affective or self-benefactive action is an action or state that affects the subject of the sentence in some way, usually to his/her benefit, but sometimes not in any clearly beneficial way. (This is what has been called 'reflexive' by other grammarians, but this is not an adequate description of many of its uses.) Sometimes the benefaction is clearly for someone else, as in (78) below. Beyond the benefaction, கோ *koo* is essentially a **completive** aspect marker as well, since whatever else happens, the implication is that the action was definitely accomplished. Compare sentences with and without கோ *koo* such as

(72) குமார் வேலெ தேடினான், ஆனா கெடெக்கல்லெ
kumaar veele teeḍinaan, aanaa keḍekkalle

'Kumar looked for a job, but didn't find one.'

(73) குமார் வேலெ தேடிக்கிட்டான்
kumaar veele teeḍikkiṭṭaan

'Kumar looked for a job **and found one**'

The latter implies completion or attainment of the goal, so cannot be followed by

...ஆனா கெடெக்கல்லெ *aanaa keḍekkalle*

'...but didn't find one'

without contradition. Other examples[35] of uses of the AM *koo* are

(74) பய்யன் தன்னெ அடிச்சுக்கிட்டான்
payyan tanne adiccu-kiṭṭaan
boy self-ACC beat-BENEF-PAST-PNG
'The boy hit himself.'

(75) ராமன் சட்டெ போட்டுக்குறான்
raaman saṭṭe pooṭṭu-kraan
Raman shirt-ACC put-BENEF-PRES-PNG
'Raman dresses himself.'

(76) நான் பணத்தெ எடுத்துக்கிட்டேன்
naan paṇatte eḍuttu-kiṭṭeen
I money-ACC take-BENEF-PAST-PNG
'I took the money for myself.'

(77) நீங்க பாத்துக்கோங்க
niinga paattu-koonga!
you see-BENEF-IMP
'Watch out (for yourself)!'

(78) நீ கொழந்தெங்களெ பாத்துக்கணும்
nii koṟandengaḷe paattu-kaṇum
you children-ACC see-BENEF-must
'You need to take care of (watch) the children.'

(79) குமார் நல்லா நடந்துக்கிட்டான்
kumaar nallaa naḍandu-kiṭṭaan
Kumar well conduct-BENEF-PAST-PNG
'Kumar behaved well.'

(80) ராமசாமி முடியெ வெட்டிக்கிட்டான்
raamasaami muḍiye veṭṭi-kiṭṭaan
Ramasamy hair-ACC cut-BENEF-PAST-PNG
'Ramasamy cut his hair (on purpose).'

(81) ராமசாமி கய்யெ வெட்டிக்கிட்டான்
raamasaami kayye veṭṭi-kiṭṭaan
Ramasamy hand-ACC cut-BENEF-PAST-PNG
'Ramasamy cut his hand (by accident).'

If the example in (76) did not have aspectual கோ *koo*, i.e. were simply நான் பணத்தெ எடுத்தேன் *naan paṇatte eḍutteen*, the meaning would be

[35] Annamalai 1981.

'I took the money (but not for myself, i.e. I transported it somewhere for someone else).' The accidental and volitional meanings of கோ *koo* are somewhat problematical, since the last two examples above can also be reversed, i.e. *R. cut his hair by accident* and *R. cut his hand on purpose*, but since this is not what one usually expects of people, the expected result is the preferred interpretation.[36] The decision as to whether an action was deliberate or accidental depends on how society valorizes the effect. In this case, South Asian society places a positive value on deliberate hair-cutting and negatively values deliberate mutilation of one's body, unless it is done for religious or ritual reasons.

3.11.19 Simultaneity

கோ *koo* is often used as an AVP (கிட்டு *kiṭṭu*) attached to one or more non-finite verbs (AVP's) to indicate that those actions are simultaneous with (either completely, or just partly) another action. Often English 'while' can be used to translate this. Sometimes simultaneity is explicitly emphasized by adding emphatic ஏ *ee*, as in the first example below.

(82) நான் சாப்பிட்டுக்கிட்டே வந்தேன்
naan saappiṭṭu-kiṭṭee vandeen
I eat-ing-EMPH came
'I was eating while I came.'

(83) செருப்பெ போட்டுக்கிட்டு கோயிலுக்குள்ளே போகக்கூடாது
seruppe pooṭṭu-kiṭṭu, kooyilukkuḷḷee pooha-kuuḍaadu
shoe-ACC wear-SIMUL temple-DAT-POSTP go-MUST-NEG-IMP
'Do not go into a temple while wearing shoes.'

(84) ஒரு கொளக்கரெயிலெ ஒரு புலி கண்ணெ மூடிக்கிட்டு
oru koḷakkareyle oru puli kaṇṇe muuḍikkiṭṭu
a tank-bank-LOC a tiger eye-ACC closed-SIMUL
ஒக்காந்திருந்தது
okkaand-irundadu
sitting-was
'(While) its eyes (were) closed, a tiger was lying by the side of a tank.'

[36] One might find a parallel to this in the English 'aspectual commentary' verbal expressions 'manage to VB' and 'go and VB', e.g. 'Ramasamy managed to cut himself in the hand' and 'Ramasamy went and cut himself in the hand.' In both of these the implication is that Ramasamy is not very competent or not very much in control of his life, whereas 'Ramasamy managed to get his hair cut' implies that the incompetent Ramasamy finally got his act together and got his hair cut.

(85) *LT* ஒரு நாள் ஒரு வியாபாரி ஒரு காட்டுவழியே முட்டையை
(*LT*) *oru naal̤ oru vyaabaari oru kaaṭṭuvar̤iyee muuṭṭaiyai*
one day a merchant a forest-path-LOC bundle-ACC
எடுத்துகொண்டு போனான்
eḍuttu-koṇḍu poon̠aan̠
take-SIMUL went

'One day a merchant was going along a forest path, carrying a bundle.'

Because of the multiple semantic interpretations of lexical and aspectual கோ *koo*, it is sometimes possible to interpret it in various ways. Sometimes 'simultaneous' கோ *koo* may be interpreted as 'self-affective', i.e. in example (79) above, போட்டுகோ *pooṭṭu koo* could also mean 'having put on' rather than 'while wearing', since கோ *pooṭṭu-koo* does mean 'wear' (this is one of those examples mentioned above where கோ *koo* has become part of the stem of the lexical entry). The sentence in example (85) could be either interpreted as the lexical verb கொண்டுபோ *koṇḍupoo* 'take (s.t.)', as simultaneous கோ *koo* 'while taking, was carrying', or self-affective கோ *koo* 'was carrying *along with* him' (for his own benefit). In sentence (82), however, emphatic ஏ *ee* serves to block this interpretation. But the ambiguity in such circumstances, if any, is usually trivial.

3.11.19.1 Durative or Continuous Action

Durative or continuous action similar to the English 'progressive' construction VERB+ING, is expressed in Tamil by combining கோ *koo* in its AVP form கிட்டு *kiṭṭu* with the 'stative' aspectual verb இரு *iru*, i.e. கிட்டிரு *kiṭṭiru*, and affixing this to the AVP of a main verb: வந்து + கிட்டிரு + ந்தேன் *vandu+kiṭṭ-irundeen* 'I was com-ing.' The expression of durative CONTINUOUS action (a semantically separate kind of aspectual contrast) will be dealt with in more detail in a later section, but a few examples are given here.

(86) எல்லாரும் பேசிக்கிட்டிருந்தாங்க
*ellaarum peesi-***kiṭṭiru***-ndaanga*
all speak-DURATIVE-were
'Everyone was talking.'

(87) ராமன் சாப்பிட்டுக்கிட்டிருக்காரு
*raaman saappiṭṭu-***kiṭṭiru***-kkaaru*
Raman eat-DURATIVE-PERF-PNG
'Raman is eating.'

(88) கமலா வந்தப்ப நான் படிச்சுக்கிட்டிருந்தேன்
kamalaa vandappa, naan paḍiccu-**kiṭṭiru**-*ndeen*
Kamala came-when, I read-DURATIVE-TENSE-PNG
'When Kamala arrived, I was reading.'

(89) கொழந்தெ ஏழு மணிக்குள்ளே தூங்கிக்கிட்டிருக்கும்
koṛande eeṛu maṇikkuḷḷee tuungi-**kiṭṭiru**-*kkum*
child 7:00 within sleep-DURATIVE-will-be
'By 7:00, the child will be sleeping.'

(90) எங்கே போய்க்கிட்டிருக்கீங்க?
engee pooy-**kiṭṭiru**-*kkiinga?*
Where go-DURATIVE-PRES-PNG
'Where are you going?'

3.11.19.2 Inchoative and Punctual Notions

We have already introduced the notion that கோ *koo* can serve as a marker of the beginning of a new state or action. This emphasizes the POINT of beginning, rather than the duration of the state. With stative verbs that require the dative (e.g. தெரி *teri* 'know', புரி *puri* 'understand'), the addition of கோ *koo* emphasizes the point (hence PUNCTUAL) of beginning to understand or know. Hitherto dative-stative verb stems with கோ *koo* affixed become nominative-subject action verbs. Examples of contrast between verbs without கோ *koo* are labelled *a* below, and examples with *koo* are labelled *b* below:

(91) a. அது எனக்கு தெரியும்
adu enakku teriyum
that to-me known
'I know that.'

b. நான் அதெ தெரிஞ்சுகிட்டேன்
*naan ade terinju***kiṭṭ***een*
I that-ACC know-INCHOAT-PAST-PNG
'I realized (came to know; found out) that.'

(92) a. அவர் சொல்றது ஒங்களுக்கு புரியுமா?
avar solradu ongaḷukku puriyumaa
he says-thing to-you understand-q
'Do you understand what he says?'

b. அவர் சொல்றது புரிஞ்சுகிட்டீங்களா?
avar solradu purinju-**kiṭṭ***iingaḷaa?*
he says-thing understand-INCHOAT-PAST-PNG-Q

'Did you (finally) understand what he is talking about? (Do you *get* it?)'

(93) a. ஒக்காருங்க
okkaarunga
sit-IMP-POL
'Please remain seated.'

b. ஒக்காந்துகோங்க
*okkaandu***koo***nga*
sit-INCHOAT-POL
'Please be/remain seated; please sit down' (Please enter the state of being seated.)

3.11.20 போடு *poodu* 'malicious intent'

For dialects where போடு *poodu* is not just a variant of விடு *(v)idu* 'completive', we place it here among the primarily attitudinal aspect markers. Note that phonologically, போட்டு *poottu* the AVP form, is often reduced to புட்டு *puttu* or ப்டு *ptu* as in விட்டுப்டு *vittuptu* 'having definitely (mischievously) left' and சாப்பிட்டுப்புட்டு *saappittuptu* 'having eaten.'

3.11.21 Lexical Problems

In modern Tamil, especially in ST, there are lexical verbs that no longer occur without what appears to be an aspectual verb, i.e. they have been relexicalized with the 'aspectual' verb incorporated, as it were, onto the stem. Since these combinations take place according to the usual compounding or verbal concatenation process, the first element has to be in the form of the AVP, and the second receives tense-marking and PNG.

LT verbs such as கா *kaa* 'wait' now occur almost exclusively with ('aspectual') கோ *koo* or 'aspectual' இரு *iru* attached, i.e காத்துக்கோ *kaattukkoo* or காத்திரு *kaattiru*. In such cases, the aspectual value of கோ *koo* is weakened (or even nullified, or at least minimized)[37] and the compound simply represents the relexicalized form of the verb. Thus there can be a sort of 'sliding scale' from lexical to grammatical, with some combinations of main verb and கோ *koo* being primarily lexical, with very little aspectual 'meaning', but at the other end of the scale the occurrence of கோ *koo* will be minimally lexical but maximally aspectual.

This is also the case with the LT verb கல் *kal* 'learn' which now in ST occurs only with கோ *koo* or இரு *iru* attached: கத்துகோங்க *kattukoonga*

[37] I would prefer a better term than this but if we see aspect as a still-variable category in Tamil, we have to place it on a continuum with two poles, and variation in between.

'(please) learn (it).' This contrasts semantically with கல் *kal* with இரு *iru* attached: கத்திரு *kattiru* 'be learning'; the illocutionary force of this combination is sarcastic or ironic, since தமிழ் எங்கெ கத்திருக்கிங்க *tamiẓ enge katt-irukkiinga* (which on the face of it appears to mean 'Where did you learn Tamil?)' can only have the illocutionary force of 'Where (in the world) did *you* learn Tamil?' (i.e. 'you don't know Tamil!'). Use of கோ *koo* with some other verbs, as noted above, also contrasts with non-use in an almost purely lexical way: போடு *pooḍu* 'put, drop' means 'put on' clothing, but போட்டுகோ *pooṭṭu-koo* implies the *result* of putting something on, i.e. 'wearing.'

3.12 Summary

Let us summarize some of what is known about Tamil aspect as follows:

- There seems to be a category of aspect that must be recognized for Tamil that involves a continuum of grammaticalization from none (i.e. pure lexical or syntactic concatenation) to aspect as a full-fledged category. In such cases, aspect can no longer be considered a syntactic process, but must be considered a morphological category of the Tamil verb (Schiffman 1993).

- Most dialects (and LT) recognize a subset of aspectual markers that are clearly aspectual, and have little or no overlap with their lexical analogs. Indeed, the lexical verb can often be followed by the corresponding aspectual verb. Furthermore, the aspectual marker is in these instances often phonologically different from its lexical analog.

- Most dialects also show a set of aspectual verbs that involve a component of aspect, but also an attitudinal (or metaphoric) notion of some sort. This set varies more from dialect to dialect, but nevertheless language-wide and even family-wide features are shared. For example, Tamil போடு *pooḍu* 'malicious intent' (lexically 'put') has as its analog in Kannada the verb *haaku*, which has the same aspectual and lexical meanings in Kannada that போடு *pooḍu* does in Tamil, even though the two verbs are quite different phonologically. This seems to be a feature of the Indian linguistic area that has been noted for many languages, i.e. the lexical-aspectual-attitudinal polarity will be found in languages as different as Tamil and Bengali; one even notes some carry-over into Indian English.

- Theories of syntax that require categorical rules, or fixed grammaticality, cannot capture generalizations about aspect in these languages.

- In the case of the aspectual auxiliaries that are unambiguously aspectual, we often find that they are phonologically different from their lexical analogs, undergoing certain phonological rules that do not apply to lexical verbs because the conditions for their application are not met there. That is, these unambiguously aspectual verbs act like grammatical morphemes, rather than separate verbs, and phonological rules that operate across morpheme boundaries of concatenated verbs do not have the same application when what is concatenated is a verb and a separate quasi-aspectual verb.

3.12.1 Pragmatic Considerations

Another variable feature of Tamil aspectual verbs is that there are pragmatic considerations that are involved in the choice of whether to mark aspect or not. Since aspect is not an obligatory category, it may or may not be present. However, there is a tendency not to mark aspectual distinctions in certain constructions, even if they might be technically grammatical. The reasons for this are pragmatic ones, having to do with politeness, shared perceptions, the nature of truth propositions, etc. There is also a tendency to use aspectual marking to add speaker commentary to the sentence, even with the 'purely' aspectual markers, but especially with the attitudinal ones.

- Aspect marking is an optional category; unlike tense or some other obligatory categories, it is not required. There is a polarity in notions such as going/coming, known/unknown, what is culturally 'correct/incorrect'.

- Aspect marking occurs most often in positive declarative sentences, rarely in negative, with the exception that it is common in both positive and negative *imperatives.*

- Even in non-attitudinal aspect-marking, use of aspectual verbs seems to be *expressive*, i.e. is used to comment, to deprecate, etc. We have already noted (∮3.12.21) the form கத்திரு (LT கற்றிரு *kaṟṟiru* 'be learning'), whose illocutionary force is sarcastic or ironic.

- Aspect may be bi-polar and paradoxical, meaning 'intentional' in one context and 'accidental' in another, as in sentences (80) and (81) ('Ramasamy cut his hair/hand')

3.12.2 Grammaticalization

The Tamil aspectual system is an incompletely grammaticalized system, in that it is open-ended, with new verbs acquiring aspectual nuances as they move from being expressive or attitudinal.[38] Most recent syntactic studies of verbal aspect in Tamil (e.g. Steever 1983, Annamalai 1978, Dale 1975) have relied on data from LT, rather than ST. Had these studies used the spoken language for data, they would, I believe, be forced to draw other conclusions, namely, that the system is in a state of variability, and categorical statements about it cannot be made.

The indicators of grammaticalization that the Tamil aspectual system exhibits many of are seen in the following:

1. The system shows great variability in syntax, morphology, and phonology. No one kind or set of rules (e.g. phonological) can account for all of the kinds of variability.

2. There are more aspectual verbs in modern ST than in LT, and they are used more frequently.

3. Aspectual verbs all have lexical analogs, but those that are more grammaticalized such as விடு *viḍu* and கோ *koo* exhibit more phonological deviance from the lexical form.

4. There is dialectal and pragmatic variation.

5. The most grammaticalized of the AM's are quite uniform and have no attitudinal or metaphoric nuances; less fully grammaticalized AM's retain semantic notions that are commentarial and judgmental, and hence highly variable. They tend to be *metaphoric* in their adaptation of the meaning of lexical verbs, e.g. the 'riddance' metaphor in தள்ளு *taḷḷu* is derived from the literal meaning of the lexical verb தள்ளு *taḷḷu* meaning 'push, displace' or 'shove.'

6. What can easily be explained as a syntactic system in LT can now best be explained as a more morphologized one in ST.

3.13 Negatives

For an outline of the negative forms of the various verb forms discussed in these sections, cf. Chapter 6.

[38] See the growing body of literature on grammaticalization (e.g. Harper and Traugott 1993) for insights on how the verbal category of aspect can be dealt with.

3.14 Defective Verb Forms

Tamil has a number of verbs that are known as 'defective' verbs; this means that they lack certain parts of the paradigm of a 'normal' verb.

3.14.1 Dative-Statives

Many defective verbs are syntactically different from verbs with complete paradigms; often, their subjects are in the dative case, because they cannot agree in PNG with first and second person subjects or third person animate subjects. However, they have some forms that regular verbs do not have, such as habitual vs. non-habitual forms. In form they resemble some of the modals, such as முடி *muḍi* 'be able.' We refer to them as 'dative-stative' verbs because they are semantically STATIVE—they refer to states (liking, wanting, sufficing, being painful, hungry, etc.) rather than actions—and because syntactically they require that their subjects be marked with the *dative* case. The most common defective verbs are புரி 'understand', வேணும் *veeṇum* 'need, want', தெரி *teri* 'know', கெடெ *keḍe* 'be available, have', and பிடி *piḍi* 'like', shown in Table 3.22.

3.14.2 Syntax of Dative-Stative Verbs

When the subject of dative-stative verbs is animate (i.e. first or second person, or third person animate), it is in the dative case. Examples:

(94)	அது	எனக்கு	பிடிக்கும்	
	adu	*enakku*	*piḍikkum*	
	that	to-me	like	
	'I like that.'			
(95)	ராஜகுமாரிக்கி	மாலெ	கெடெச்சது	
	raajakumaarikki	*maale*	*keḍeccadu*	
	princess-to	necklace	be-gotten	
	'The princess got her necklace (back)'			
(96)	அவனுக்கு	மொழி	புரியாட்டாலும்	போயிடுவான்
	avanukku	*moẓi*	*puriyaaṭṭaalum*	*pooyiḍuvaan*
	him-to	language	even-if-not-understood	go-DEF-FUT-PNG
	'Even if he doesn't understand the language, he'll go.'			
(97)	என்	தம்பிக்கி	காப்பி	வேண்டாம்
	en	*tambikki*	*kaappi*	*veeṇḍaam*
	my	ygr-brother-to	coffee	not-wanted
	'My younger brother doesn't want coffee.'			

It may seem in the examples in Table 3.22 that the dative subject nouns are not actually subjects, since the other nouns (which would be objects in English) are in the nominative. However, this is shown not to be the case by the following examples: If the 'object' noun is *animate*, it must as always be marked *accusative*. Thus some sentences may seem to have no subject, since one noun is the dative and the other is the accusative. It is easier, therefore, to consider the dative case noun to be the semantic subject:

(98) அவரெ எனக்கு தெரியல்லெ
avar-e enakku teriyalle
'him to-me not-known
'I didn't know him'

No-one would consider அவரு *avaru* 'he' to be the subject, since it is marked accusative. The nouns in the other examples are merely neuter nouns unmarked for accusative, rather than subject-nominatives.

3.14.3 Modality and Dative-Stative Verbs

Dative-stative verbs can have modals affixed to them, like other verbs, and as always, they are attached to the infinitive. Examples:

(99) அந்தக் கடெய்லெ காப்பி கெடெக்கலாம்
anda kaḍeyle kaappi keḍekkalaam
that shop-in coffee available-may-be

'Coffee may be available in that shop (You may be able to get/find a cup of coffee in that shop).'

(100) நீங்க கேட்டா, தெரியலாம்
niinga keeṭṭaa teriyalaam
'If you ask, you might find out.'

3.14.4 Complex Morphology and Dative-Statives

Some other derived verbal forms, such as verbal nouns, verbal participles (particularly negative), and conditional, are possible with these dative-stative verbs.

(101) அது தெரிஞ்சுகுறதுக்கு, ஊருக்கு போய்ட்டேன்
adu terinjukradukku uurukku pooyṭṭeen

'In order to know that, I went to (my home)town.'

Table 3.22: Paradigms of Dative-Stative Verbs, all Tenses and PNG

STEM	INFINITIVE	HABITUAL	NEGATIVE NABITUAL	PAST, NON-BABITUAL:	NEG PAST, NON-HABITUAL
பிடி *piḍi* 'like'	பிடிக்க *piḍikka* 'to like'	பிடிக்கும் *piḍikkum* 'is liked'	பிடிக்காது *piḍikkaadu* 'not liked'	பிடிச்சது *piḍiccadu* 'was liked'	பிடிக்கல்லெ *piḍikkalle* 'wasn't liked'
புரி *puri* 'understand'	புரிய *puriya* 'to understand'	புரியும் *puriyum* 'understood'	புரியாது *puriyaadu* 'isn't understood'	புரிஞ்சது *purinjadu* 'understood'	புரியல்லெ *puriyalle* 'wasn't understood'
தெரி *teri* 'know'	தெரிய *teriya* 'to know'	தெரியும் *teriyum* 'is known'	தெரியாது *teriyaadu* 'is not known'	தெரிஞ்சது *terinjadu* 'knew'	தெரியல்லெ *teriyalle* 'wasn't known'
கெடெ *keḍe* 'be available'	கெடெக்க *keḍekka* 'to be available'	கெடெக்கும் *keḍekkum* 'is available'	கெடெக்காது *keḍekkaadu* 'isn't available'	கெடெச்சது *keḍeccade* 'was 'available'	கெடெக்கல்லெ *keḍekkalle* 'wasn't available'
வேண்டு *veeṇḍu* 'want, need'	வேண்டிய *veeṇḍiya* 'to be wanted'	வேணும் *veeṇḍum* 'is wanted'	வேண்டாம் *veeṇḍaam* 'isn't wanted'	வேண்டியது *veeṇḍiyadu* 'was needed'	வேண்டியதுல்லெ *veeṇḍiyadille* 'wasn't wanted'

(102) கெடெக்காட்டாலும் அவன் கேப்பான்
keḍekkaaṭṭaalum avan keeppaan

'Even if it's not available, he'll ask.'

(103) மொழி தெரியாம இந்த்யாவுக்கு வந்தேன்
moṛi teriyaama indyaavukku vandeen
language knowing-not India-to came-I

'I came to India *without knowing* the language.'

3.15 Verbalizers and Compound Verbs

Tamil can combine nouns with verbs and make 'compound verbs', that is, compounded expressions that are equivalent to a verb in another language. The nominal part of this compound is *not* marked for case though it may in fact be the semantic object of the verbal action. These compound verbs are on the borderline between being independent verbs, and being phrases containing a noun and a verb.

3.15.1 Transitive Absolutes

An example of these phrasal or compound verbs is the verb பதில் சொல் *padil sollu* 'answer', (i.e. lit. tell the answer) which combines a nominal object with a verb stem in a kind of compound, equivalent to the English verb 'to reply.' The noun, though functioning as the object of the verb, is not marked with the expected accusative marker. Though no accusative is marked, no other noun in the sentence may be marked as the object of that verb either, so that the structure of English 'he answered his sister (when she asked a question)', with 'sister' as the object of the verb 'reply', cannot be exactly replicated in Tamil. In Tamil the object of the verb பதில் சொல் *badil sollu* must be marked with some other case; one possibility would be the 'dative' or locative–human, as in (104):[39] Such structures, with an incorporated object but NO object marking, are referred to by some grammarians as TRANSITIVE ABSOLUTES.

(104) அவன் தன் தங்கெச்சிகிட்டெ அவளோட கேள்விக்கி பதில் சொன்னான்
avan tan tangecci-kiṭṭe avaḷooḍa keeḷvi-kki badil sonnaan
he his sister-LOC her-GEN question-DAT answer said
'He answered his sister (in reply to her question).'

This matter is somewhat confused by the fact that in English one can say either 'He answered his sister (in reply to her question)', or 'He answered his sister's question', or 'He replied to the question his sister asked' which are all more or less equivalent, but which have 'different' objects, whereas in Tamil பதில் சொல் *badil sollu* requires various case markers, but never the accusative.

It should be obvious that verbs like these 'incorporated-object transitives' or transitive 'absolutes' are problematical, and really need a case-frame to indicate who or what is the semantic target, if not the syntactic target, of the action. In fact many researchers feel that verbs must be scaled for degree of transitivity, since 'blaming' or 'seeing' is in some sense less transitive than 'breaking' or 'killing', actions which have a definite effect on an object, whereas to be blamed or seen does not affect the 'target' of the action in the same physical way.

Thus to refer to உடை II INTR as an intransitive kind of *breaking* since the process or person who caused the breaking is not known is also not as neat a distinction as one would like, even though the morphology of Tamil gives us two உடை's, one 'intransitive', i.e. without known agent, as in கண்ணாடி உடைந்தது *kaṇṇaaḍi oḍenjadu* 'the glass broke', the other 'transitive', as in அவன் கண்ணாடியை உடைத்தான் *avan kaṇṇaaḍiye oḍeccaan* 'He

[39] The LT version of this sentence would be with இடம், i.e. அவன் தன் தங்கையிடம் அவளுடைய கேள்விக்கு பதில் சொன்னான்.

broke the glass.' These 'intransitives' are also usually possible only with a third person, often neuter, 'subject', i.e. 'glass'. Yet to think of glass as the 'subject' of 'intransitive' breaking but as the object or target of transitive breaking (when the agent of the action is known), is problematical.[40]

3.15.2 Common Verbalizers

Tamil uses a number of ordinary verbs that combine with other words, usually nouns, to make new verbs. Tamil cannot otherwise borrow *verbs* from other languages, so this process borrows verbs, nouns and other forms *as if they were nouns* and then makes compound verbs out of them. The commonest verbs involved in this process are அடி *aḍi*, எடு *eḍu*, பண்ணு *paṇṇu*, செய்யி *seyyi*, பாரு *paaru*, படு *paḍu*, பிடி, *piḍi*, and சொல்லு *sollu*, though we have also seen that கோ *koo* and இரு *iru* can also be used to verbalize or reverbalize another verb (see ∮3.12.21).

3.15.3 பண்ணு *paṇṇu* 'make, do'

The commonest and most general of these verbs is பண்ணு *paṇṇu* 'make, do.' It can be added to a noun to make a verb, and is the most common way of making verbs out of borrowed *English* words. Sometimes Tamil even borrows words for lexical items it already has.

- ட்ரைவ் பண்ணு *ḍraiv paṇṇu* 'Drive (a car)' (lit. 'make drive')
- வாக்கிங் பண்ணு *vaakking paṇṇu* 'take a walk, go walking'
- காப்பி பண்ணு *kaappi paṇṇu* 'copy, make a copy'
- போர் பண்ணு *boor paṇṇu* 'bore, make a hole'
- வர்க் பண்ணு *vark paṇṇu* 'work, do work' (வேலெ பாரு cf. *veele paaru* 'work')

பண்ணு *paṇṇu* can be attached to both nouns and verbs (usually borrowed from English), but always with the net effect of having been added to nouns; that is, what precedes பண்ணு *paṇṇu* is an NP in Tamil, regardless of whether it is an NP or a VP in English. Thus, ட்ரைவ் *ḍraiv* in the above example, though a verb in English ('drive') is treated as if it is a noun in Tamil.

[40] But as anyone who has dealt with young children knows, an argument is often likely to ensue between the parent and the child over who the agent of the breaking was, with the parent claiming that the action was transitive and that there had to be an agent, while the child argues that the action had no cause and no agent—'it just *broke*'. Parents typically contend this is not the case, and that responsibility or blame has to be assigned; children, even when found with rocks in their hands, attempt to deny this contention.

3.15.4 அடி *aḍi* 'pejorative action'

The main verb அடி *aḍi* 'beat, strike' may be used as a verbalizer to create verbs whose actions are metaphors for pejorative, inappropriate, or unpleasant states or activities, i.e. the speaker disapproves of the action in some way.

(105) போர் அடி
boor aḍi
'be boring'

(106) நான் அங்கெ போகமாட்டேன்; ரொம்ப போர் அடிக்குது
naan ange poohamaaṭṭeen; romba boor aḍikkudu
'I won't be going there; it's really boring.'

(107) டல்லடி
ḍall aḍi
'be dull, morose; be depressed'

(108) என்ன ஸார், ரொம்ப டல்லடிக்குறீங்க
enna saar, rompa ḍallaḍikkriinga
'What's the matter, man? You seem really depressed.'

Other examples are:

- வெரெட்டி அடி *vereṭṭi aḍi* 'drive out'
- காப்பி அடி *kaappi aḍi* 'cheat, copy (illegally)'
- தண்ணி அடி *taṇṇi aḍi* 'drink excessively; abuse alcohol ('beat water')'

Note the contrast between அடி *aḍi* and பண்ணு *paṇṇu* as a regular verbalizer for 'ordinary' (non-pejorative) actions in the constructions above, where போர் அடி *boor-aḍi* and காப்பி அடி *kaappi aḍi* using the English borrowed verbs 'to bore' and 'to copy' (as if they were nouns) means 'to do something unpleasant or wrong', whereas போர் பண்ணு *boor-paṇṇu* and காப்பி பண்ணு *kaappi paṇṇu* mean 'to make legitimate and proper holes, copies, etc.'

In some other combinations, however, the use of அடி aḍi is not to be construed as particularly pejorative or unpleasant.

- தந்தி அடி *tandi aḍi* 'send a telegram' (lit. 'beat wire')
- டைப் அடி *ṭaip aḍi* 'type' (i.e. 'operate a typewriter')
- வெயில் அடிக்குது *veyil aḍikkudu* 'The sun is beating down.'

அடி *aḍi* is normal in these phrases because of the action of tapping the telegraph key or typewriter keys, and because in South India standing in the direct heat of the sun can be routinely uncomfortable during most of the year.

3.15.5 எடு *eḍu* 'inchoative'

எடு *eḍu* is used as a verbalizer to express the notion 'inchoative' or the beginning of an action. They are 'dative-stative' in syntax.

1. பசி எடு *pasi eḍu* 'begin to get hungry' (lit. 'take hunger')

   எனக்கு பசி எடுக்குது *enakku pasi eḍukkudu*

   'I'm beginning to get hungry'

2. வலி எடு *vali eḍu* 'begin to feel pain, hurt'

   எனக்கு வலி எடுக்குது *enakku vali eḍukkudu*

   'It's beginning to feel painful'

3. தாகம் எடு *daaham eḍu* 'begin to get thirsty'

   அவனுக்கு தாகம் எடுத்தது *avanukku daaham eḍuttadu*

   'He was beginning to get thirsty'

Note that 'getting sleepy', however, is expressed with வா *vaa* 'come:'

எனக்குத் தூக்கம் வரது *enakku tuukkam varadu*
'I'm getting sleepy'

3.15.6 படு *paḍu* 'experience emotions' and 'passive'

3.15.6.1 படு *paḍu* 'experience emotions'

படு paḍu is used with nouns expressing the notion of feeling and experiencing emotions:

1. கஷ்டப்படு *kaṣṭap-paḍu* 'experience difficulty'

   நான் ரொம்ப நாளா கஷ்டப்பட்டேன்

   naan romba naaḷaa kaṣṭap-paṭṭeen

   'For a while there I was having a lot of trouble.'

2. சந்தோஷப்படு *sandooṣap-paḍu* 'feel pleasure'

   அதெக் கேட்டா, ரொம்ப சந்தோஷப்பட்டேன்

   ade keeṭṭaa, romba sandooṣappaṭṭeen

   'When I heard that, I was really happy.'

3. கவலெப்படு *gavale-paḍu* 'worry, be troubled'

   அதெத் பத்தி கவலெப்படாதெங்க

   ade patti gavalep-paḍaadenga

   'Don't worry about that.'

4. பெருமெப்படு *perume-paḍu* 'feel pride'

5. ஆசெப்படு *aasep-paḍu* 'desire'

6. வெக்கப்படு *vekkap-paḍu* 'feel shame'

3.15.7 படு *paḍu* with Other Verbs: 'passive'

When படு paḍu follows the infinitive of another verb, the notion is similar to the English 'passive':

(109) ராமன் அவனாலெ கொல்லப்பட்டான்
raaman avanaale kollap-paṭṭaan
Raman him-by kill-experience
'Raman was killed by him.'

As in English, the subject (semantic subject) is in the nominative, with the agent marked by ஆலெ *aale* 'instrumental.' There is some debate among grammarians as to whether this construction is a 'true passive' in the sense of the passive in Indo-European languages. There is some evidence that the construction is somehow borrowed, since it does not occur in most colloquial speech, but is found usually only in more LT usage. If found in ST, it represents the influence of the LT dialect.

3.15.8 பிடி *piḍi* 'increase, augment'

பிடி *piḍi* 'seize, hold, grasp' is used with certain nouns to indicate an increase or augmentation of something.

- மழெ பிடிக்குது *maẓe piḍikkudu* 'The rain is picking up (falling harder, beginning to really come down).'
- திமிர் பிடிக்குது *timir piḍikkudu* 'get smart, get wise'

3.15.9 சொல்லு *sollu* as a Performative Verb

When சொல்லு *sollu* 'say' is used with certain nouns, a number of performative verbs are formed.[41]

1. பொய் சொல்லு *poy sollu* 'tell a lie'
2. பதில் சொல்லு *badil sollu* 'answer, retort, reply'
3. வரச் சொல்லு *vara sollu* 'order (s.o.) to come; summon'

    நான் அவனெ வரச்சொன்னேன்

    naan avane vara sonneen

    'I ordered him to come, I summoned him.'
4. குத்தம் சொல்லு *kuttam sollu* 'blame, accuse'

    நீங்க என்னெ குத்தம் சொல்லுறீங்களா?

    niinga enn-e kuttam solriingaḷaa?

    'Are you putting the blame on me?'

[41] Performative verbs are verbs that, once uttered, 'do' something, such as confer a status or commit the speaker to some action, expectation, or outcome. English verbs like 'pronounce (someone) married)', 'promise', 'swear, take an oath', 'order' etc. are performative in that they have legal, ritual, ceremonial, and other consequences. Especially when preceded by 'hereby', they are irrevocable in the sense that they commit the speaker to some outcome.

Chapter 4

Pronouns and Pro-Forms

4.1 Pronouns and Agreement

Tamil sentences that contain finite verbs are marked with person-number-gender (PNG) suffixes to agree with the person, number and gender of the noun or pronoun that is the subject of the verb. PNG markers are the same for all tenses, except for the neuters, which are somewhat idiosyncratic (see below). The finite verb consists of a verb *stem* (usually the same as the imperative singular) a tense-marker, and PNG.

Note that the third singular honorific form அவரு *avaru*, though it is not specifically 'marked' as masculine (and could therefore be interpreted as possibly singular feminine honorific also), is in actuality not used for the latter. Instead, அவங்க *avanga* a form identical to the third plural animate is used for honorific feminine singular.

4.1.1 Inclusive and Exclusive

The first person plural may be either inclusive (the addressee is included in the reference) or exclusive (speaker excludes the addressee, referring to him/herself and others, but not the addressee). But the PNG marker on the verb is the same for inclusive and exclusive: ஓம் *oom*.

4.1.2 Neuter Forms

Neuter PNG markers are somewhat idiosyncratic; there are different forms for some neuter pasts (cf. ∮3.7.2-3) and the neuter *future* form is உம் *um* and is attached to the infinitive, rather than the future tense marker.

Table 4.1: Structure of Finite Verbs

Stem	Tense Marker	PNG	Gloss
இரு *iru* 'be located'	க்குற் *kur* 'present'	ஏன் *een* '1st person SG'	
நான் இருக்குறேன் *naan irukkreen*			'I am located'
வர் *var* 'come'	ந்த் *nd* 'past'	ஆரு *aaru* '3 hon'	
அவரு வந்தாரு *avaru vandaaru*			'He came'
போ *poo* 'go'	வ *v* 'future'	ஈங்க *iinga* '2nd PLpol'	
நீங்க போவீங்க *niinga pooviinga*			'You will go'

Table 4.2: Pronouns and PNG-markers

Person	Singular	Pronoun	English	PNG
I		நான் *naan*	'I'	ஏன் *-een*
II	(NON-POL)	நீ *nii*	'you'	ஏ *-ee*
III	M F M HON	அவன் *avan* அவ(ள்) *ava(ḷ)* அவரு அவரு	'he' 'she' 'he, she*' (POL)	ஆன் *-aan* ஆ(ள்) *-aa(ḷ)* ஆரு *-aaru*
	F HON	அவங்க(ள்) *avanga(ḷ)*	'she' (POL)	ஆங்க(ள்) *-aanka(ḷ)*
	N	இது/அது *idu/adu*	'it'	அது *adu**
Person	*Plural*	*Pronoun*	*English*	PNG
I	PL EXCL PL INCL	நாங்க(ள்) *naanga(ḷ)* நாம *naama*	'we (EXCL)' 'we (INCL)'	ஓம் *-oom* ஓம் *-oom*
II		நீங்க(ள்) *niinga(ḷ)*	'you (POL)'	ஈங்க(ள்) *-iinga(ḷ)*
III		அவங்க(ள்) *avanga(ḷ)*	'they' (ANIM)	ஆங்க(ள்) *-aanka(ḷ)*

4.1.3 Sandhi

The consonants in parentheses are deleted when in word-final position, e.g. அவ போறா *ava pooraa* 'she goes', but are present if suffixes are added, e.g. அவளுக்கு *avaḷukku* 'to her' or அவ போறாளா? *ava pooraaḷaa*? 'Does she go?' Inanimate nouns are never marked for plural, but always take the neuter singular—there is no way of referring to more than one such noun without numerals or (optional) plural marker, e.g. அந்த ரெண்டு பஸ்ஸும் அங்கெ போச்சு *anda reṇḍu bassum ange pooccu* 'Both of those buses went that way.' Note that the verb '(to) be' இரு *iru* has a different PNG form than other verbs in the neuter present, i.e. the expected form இருக்குறது **irukkradu* is usually replaced by *irukku* 'it is' or by இருக்கது *irukkadu.* (In the past the expected form இருந்தது *irundadu* 'it was' is unproblematical.)

4.2 Pronoun Deletion

Pronouns in the NOMINATIVE case may often be deleted from a sentence since their semantic information is repeated by the PNG marker of the verb. When there is ambiguity, as in the first person plural (both நாங்க *naanga* 'exclusive' and நாம *naama* 'inclusive' take the same PNG marker ஓம் -*oom*), deletion is rarer. However, it may still occur, even with modals and negatives, where there is no PNG marking on the verb. Thus in a sentence like நான் போறேன் *naan pooreen* 'I am going' the நான் *naan* can be deleted to get just போறேன் *pooreen*, which is still unambiguously 'I go.' But a sentence like நான் போகலாமா? *naan poohalaamaa* 'May I go?' or நான் போகல்லெ *naan poohalle* 'I didn't go' may also have the pronoun deleted, with the resulting போகலாமா? *poohalaamaa* 'May (someone) go?' and போகல்லெ *poohalle* '(Someone) didn't go' ambiguous as to person; mother-tongue speakers know from the context what or who is meant.

As a rule of thumb, non-native speakers are wise to delete only when no ambiguity will result. For emphasis, the pronoun is left in, e.g. நான் போறேன் *naan pooreen* '**I** will go.'

4.3 Genitive and Oblique Forms

The possessive forms of the pronouns, and the oblique forms (with addition of case) differ from the nominatives in the first and second persons, but not in the third person. (See ∮2.1.5, Chapter 2, for a discussion of case and oblique forms.)

Things to note: dative forms for the first and second persons singular, have the shape அக்கு *-akku* instead of உக்கு*-ukku*, which is normal

Table 4.3: Pronouns and Oblique forms

Person	Pronoun	Gloss	Gen./Oblique	Dative
1 SG	நான் *naan*	'I'	என் *en*	எனக்கு *enakku*
2 SG	நீ *nii*	'you (SG)'	ஒன் *on*	ஒனக்கு *onakku*
3 M	அவன் *avan*	'he'	அவன் *avan*	அவனுக்கு *avanukku*
3 F	அவ(ள்) *ava(ḷ)*	'she'	அவ(ள்) *ava(ḷ)*	அவளுக்கு) *avaḷukku*
3 M HON	அவரு *avaru*	'he (POL)'	அவர் *avar*	அவருக்கு *avarukku*
3 F HON	அவங்க(ள்) *avanga(ḷ)*	'she (POL)'	அவங்க(ள்) *avanga(ḷ)*	அவங்களுக்கு *avangaḷukku*
3 N.	இது/அது *idu/adu*	'it'	இது/அது * *idu/adu*	இதுக்கு/அதுக்கு *idukku/adukku*
1 PL EXCL	நாங்க(ள்) *naanga(ḷ)*	'we (excl.)'	எங்க(ள்) *enga(ḷ)*	எங்களுக்கு *engaḷukku*
1 PL INCL	நாம *naama*	'we (incl.)'	நம்ம *namma*	நமக்கு *namakku*
2 PL	நீங்க(ள்) *niinga(ḷ)*	'you (POL)'	ஒங்க(ள்) *onga(ḷ)*	ஒங்களுக்கு *ongaḷukku*
3 PL	அவங்க(ள்) *avangaḷ*	'they' (ANIM)	அவங்க(ள்) *avangaḷ*	அவங்களுக்கு *avangaḷukku*

with nouns and third person pronouns. The third neuter may have the genitive/oblique form அதன் *adan-* before some case forms, e.g. அதனாலெ *adanaale*, originally the instrumental form, but now a lexical item meaning 'therefore.' Otherwise the 'genitive' of அது *adu* is அதோடெ *adoo̤de*, as in அதோடெ தலெ *adoo̤de tale* 'its head'.[1]

4.4 Demonstrative Pronouns

Table 4.4: Structure of Demonstrative Pronoun Sets

Proximate இ *i*	Distant அ *a*	Interrogative எ *e*
இது *idu* 'this thing'	அது *adu* 'that thing'	எது *edu* 'which thing?'
இவரு *ivaru* 'this person'	அவரு *avaru* 'that person'	யாரு *yaaru* (எவரு) (*evaru*) 'which person? who?'
இவ(ள்) *iva(ḷ)* 'this (F)'	அவ(ள்) *ava(ḷ)* 'that (F)'	எவ(ள்) *eva(ḷ)** 'which (F)'
இவன் *ivan* 'this male'	அவன் *avan* 'that male'	எவன் *evan** 'which male'
இவங்க *ivanga* 'these persons'	அவங்க *avanga* 'those persons'	எவங்க *evanga** 'which persons?'
இவங்க *ivanga* 'this woman (POL)'	அவங்க *avanga* 'that woman (POL)'	எவங்க *evanga** 'which woman (POL)?'

All Tamil third person pronouns contain a prefixed phonetic element that indicates whether one is referring to something proximate, distant, or whether a question is being asked about someone or something. This is similar to sets in English like 'here, there' and 'where', or 'this, that,' and 'what.' In English the only portion of these sets that replicates itself reliably is the **wh-** element, so in English these are referred to as wh-interrogatives by linguists. In Tamil, the first vowel of the adjective or pronoun, இ *i*, அ *a* and எ *e*, represent the meanings 'proximate' (this, here), 'distant' (that, there) and 'interrogative' (what, where). These sets (shown in Table 4.4) are quite regular (more so than in English), with only a few deviations from

[1] Some dialects even have a forms that resemble the dative, i.e. அதுக்கு *adukku* or அதுக்க *adukka*; thus அதுக்கு தலெ *adukku tale* 'its head' or அதுக்க தலெ *adukka tale*, 'ibid.' for LT அதன் தலை.

this vowel pattern.[2] Some grammarians refer to these kinds of pronouns etc. as 'deictic' pronouns (from the Greek *deixis* meaning 'pointing'). Cf. also ∮5.2 (Demonstrative Adjectives).

Note that in the cases of எவ(ள்) *eva(l̥)* 'which (female)?', எவன் *evan* 'which (male)?', எவரு *evaru* 'which (HON) person?' and எவங்க *evanga* 'which people?' these forms are only used when it is known that the person(s) in question is/are (a) (low-status) male(s) or female(s), or something particular is known about the person/people. Otherwise, யாரு *yaaru* 'who' is used in place of all these forms. Furthermore, எது *edu* is also used only when something is known about a thing; if nothing is known, என்ன *enna* is used.

(110) எவன் வந்தான்
evan vandaan
which-man came

'Which fellow was it that came? ('We know that somebody came; we just don't know anything about him.)'

(111) யாரு வந்தாரு?
yaaru vandaaru?

'Who came?'

(112) புஸ்தகம் எது
pustaham edu?
book which-thing

'Which (of those things) is a book?
('We know that one of the things is a book, but not which one.)'

(113) புஸ்தகம் என்ன
pustaham enna?
book what

'What (in the world) is a book?'

4.4.1 Pronouns and Case

Case markers (cf. ∮2.3) are the same for pronouns as for nouns. But pronouns in most instances refer to animate beings, so rules about co-occurrence of certain postpositions (e.g. the locative) with animates, apply.

[2] In older LT, there was a further distinction, 'yonder, out of sight' provided by the vocalic element உ *u*, but this is no longer in use, even in modern LT.

4.4.2 The Reflexive Pronoun

LT has a reflexive pronoun தான் *taan* which refers to the subject of the sentence, and often is used pragmatically for emphasis:

(114) நான் தான் வந்தேன்
naan taan vandeen
I self came
'I myself came; only I came.'

Many dialects of ST do not use this pronoun (except as an emphatic marker), substituting third person pronouns in its place. For those that do use தான், it may be marked for case; it has an oblique form தன் *tan-* which can function as a genitive/possessive form, and then other case markers may be added. It behaves like other short-vowel (CVC) patterning pronouns, with doubling of ன் *n* before case: தன்னெ *tanne* 'itself-ACC' Like என் *en* and other similar pronouns, it has the dative form அக்கு *akku* instead of உக்கு *ukku*.[3]

One common usage of this pronoun, even in dialects which do not use any other parts of the paradigm elsewhere, is the dative form தனக்கு *tanakku* 'to oneself', as in

(115) தனக்குள்ளெ அதே மாதிரி நெனெச்சுகிட்டிருந்தேன்
tanakkuḷḷe adee maadiri neneccukiṭṭirundeen
self-to same way think-DUR-PAST-PNG
'I was thinking the very same thing (to) myself.'

[3]In LT there is a non-polite plural of this pronoun தாம் *taam* as well as a polite plural தாங்கள் *taankaḷ*; the latter is used in LT as a very polite pronoun equivalent to English 'your honour' or 'your grace.' These forms are declinable in LT; they are not used in ST.

Chapter 5

Adjectives

With a very few exceptions, Tamil does not have what are considered to be 'true' adjectives, i.e. there are very few lexical items that one would enter into a dictionary under the rubric 'adjective'; there are lexical items that act like adjectives in other languages, but most are derived from verbs or from nouns (cf. ∮5.4 and ∮6.3). The few adjectives that are not derivable from something else form a very small list, as follows:

- பெரிய *periya* 'big'
- சின்ன *cinna* 'small'
- நல்ல *nalla* 'good'
- கெட்ட *keṭṭa* 'bad'[1]
- புது *pudu* 'new'
- பழய *par̤aya* 'old'
- பச்செ *pacce* 'green; fresh, cool (as water)'
- கறுப்பு *karuppu* 'black'
- வெள்ள *veḷḷa* 'white'

Most adjectives (though not all), whether 'basic' (as above) or derived from nouns or verbs, have a final அ *a*. Other color terms such as நீலம் *niilam* 'blue' and செம்பு *cembu* 'red' are nouns and must be converted into

[1] கெட்ட *keṭṭa* although included above, is not a 'true' adjective, since it is derivable from the verb *keḍu* 'spoil, go bad.'

adjectives by derivational suffixing (see below). Some color names are borrowed (from English, Sanskrit, Hindi, etc.), or the color concept is borrowed, and are formed by addition of கலர் *kalar* 'color' to the word: மஞ்சள் கலர் *manjaḷ kalar* 'turmeric color' (yellow); காப்பி கலர் *kaappi kalar* 'coffee color' (brown); பச்செ *pacce* 'green' is an indigenous color term that covers some greenish-yellow tints that speakers of other languages would classify as yellow. பச்செ *pacce* also means 'fresh' as in பச்செ தண்ணி *pacce taṇṇi* 'fresh (unboiled/cool/raw) water, drinking water.'

5.1 Use in the Sentence and with Nouns

Adjectives immediately precede the noun: சின்ன பய்யன் *cinna payyan* 'small boy'; புது வீடு *pudu viiḍu* 'new house'; பச்செ தண்ணி *pacce taṇṇi* 'fresh, cool water'; etc. Adjectives are indeclinable and invariable for PNG; ரெண்டு புது வீட்டுக்கு *reṇḍu pudu viiṭṭukku* 'to the two new houses'; மூணு நல்ல பொம்பிளெங்க *muuṇu nalla pombuḷenga* 'three good women.'

5.1.1 Predicate Adjectives: து *tu* and சு *cu* Suffixes

If the adjective is in the predicate and not preceding any noun, as in English 'this house is **new**', it must be nominalized in Tamil by the addition of து *du* or in some cases, சு *su*. Example: இந்த வீடு புதுசு *inda viiḍu pudusu* 'this house is (a) new (one).' In some cases, the consonants of the stem also undergo morphophonemic alternation when nominalized: சின்ன *cinna* ⟶ சிறுசு *sirisu*. The following is a list of nominalized forms of 'true' adjectives:

- பெரிசு *perusu* 'big one/thing'
- சிறிசு *sirusu* 'small thing/one'
- நல்லது *nalladu* 'good thing'
- கெட்டது *keṭṭadu* 'bad one/thing'
- புதுசு *pudusu* 'new one/thing'
- பழயது *paẓayadu* 'old thing/one'

Nominalizations of the sort in English 'good man' are also possible, by suffixing the third person pronouns directly to the adjectival stem: பெரியவ *periyava* 'big woman', சின்னவன் *cinnavan* 'small man', நல்லவரு *nallavaru* 'good man', கெட்டவங்க *keṭṭavanga* 'bad people', etc.[2]

[2] Arden (1942) refers to these as 'participial nouns.'

Table 5.1: Structure of Demonstrative Adjective Sets

Proximate இ *i*	Distant அ a	*Interrogative* எ *e*
இந்த *inda* 'this'	அந்த *anda* 'that'	எந்த *enda* 'which?'

5.2 Demonstrative Adjectives

Tamil has demonstrative adjectives, pronouns and other pro-forms which form sets of three, differing only in the initial vowel, which indicates whether one is referring to something proximate from the speaker, something distant, or whether a question is being asked about someone or something. In these sets in Tamil, the first vowel of the adjective or pronoun, இ *i* represents the meaning 'proximate' (this, here), அ *a* represents the meaning 'distant' (that, there), and எ *e* represents the meaning 'interrogative' (what?, where?). These sets are quite regular (more so than in English), with only a few deviations from this vowel pattern.[3] Some grammarians refer to these kinds of pronouns etc. as 'deictic' pronouns (from the Greek *deixis* meaning 'pointing.')

Thus இது *idu* '**this** thing', அது *adu* '**that** thing', எது *edu?* '**which** thing?' This contrasts with purely 'adjectival' இந்த *inda* 'this', அந்த *anda* 'that' and எந்த *enda* 'which?' The latter forms must always be followed by some kind of nominal element, or be nominalized; the former (இது *idu* etc.) cannot be followed by a nominal element, unless in a NOUN–NOUN construction (cf. ∮6.1). Example: அது நல்ல வீடு *adu nalla viiḍu* 'That is a good house' vs. அந்த வீடு நல்லா இருக்கு *anda viiḍu nallaa irukku* 'That house is (looks) good.' In the first example, one must assume that it is an equational sentence with a deleted element 'be' or else the statement that *adu* cannot be followed by a noun is contradictory.

5.2.1 Other Variations, Other Deictic Sets

In Table 5.2. we list இப்ப *ippa* etc. for 'now' etc. but the form of this set varies widely in ST. The older LT form இப்பொழுது *ippoẕutu* does not occur in ST, but a more modern form இப்போது *ippoodu* 'now' is used by some in ST. Other speakers use இப்பொ *ippo* 'now' (அப்பொ *appo* 'then', and எப்பொ *eppo* 'when'?); some others have the forms இப்பம் *ippam* அப்பம் *appam*, and எப்பம் *eppam* 'when'?

[3] In older LT, there was a further distinction, 'yonder, out of sight' provided by the prefixed vocalic element உ *u*, but this is no longer in use, even in modern LT.

Table 5.2: Structure of Other Deictic Sets

Proximate இ *i*	Distant அ *a*	Interrogative எ *e*
இப்ப *ippa* 'now'	அப்ப *appa* 'then'	எப்ப *eppa* 'when'?
இவ்வளவு *ivvaḷavu* 'this much'	அவ்வளவு *avvaḷavu* 'that much'	எவ்வளவு? *evvaḷavu?* 'how much'?
இங்கெ *inge* 'here'	அங்கெ *ange* 'there'	எங்கெ? *enge?* 'where'
இண்ணெக்கி *iṇṇekki* 'today'	அண்ணெக்கி *aṇṇekki* 'that day'	எண்ணெக்கி? *eṇṇekki?* 'which day?'
இவரு *ivaru* 'this person'	அவரு *avaru* 'that person'	யாரு *yaaru* 'which person? who?'
இவங்க *ivanga* 'these persons'	அவங்க *avanga* 'those persons'	எவங்க *evanga** 'which persons?'
இத்தனெ *ittane* 'this many'	அத்தனெ *attane* 'that many'	எத்தனெ? *ettane?* 'how many?'

LT is capable of making other sets of words by prefixing இ *i*, அ *a* and எ *e* to nouns of various sorts (and doubling the first consonant): இந்நாள் *innaaḷ* 'this day', இக்காலம் *ikkaalam* 'this time; the contemporary period', etc. This is rare in ST, but some dialects may occasionally produce such forms.

5.3 Comparison of Adjectives

Adjectives in Tamil do not have morphological forms for the 'comparative' and 'superlative' degrees like English and many other European languages (-er, -est, etc.). Adjectives can be compared, however, with the use of விட *viḍa* (the infinitive of the verb விடு *viḍu* 'leave, let'). The rule for this construction on the model of English '**A** is bigger than **B**' would be

'**B** ACC விட viḍa **A** NOUN + ஆ இருக்கு *-aa irukku*'

The noun in this construction is adjectivalized and made comparative by the addition of the so-called ADVERBIAL suffix ஆ *aa* (from LT ஆக/ஆய் *aaha/aay*), which are both reduced to *aa* in ST. This, in combination with the copula, makes a 'temporary-state' adjective.[4]

[4] Note that ஆக *aaha* is the INFINITIVE of ஆகு *aahu* 'become', and ஆய் *aay* is the AVP (past participle) of the same.

(116) அந்த வீட்டெ விட இந்த வீடு பெருசா இருக்கு
anda viiṭṭe viḍa inda viiḍu perusaa irukku
that house-ACC than this house big-ADV be
'This house is bigger than that house.'

Note that in the Tamil the order of the two items compared is **B: A**, while in English the order is **A: B**.

5.3.1 Superlatives of Adjectives: Locative plus Emphatic

In Tamil, superlatives may be formed by use of the locative case plus emphatic ஏ *ee*. For example, English 'This is the biggest house in (all of) Madurai' is expressed in Tamil, 'This in-all-Madurai-EMPH big house.'

(117) இது மதுரெய்லெயே பெரிய வீடு
idu madurey-le-yee periya viiḍu
this-thing Madurai-in-EMPH big house
'This is the bigg**est** house in (all of) Madurai.'

Note that in English the *realm* or *domain* of the superlative degree can be omitted, i.e. 'This is the biggest house.' In Tamil the realm cannot be omitted because the locative and emphatic are attached to the word defining the realm, i.e. in all of *Madurai*, in this *school*, in *America*, etc.

5.4 Adjectives Derived from Other Constituents

Since Tamil lacks large sets of true adjectives, it must form adjectives by deriving them from other constituents. This is done in various ways.

5.4.1 Denominal Adjectives

Tamil can make adjectives from nouns by various processes. One is to take the OBLIQUE form of nouns (those that have them) and prepose it to the noun being modified:

- கொளம் *koḷam* 'pond, tank' ⟶ கொளத்து *koḷattu* 'fresh-water' + மீனு *miinu* 'fish' ⟶ கொளத்து மீனு *koḷattu miinu* 'fresh-water fish'
- வீடு *viiḍu* 'house' ⟶ வீட்டு *viiṭṭu* + காரன் *kaaran* 'one who does s.t.' ⟶ வீட்டுக்காரன் *viiṭṭukaaran* 'landlord; husband'

Other nouns can be prefixed to nouns to form new nouns:

- பொண்ணு *poṇṇu* 'girl' + பிள்ளெ *piḷḷai* 'child' ⟶ பொம்பிள்ளெ *pombuḷḷe* 'female, woman; girl'
- புஸ்தகம் *pustaham* 'book' + நிலையம் *nilayam* 'place' ⟶ புஸ்தகநிலையம் *pustahanilayam* 'library'
- கண்ணாடி *kaṇṇaaḍi* 'glass' + ஜாடி *jaaḍi* ⟶ கண்ணாடிஜாடி *kaṇṇaaḍi jaaḍi* 'glass jar'

5.4.2 Deverbal Adjectives

Another way to form adjectives is to derive them from verbs. This can be done very simply by taking the tense-marked form of a verb, removing the PNG, add அ *a*, and preposing it before the noun. This form of the verb is known as the adjectival participle, or AJP. Only the past and present forms of the AJP are available in ST; in LT, future forms are also used.

(118) நேத்து வாங்குன பணம்
neettu vaanguna paṇam
yesterday taken money
'The money (that was) taken (borrowed) yesterday.'

(119) போன வாரம்
poona vaaram
gone week
'The week (that) went; last week'

(120) நாளெக்கி வர்றவங்களுக்கு திருப்பி குடுக்கணும்
naaḷekki varravangaḷukku tiruppi kuḍukkaṇum
tomorrow coming-people-DAT back give-must
'(We'll) have to give (it) back to the people who will come tomorrow.'

Many of these AJP's translate better in English as relative clauses, since English cannot generally prepose long adjectival phrases before nouns like Tamil can. However English does have certain 'phrasal' adjectives, such as 'rat-infested (house)', 'moth-eaten (coat)', 'newly constructed (building)' etc. that are more likely to occur than the simpler forms 'infested (house)' or 'eaten (coat)', etc.

Note that the Tamil equivalents of English adjectives 'next' and 'last' are only derivable from AJP's: அடுத்த *aḍutta* 'next', from அடு *aḍu* 'approach, be close'; போன *poona* 'last' from போ *poo* 'go.'

5.4.3 Adjectives Derived from Nouns with ஆன *aana*

Yet another way to form adjectives from nouns is to take ஆன *aana*, the past AJP of ஆகு *aahu* 'become', and suffix it to a noun in order to form an adjective.

- அழகு *arahu* 'beauty' + ஆன *aana* ⟶ அழகான *arahaana* 'beautiful'
- நீளம் *niiḷam* 'length' + ஆன *aana* ⟶ நீளமான *niiḷamaana* 'long'
- நீலம் *niilam* 'blue color' + ஆன *aana* ⟶ நீலமான *niilamaana* 'blue'
- உரிமெ *urime* 'right' + ஆன *aana* ⟶ உரிமெயான *urimeyaana* 'rightful'

In LT, another suffix, உள்ள *uḷḷa*, a form derived from a verb உள் *uḷ* 'be inherent, be within' is also used to form derived adjectives; for some speakers these two forms are equivalent, but for others there may be a contrast in meaning.

5.5 Quantifiers and Numerals

5.5.1 Quantifiers

Words that express quantities of things, such as English 'many, much, few, a lot' as well as interrogative quantifiers such as 'how many, how much' have equivalents in Tamil that in general resemble the adjectives we have seen in previous sections of this chapter. That is, they in general end in the vowel அ *a* and precede nouns or noun phrases. Examples:

- நெறெய *nereya* 'many, lots of, much'
- கொஞ்ச *konja* '(a) few, some'
- செல *sela* '(a) few, some'
- பல *pala* 'many, several'
- எவ்வளவு *evvaḷavu* 'how much?'
  அவ்வளவு *avvaḷavu* 'that much'
  இவ்வளவு *ivvaḷavu* 'this much'
- எத்தனெ *ettane* 'how many?'
  அத்தனெ *attane* 'that many'
  இத்தனெ *ittane* 'this many'

- ரொம்ப *romba* 'many, lots of; very'
- அதிக *adiha* 'much, lots of'
- ஒவ்வொரு *ovvoru* 'each'
- எல்லா ... உம் *ellaa ... um* 'all, every'

There are many lexical differences between LT and ST, with forms used in LT that are rarely or never used in ST. When it comes to quantifiers, many of the above list are not used by all speakers in ST, especially the forms செல (LT சில) *sela* '(a) few, some' and பல *pala* 'many, several' or are only used in certain frozen phrases, such as செல சமயம் *sela samayam* 'sometimes, many times'. LT quantifiers such as மிக *miha* 'many, much' and அநேக *aneeha* 'several, some' are not used in ST at all, whereas some of the other quantifiers have LT forms that are phonologically more conservative but are essentially the same item. As with many adjectives, some of these forms are derived from nouns or verbs; கொஞ்ச *konja* '(a) few, some' and அதிக *adiha* 'much, lots of' are derived from the nouns கொஞ்சம் *konjam* 'little' and அதிகம் *adiham* 'much, plenty' respectively. The forms நெறெய *nereya* 'many, lots of, much' and ரொம்ப *romba* 'many, lots of; very' are ST infinitive forms of the LT verbs நிறை *nirai* 'fill; be full' and நிரம்பு *nirampu* 'fill, complete, satisfy,' respectively. And there are forms that express amounts, especially regarding prices, that are not used attributively (i.e. pre-nominally) but are used in predicates, such as ஜாஸ்தி *jaasti* '(too) much; high (in price)' and its opposite, கம்மி *kammi* 'cheap, (too) low', such as:

- அங்கே வெலெவாசி ரொம்ப ஜாஸ்தி *ange velevaasi romba jaasti*
  'The cost of living is very high there'
- அவங்க சொன்ன வெலெ ரொம்ப கம்மி *avanga sonna vele romba kammi*
  'The price they quoted was very cheap'

The use of attributive quantifiers in sentences is illustrated by the following:

(121) நெறெய பெரிய வீடு அந்த வீதியில் இருக்கு
nereya periya viiḍu anda viidiyle irukku
many big house that street-in is
'There are many big houses in that street'

(122) எத்தனெ சின்ன கொழந்தெங்க ஒங்க குடும்பத்தில் இருக்குறாங்க
ettane cinna kor̤andenga onga kuḍumbattule irukkraanga
how-many small children your family-in are
'How many little children are there in your family?'

(123) அவ்வளவு நேரம் வேண்டாம்
avvaḷavu neeram veeṇḍaam
that-much time non-needed
'That much time is not necessary'

(124) எல்லா வீட்டுலெயும் தேடினேன்
ellaa viiṭṭleyum teeḍineen
all house-in searched-I
'I searched (in) every house'

Since Tamil inanimate nouns are usually not marked for number, it is only the quantifier நெறெய *nereya* 'many' that marks plurality in the first sentence, and எல்லா (... உம்) *ellaa ... um* in the third. Note that quantifiers PRECEDE the (other) adjectives in the sentences; note also that எல்லா (... உம்) *ellaa ... um* is disjunctive; உம் *um* is suffixed to the noun that precedes it; if a noun is not present, எல்லா (... உம்) *ellaa ... um* becomes எல்லாம் *ellaam* 'all (things); the whole (thing); everything' and the meaning is then singular:

வீட்டுலெ எல்லாம் தேடினேன் *viiṭṭleyellaam teeḍineen*
'I searched all over the whole house.'

In referring to humans, எல்லாம் *ellaam* is replaced, in some dialects, with the form எல்லாரும் *ellaarum* 'everybody, all (people)'

எல்லாரும் கவனிச்சுகிட்டேயிருந்தாங்க
ellaarum gavaniccukiṭṭeeyirundaanga
'Everybody was staring'

If the focus is on individuals, rather than on an undifferentiated group, the form ஒவ்வொரு ... உம் *ovvoru ... um* 'each; each and every' can be pronominalized, to get ஒவ்வொருத்தனும் *ovvoruttanum* 'each male', ஒவ் வொருத்தியும் *ovvoruttiyum* 'each woman" and ஒவ்வொருத்தரும் *ovvoruttarum* 'each person (HON)'.

அந்த வீட்டுலெ, ஒவ்வொருத்தருக்கும் ஒரு தனி கார் இருக்கு
anda viiṭṭule, ovvoruttarukkum oru tani kaar irukku
'Every person (irrespective of gender) in that household has his or her own (individual) car'

Table 5.3: Basic Tamil Cardinal Numerical Morphemes

ஒண்ணு	*oṇṇu*	'one'	நூறு	*nuuru*	'hundred'
ரெண்டு	*reṇḍu*	'two'	ஆயிரம்	*aayiram*	'thousand'
மூணு	*muuṇu*	'three'	லக்ஷம்	*lakṣam*	'lakh'
நாலு	*naalu*	'four'	கோடி	*kooḍi*	'crore'
அஞ்சு	*anju*	'five'			
ஆறு	*aaru*	'six'			
ஏழு	*eeṛu*	'seven'			
எட்டு	*eṭṭu*	'eight'			
ஒம்பது	*ombadu*	'nine'			
பத்து	*pattu*	'ten'			

5.5.2   Cardinal Numerals

The Tamil numerical system has terms for the numerals 1 to 10, 100, 1000, 100,000 (the 'lakh') and 10,000,000 (the 'crore'). These are combined in various ways to get teens, multiples of 10 and all the other possibilities a numerical system would need. The basic numerals are as shown in Table 5.3.

The numerals from one to ten are unproblematical; like adjectives, they are invariable (are not marked for PNG); syntactically, they occur at the beginning of noun phrases, before any adjectives (with one or two exceptions to this rule, see below) but following deictic adjectives such as இந்த, அந்த, எந்த *inda, anda, enda* (cf. §5.2).

When the basic numerals are combined, however, to get larger integers such as '12' '42' '542' '1963', there are a number of complexities to be observed.

The first complexity is that the basic Tamil numerals seem to have, in their form, similarities to Tamil NOUNS, rather than adjectives. When combined with other numerals, any form that precedes another takes on what we might consider to be an ADJECTIVAL FORM; we could also refer to this as an OBLIQUE form (cf. §2.1.5). The numeral 'ten' பத்து *pattu* also has various allomorphs, depending whether it is combining with basic numbers to form 'teens', in which case its form is பதி *padi-* (or sometimes பத *pada-* or பன் *pan-*), or to form multiples of ten, where it has the form பது *padu* (or in some dialects வது *vadu*). Other numerals also have oblique or adjectival forms, as seen in Table 5.4.

Such a table does not explain the complexities of the system. What we can observe is that the ADJECTIVAL or OBLIQUE form seems to be a

Table 5.4: Oblique or Adjectival Forms of Numerals

Basic form of numeral			Oblique or adjectival form
ஒண்ணு	*oṇṇu*	'one'	ஒரு *oru*
ரெண்டு	*reṇḍu*	'two'	இர *ira-*, இரு *iru-*, ஈர் *iir-*
மூணு	*muuṇu*	'three'	மூ *muu-*, மு *mu-*
நாலு	*naalu*	'four'	நா *naa-*
அஞ்சு	*anju*	'five'	ஐ *ai-*, அம் *am-*
ஆறு	*aaru*	'six'	அறு *aru-*
ஏழு	*eeṛu*	'seven'	எழு *eṛu*
எட்டு	*eṭṭu*	'eight'	எண் *eṇ-*, எம் *em-*
ஒம்பது	*ombadu*	'nine'	(no special form; cf. below)
பத்து	*pattu*	'ten'	பதி *padi-*, பத *pada-*
நூறு	*nuuru*	'hundred'	நூத்தி *nuutti*
ஆயிரம்	*aayiram*	'thousand'	ஆயிரத்தி *aayiratti*
லக்ஷம்	*lakṣam*	'lakh'	(no special form; cf. below)
கோடி	*kooḍi*	'crore'	(no special form; cf. below)

truncated form of the basic cardinal number, minus what in some cases appears to be a 'nominal' suffix.[5] The oblique form, however, undergoes various sandhi phenomena in combining with the other morphemes, and the output of these is not very predictable. Essentially, the system is irregular enough that we must specify all the permutations, as shown in Table 5.5.

The generalizations that can be made about the data in Table 5.5 are the following:

- Long vowels in the basic numerals become shortened in combinations that give multiples of tens; ஆறு *aaru* 'six' ⟶ அறு *aru-*, as in அறுபது *aru+badu* 'six+ty'; in other cases the form is so truncated that it is difficult to see its relationship to the basic numeral, as in அம்பது *ambadu* 'fif+ty' and எம்பது *embadu* 'eighty'.[6]

- In the combinations with higher numerals, such as with hundreds and thousands, other sandhi forms appear, which seem even less regular.

- The forms for 'nine', ninety' and 'nine hundred' are extremely irregular; a hitherto unmentioned morpheme தொள் *toḷ-* appears in combination with the next-highest decimal place in the case of 'ninety' and

---

[5] This is clearer in LT than in ST; cf. Schiffman 1968 for more details.

[6] Some dialects retain a more LT-like form for 'eighty': எண்பது *eṇbadu*; others have an unpredictable form எம்ப்ளது *embḷadu*.

'nine hundred' while the form for 'nine' appears to be a combination of 'one' and 'ten.'[7]

It should also be noted that some alternatives to the forms in Table 5.6 occur:

- For எரனூறு *eranuuru* '200' some speakers say இரனூறு *iranuuru*
- For ஐனூறு *ainuuru* '500' some speakers say ஐஞ்ஞூறு *aiññuuru*
- For அஞ்சாயிரம் *anjaayiram* '5,000' some speakers have ஐயாயிரம் *aiyaayiram*
- For ரெண்டாயிரம் *reṇḍaayiram* '2,000' some speakers say ஈராயிரம் *iiraayiram*

Some of these forms are forms closer to LT forms; Tamil numerals are rarely written out; the 'international' forms of the numerals[8] are in standard usage in Tamilnadu (though Tamil forms of the numerals may still be found in old manuscripts), so most speakers never see other speakers' 'spellings' of numerals, and never notice the differences. Indeed, among educated speakers, English names of numerals are in such common usage, especially for dates, that instead of using the Tamil form of the date, many speakers use the English.

- ஆயிரத்து தொள்ளாயிரத்து தொண்ணூத்தெட்டாம் வருஷத்துலெ அங்கே இருந்தேன்

  aayirattu toḷḷaayirattu toṇṇuuttettaam varuṣattule ange irundeen

  'I was there in 1998.'
- ⟶ நைண்டியேட்டுலெ அங்கே இருந்தேன் *naintiyeytle ange irundeen*

  'I was there in (19)98.'

5.5.3 Numbers of Persons

The numerals can be used to refer to quantities of people, but if pronominalized, the following forms are used for a single person.

> ஒருத்தன் *oruttan*, ஒருத்தி *orutti*, ஒருத்தரு *oruttaru*
> 'one male, one female, one person (hon)'

[7] The system gives the appearance of having originally been an 'octenary' (eight-base) system, with no words for 'nine', ninety' and 'nine hundred' so that when the system became decimalized, something ad hoc had to be invented for these integers.

[8] What we call in English the 'Arabic' numerals.

For numbers higher than one, the regular number plus the word பேரு *peeru* 'name' is used:[9]

> அந்த வீட்டுலெ, ரெண்டு பேருக்குத் தான் இங்க்ளிஷ் தெரியும்
> *anda viiṭṭule, reṇḍu peerukku taan ingliṣ teriyum*
> 'In that house, only two persons know English'

These forms may also be postposed to a noun, in which case they mean a certain (one); one of (a set)':

> என் ஸ்னேய்தரு-ஒருத்தரு மதுரெய்லெருந்து வந்திருக்காரு
> *en sneydar-oruttaru madureylerundu vandirukkaaru*
> 'A (certain) friend of mine has come from Madurai (one of my friends has come . . .).'

5.5.3.1 Indeterminate Quantities

To express indeterminacy of quantities, a number of syntactic devices are possible, such as ஒரு *oru* plus another number:

> ஒரு பத்து பேரு அங்கே இருந்தாங்க
> *oru pattu peeru ange irundaanga*
> 'Around ten people were there; ten people or so were there'

The expression நாலு பேர் *naalu peer*, though it literally means 'four people', is often used to mean 'an indeterminate number of people; a bunch of people; a group' much the way English 'a couple' does not always refer to exactly 'two.' Indeterminate or approximate quantities can also be expressed by combining numerals, e.g. நாலஞ்சு *naalanju* 'four or five' etc.:

> ரெண்டுமூணு வருஷம் அங்கே இருக்கணும்
> *reṇḍumuuṇu varuṣam ange irukkaṇum*
> '(I'll) have to stay there two or three years or so'

If the focus is on the inclusivity of something, the clitic உம் *um* (cf. §7.8.3) is added to the noun: ரெண்டு பேரும் *reṇḍu peerum* 'both (of the people)'; நாலு பேரும் *naalu peerum* 'all four of the people'; பத்து பேரும் *pattu peerum* 'all ten of them.' If பேர் *peer* is omitted, the numeral plus clitic means 'both things' but then the verb will be marked for neuter (and perforce singular) as in

[9] In LT, there are pronominalized forms for persons up to five, i.e இருவர் *iruvar* 'two persons', மூவர் *muuvar* 'three people', நால்வர் *naalvar* 'four people', and ஐவர் *aivar* 'five persons' but ST does not usually use these forms.

- ரெண்டும் வந்தது *reṇḍum vandadu* 'Both (things) came'

- எப்ப பாத்தாலும், நாலு பேரு எங்க சொவத்து-கிட்டெ நிண்ண மயமா தானே இருக்காங்க

  eppa paattaalum, naalu peeru enga sovattu-kiṭṭe niṇṇa mayamaa taane irukkaanga

  'Whenever you look, there's a bunch of people hanging around our wall, gawking (as if in a trance)'

5.5.4 Ordinal Numbers

The above cardinal numerals can be made into 'ordinal' numerals by the addition of suffixes, either ஆம் *-aam* or ஆவது *-aavadu* though these two suffices do not always 'mean' the same thing, nor is their use interchangeable. ஆவது *aavadu* may also be suffixed to எத்தனெ *ettane* to mean 'how many-eth':

> இது எத்தனாவது தடவெ *idu ettanaavadu taḍave*? 'This is the how-many-eth time? (How many times has this been?)'

For dates, ஆம் *aam* is usually the preferred usage:

> இது அஞ்சாம் (அஞ்சாவது) தேதி *idu anjaam (anjaavadu) teedi*
> 'This is the fifth (day) of the month'

ஆவது *-aavadu* together with நம்பர் *nambar* 'number' usually means 'that which is designated with that number' whereas ஆம் *aam* means 'that number in a series'. Compare:

- இது அஞ்சாவது நம்பர் வீடு *idu anjaavadu nambar viiḍu* 'This is house No. 5'

- இது அஞ்சாம் நம்பர் வீடு *idu anjaan nambar viiḍu* 'This is the fifth house (in a series)'

Most numerals take these two suffixes without problems, but the number 'one' has other forms:

- மொதல் *modal*, as in மொதல் மொதலா *modal-modalaa* 'at first, from the very beginning'

  மொதல் வகுப்பு *modal vahuppu* 'first class'

  இது மொதலாவது தடவெ *idu modalaavadu taḍave*

  'This is the first time'

- ஒண்ணாம் *oṇṇaam* as in ஒண்ணாம் தேதி *oṇṇaan teedi* 'the first of the month'

For further details about the idiosyncracies of numerals, see Asher (1982:191).

Table 5.5: Regular and Irregular Combined Forms of Numerals

'Teen' Forms		
பதநொண்ணு	*padinoṇṇu*	'eleven'
பன்னெண்டு	*panneṇḍu*	'twelve'
பதிமூணு	*padimuuṇu*	'thirteen'
பதனாலு	*padanaalu*	'fourteen'
பதனஞ்சு	*padananju*	'fifteen'
பதனாறு	*padanaaru*	'sixteen'
பதனேழு	*padaneeṟu*	'seventeen'
பதனெட்டு	*padaneṭṭu*	'eighteen'
பத்தொம்பது	*pattombadu*	'nineteen'
Multiples of Ten		
இருபது/(இருவது)	*irubadu*, (*iruvadu*)	'twenty'
முப்பது	*muppadu*	'thirty'
நாப்பது	*naappadu*	'forty'
அம்பது	*ambadu*	'fifty'
அறுபது/(அறுவது)	*arubadu*, (*aruvadu*)	'sixty'
எழுபது/(எழுவது)	*eṟubadu*, (eṟuvadu)	'seventy'
எண்பது/(எம்பது)	*eṇbadu*, (*embadu*)	'eighty'
தொண்ணூறு	*toṇṇuuru*	'ninety'

Table 5.6: Multiples of Hundreds and Thousands

Hundreds		
எரனூறு	*eranuuru*	'200'
முன்னூறு	*munnuuru*	'300'
நானூறு	*naanuuru*	'400'
ஐனூறு	*ainuuru*	'500'
அறுனூறு	*arunuuru*	'600'
எழுனூறு	*eṟunuuru*	'700'
எண்ணூறு	*eṇṇuuru*	'800'
தொள்ளாயிரம்	*toḷḷaayiram*	'900'
Thousands		
ரெண்டாயிரம்	*reṇḍaayiram*	'2,000'
மூவாயிரம்	*muuvaayiram*	'3,000'
நாலாயிரம்	*naalaayiram*	'4,000'
அஞ்சாயிரம்	*anjaayiram*	'5,000'
ஆறாயிரம்	*aaraayiram*	'6,000'
ஏழாயிரம்	*eeṟaayiram*	'7,000'
எட்டாயிரம்	*eṭṭaayiram*	'8,000
ஒம்பதாயிரம்	*ombadaayiram*	'9,000

Chapter 6

Syntax: Introduction

The basic order of constituents in a simple Tamil sentence is subject-object-verb (SOV). Other orders can be found, but they range from simple stylistic variation to unusual 'afterthought' word order, where the speaker has not formed the sentence well and adds things after the basic order has been established (usually after the verb has been made finite). Compared to English, Tamil syntax is often the mirror-image of the order in an English sentence, particularly when there are relative clauses, quotations, adjectival and adverbial clauses, conjoined verbal constructions, aspectual and modal auxiliaries, and other complexities.

6.1 Nouns

The simplest sentence can consist of two noun phrases, with no verb present in the surface structure. This is known as an equational sentence and functions to make identity statements:

இது புஸ்தகம் *idu pustaham* 'This (is a) book.'

Such NOUN-NOUN constructions can also be very complex, with embedded verbal constructions, adjectival participles and what-not:

(125)	நாங்க	தீவெட்டி	கொள்ளித்திரிறவங்க	இல்லெ
	naanga	*tiiveṭṭi*	*koḷḷittiriravanga*	*ille*
	We	torch	prowlers	not

'We are not night-prowlers'

Nouns that are the subject of a sentence are usually in the nominative case, except in certain constructions involving stative and/or defective verbs, and in constructions involving இரு *iru* when it means 'have.'

Noun phrases which are the subject of a sentence are generally the first constituent in the sentence. Adjectives and other members of the NOUN PHRASE precede the noun. Case markers, plural markers, and certain quantifiers follow the Noun, as in:

- அவனுக்கு *avan-ukku* 'to him'
- கொழந்தெங்க *kor̤andenga* 'children'
- பால் எல்லாம் *paal-ellaam* 'all the milk'

6.2 Verbal Syntax

As mentioned above, verb phrases containing finite verbs are generally the last constituent in the surface structure of a Tamil sentence. The order of various constituents of the verb phrase is basically as follows.

$$= \left\{ \begin{array}{llllll} VBSTEM & TNS & (INF) & (ASP) & (MODAL) & PNG \\ & & (COND) & (NEG) & & \end{array} \right\}$$

This can be expanded somewhat as follows:

$$= VBSTEM \left\{ \begin{array}{lll} TNS & (ASP) & (MODAL) \\ (INF) & (MODAL) & (NEG) \\ & (COND) & \end{array} \right\}$$

That is, a verb phrase (VP) consists of a verb stem (VBSTEM) plus tense, plus optional infinitive (INF) plus optional aspect (ASP) and optional modal (MODAL) and person-number-gender. If a conditional mode (COND) is chosen, it is attached to tense; negation (NEG) must be attached to an infinitive, in which case there is no PNG. When aspect (ASP) is present, the AVP or past-marked verb stem must be used; aspectual verbs have their own tense markers as well, or modal/negative; PNG is present if modal and negative are not. (Cf. individual sections on these categories for a discussion of the syntax of various categories.)

In general, the order of constituents in a Tamil verb phrase is the mirror image of English order. Compare:

(126) வந்து கிட்டிருந்த் இருக்க ணும்
vandu kiṭṭirund irukka ṇum
come -ing be-INF must

'Must have been com-ing'

Table 6.1: Nominalized and Adverbial Adjectives

	Nominalized adjectives	Adverbial Phrases
1.	இந்த வீடு புதுசு *inda viiḍu pudusu* 'This house is new'	இந்த வீடு புதுசா இருக்கு *inda viiḍu pudusaa irukku* 'This house is quite new'
2.	இது சரி *idu sari* 'This is fine'	இது சரியா இருக்கு *idu sariyaa irukku* 'This is okay now'
3.	இது நல்லது *idu nalladu* 'This is (a) good (thing)'	இது நல்லா இருக்கு *idu nallaa irukku* 'Now it's good; it looks good'
4.	இந்தக் காலம் ரொம்ப மோசம் *inda kaalam romba moosam* 'This weather is very bad' (or: 'Times are bad')	இந்தக் காலம் ரொம்ப மோசமா இருக்கு *inda kaalam romba moosamaa irukku* 'This weather is bad right now'

6.3 Adjectival Syntax

Within the NOUN PHRASE, adjectives **always** precede a noun. If there is no nominal form present, there can be no adjective. That is, a sentence like English 'this is good' is not possible in Tamil; rather a Tamil sentence must have the form 'this thing is a good thing' or 'this one is a good one.'

இது நல்லது *idu nalladu* 'This thing is (a) good thing.'

(For the formation of adjectival clauses, cf. ∮5.1.)

6.4 Adverbs

There are no true adverbs in Tamil, i.e. none that one would list as such in the dictionary. All adverbs are formed by the addition of ஆ(ய்) *-aa(y)* to nouns or NOMINALIZED adjectives, with one exception: நல்ல *nalla* 'good' + ஆ *aa* ⟶ *nallaa* 'well' (although நல்லதா *nalladaa* also occurs).[1]

Adverbial forms of adjectives occur in identity statements with copula இரு *iru*. The contrast between the two forms is given in Table 6.1.

[1] In Brahmin dialect this item is regular, i.e. *nallaa* does not occur, but the nominalization of *nalla* is *nannaa*; *nalladaa* also occurs.

The two columns in Table 6.1. differ in meaning; the sentences with nominalized adjectives mean 'habitually (so-and-so)' while the sentences with adverbial phrases ஆ இரு *-aa iru-* mean 'temporarily, at the moment (so-and-so).' Or, it can mean that something has recently *become* or attained the state in question: இது சரி *idu sari* 'This is all right, this is permanently all right' versus இது சரியா இருக்கு *idu sariyaa irukku* 'This is all right NOW, at the moment (but it wasn't before).'

With certain noun phrases marked with ஆ இரு *aa iru* the meaning may be 'temporarily serving as, functioning as', e.g. இது வகுப்பு சாலெ, ஆனா இப்ப ஆப்பீஸா இருக்கு *idu vahuppu saale, aanaa ippa aaffiisaa irukku* 'This is (usually) a classroom, but now it's (serving as) an office.'

6.5 Negative Forms

Negation in Tamil is a rather complex phenomenon, and not simply a matter of taking some negative element (such as English 'not') and adding it to a sentence. In some ways the Tamil system is *skewed*, with distinctions found in affirmative sentences not found in the 'equivalent' negative sentences, and vice-versa. There is, of course, a simple negative particle இல்லெ *ille* which occurs in equational sentences (∮6.1):

(127) இது என் வீடு இல்லெ
idu en viiḍu ille
this my house not
'This is not my house.'

(128) நாங்க தீவெட்டி கொள்ளித்திரிறவங்க இல்லெ
naanga tiiveṭṭi koḷḷitiriravanga ille
We torch prowlers not
'We are not night prowlers.'

6.5.1 Ordinary Verbal Negation (Non-Future, Non-Habitual)

The simplest kind of Tamil verbal negative is formed by adding ல்லெ *-lle* to the infinitive of the verb. This form means, in general, non-future and non-habitual, i.e. beginning in the past and extending into the present.[2]

[2]The LT form இல்லை *illai* when added to the infinitive requires a morphophonemic வ *v* but this is deleted in ST, under complicated conditions (cf. Schiffman 1993). The resultant ல்லெ *lle* may in many cases be phonetically non-geminate, i.e. போகல்லெ *poohalle* is phonetically really [poːhalɛ] but to avoid confusion with other morphology we

- போகல்லெ *poohalle* 'didn't go, isn't going'
- வரல்லெ *varalle* 'didn't come, isn't coming'

In the case of the verb இரு *iru* 'be located, stay, reside', the negative is simply இல்லெ *ille*. The form involving the infinitive, i.e. *irukkalle*, is found only when இரு *iru* is suffixed to another verb, e.g. as an aspect marker (cf.∮3.9).

- நான் வந்திருக்கல்லெ *naan vand-irukkalle* 'I didn't, haven't come; it's not that I've come (it's that I've done something else).'
- அவன் சாப்பிட்டுக்கிட்டிருக்கல்லெ *avan saappiṭṭu-kiṭṭ-irukkalle* 'he hasn't been eating; it's not that he's been eating.'

6.5.2 Habitual Negative

The Habitual Negative is the only productive negative form in Tamil that is not formed by affixing some negative morpheme to the INFINITIVE. Rather, it is a SENTENTIAL negative, formed by adding *-lle* to the present verbal noun.

(129) அவன் பொதுவா படத்துக்கு போறதுல்லெ
avan poduvaa paḍattukku pooradulle
he generally picture-DAT going-NEG
'He doesn't usually go the movies.'

(130) நான் சாதாரணமா மாமிசம் சாப்பிடுறதுல்லெ
naan saadaaranamaa maamsam saappiḍradulle
I usually meat eating-NEG
'I don't usually eat meat.'

Note that this form only means habitual negative when there is a time adverb like பொதுவா *poduvaa* 'generally' or சாதாரணமா *saadaaraṇamaa* 'usually' in the sentence. Without these adverbs, the sentence is interpreted to mean IMMEDIATE FUTURE NEGATIVE:[3]

(131) நான் இண்ணெக்கி சினிமாவுக்கு போறதுல்லெ
naan iṇṇekki sinimaavukku pooradulle
'I'm not going to the movie today.'

hold to the doubled form.

[3]For some speakers, an immediate future negative interpretation is only possible if the form is embedded, e.g. in நான் இண்ணெக்கி சினிமாவுக்கு போறதுல்லெ-ண்ணு முடிவு பண்ணிட்டேன் *naan iṇṇekki sinimaavukku pooradulle-ṇṇu muḍivu paṇṇiṭṭeen* 'I have decided that I'm not going to the movie today.'

6.5.2.1 Past Habitual Negative

It is also possible to form a past habitual negative by embedding the habitual negative form before ண்ணு -*ṇṇu irund*-PNG. We gloss this as 'never intended to (do s.t.)', meaning that it was their habit *not* to do such-and-such, but now circumstances have changed.

(132) முழு ஸ்காலர்ஷிப் குடுக்குறதுல்லெண்ணு இருந்தாங்க
muẓu skaalarṣip kuḍukkradulleṇṇu irundaanga

'They never intended to give full scholarships.'

(133) இது வரெக்கும் நான் ஹிந்தி படத்துக்கு போறதுல்லெண்ணு
idu varekkum naan hindi paḍattukku pooradulleṇṇu
இருந்தேன்
irundeen

'Up until recently I made a habit of never going to Hindi movies.'

6.5.2.2 Alternative Form of Negative Past Habitual

Another form, contrasting with that in ∮6.5.2.1, and used perhaps in different dialects, is a form where the modal கூடாது ***kuuḍaadu*** 'should not, must not' is affixed to the verb and embedded before ண்ணு இருந்த் *ṇṇu irund* + PNG.

(134) போன வருஷம் நான் ஹிந்தி படத்துக்கே போககூடாதுண்ணு
poona varuṣam naan hindi paḍattukkee poohakuuḍaaduṇṇu
இருந்தேன்
irundeen

'Last year I managed to totally avoid seeing any Hindi movies.'

This form indicates a slightly higher degree of intentionality, and an emphatic ஏ *ee* is suffixed to படத்துக்கு ***paḍattukku*** 'to the movies' to signal this.

6.5.3 Future Negative

Unlike most other negative forms, the future negative is marked for person, number and gender (PNG). Being a negative, the formation involves the use of the infinitive of the verb, plus the future negative morpheme மாட்ட் *maaṭṭ* to which are attached regular PNG markers which agree with the subject. When the subject is neuter, ஆது ***aadu*** is used instead of மாட்ட் *maaṭṭ*.

- அவன் வரமாட்டான் *avan varamaaṭṭaan* 'he will-not come'

- நீங்க தூங்க மாட்டீங்க *niinga tuunga maaṭṭiinga* 'you will-not sleep'

The morpheme ஆது *-aadu* is a 'portmanteau morph' that functions both as a neuter and the future negative and, like மாட்ட் *maaṭṭ-*, is attached to the infinitive.

அது வராது *adu varaadu* 'it won't come'

The அ *-a* of the infinitive is deleted before ஆது *-aadu*. Note that this negative is not a HABITUAL negative; since the future positive form is identical with the habitual form (e.g. அவ போவா *ava poovaa* means both 'she will go' *or* 'she would habitually go', 'she used to go'), it is important to note that the negative of the habitual is formed by a different process. (Cf. ∮6.5.2 for the form used to express habitual negative action.)

6.5.4 Negative Result Clauses: Verbal Noun + அனாலெ *anaale*

Negative result clauses are formed by taking the verbal noun, e.g. பேசினது *peesinadu* and adding the instrumental அனாலெ *anaale* which translates as 'since, because, as a result.' The positive forms occur with either the past or non-past verbal nouns.

மழெ பேஞ்சதனாலெ, நான் சினிமாவுக்கு போகல்லெ *maṟe peen-jadanaale, naan sinimaavukku poohalle* 'Because it rained, I didn't go to the movies'

The negative result clause is formed the same way, except that the NEGATIVE verbal noun is used:

வராதது + அன் + ஆலெ *varaadadu + an + aale* ⟶ வராததனாலெ *varaadadanaale* 'since (it) did not come'

The negative verbal noun is tenseless, like all good negatives in Tamil; it is formed by taking the infinitive and adding ஆத் *-aad-* + அது *-adu*:

வர *var(a)* 'come' + ஆத் *aad-* (NEG) + அது *-adu* ⟶ வராதது *varaad-adu* 'that which does not come'

This is true for all verbs except இரு *iru* which has இல்ல் *ill-* as the stem instead, i.e. இல்லாதது *illaad-adu* 'That which is not.' The negative result form of இரு *iru* is thus இல்லாததனாலெ *illaad-ad-anaale* 'as a result of not being' or 'since there wasn't (s.t.).' Note that this negative, like all other negatives, is formed with the infinitive base, with deletion of அ *a* before ஆது *aadu*.

- வராது *var-aadu* 'not coming'
- போகாது *pooh-aadu* 'not going'
- சாப்பிடாது *saappiḍ-aadu* 'not eating'

Therefore, the formation of the negative result clause involves taking the infinitive, adding ஆது *aadu*, then deleting one உ *u*; then adding அது *adu* and deleting உ *u*; then adding அனாலெ *anaale*.

> வர + ஆது + அது + அன் + ஆலெ *vara + aadu + adu + an + aale* ⟶ வராததனாலெ *varaadadanaale* 'since (s.o.) didn't/wasn't coming'

6.5.5 Negative Simultaneity: VB[1] ஆமெ *-aame* VB[2]

To express the notion that two actions are simultaneous but one is negated (i.e. they are mutually exclusive), a construction that we call the simultaneous negative is used. The simultaneous negative is formed by adding the suffix ஆமெ *-aame* 'without' to the infinitive forming the so-called 'negative adverbial participle.' It simply means 'without verb-ing.'[4] Used with another finite verb, the notion is 'do VB[1] without doing VB[2].

- சாப்பிடாமெ வந்தேன் *saappiḍaame vandeen* 'I came without eating' (or 'without having eaten.')
- பேசாமெ ஒக்காந்தேன் *peesaame okkaandeen* 'I sat without speaking'

As these examples above, the subject of the two verbs is the the same. However, when the subject is not the same, a causal relationship is implied:

> அவரு வராமெ நான் போனேன் *avaru varaame, naan pooneen* 'Since he didn't come, I left'

In this example there are two different subjects, அவரு *avaru* and அவன் *avan*; consequently, there is a cause-and-effect relationship implied: 'A doing VB[1] resulted in B doing VB[2].' When ஆமெ *-aame* is used with two non-coreferential subjects (the two subjects are NOT identical), ஆமெ *-aame* forms are synonymous with ஆததனாலெ *-aadadanaale* forms. That is, the following is synonymous with the immediately previous example:

> அவரு வராததனாலெ நான் போனேன் *avaru varaadadanaale, naan pooneen* 'Since he didn't come, I left'

[4] LT has two forms, ஆமல் *aamal* and ஆமை *aamai*, which, by various changes and deletions, come out the same in ST, pronounced [aːmɛ].

Since the negative habitual form often translates as 'not VERB-ing', instead of VERB-ing, without VERB-ing', with certain lexical items the meaning can be equivalent to English adverbs, e.g. எதிர்பாராமெ *edirpaaraame* can mean 'unexpectedly':

(135) யாரும் எதிர்பாராமெ புத்து நோய்லெருந்து
yaarum edirpaaraame puttu nooylerundu
everybody not-expecting cancer disease-from
கொணமடெஞ்சுட்டான்
goṇamaḍenjuṭṭaan
recovered-he

'Against all expectations, he recovered from cancer.'

The form எதிர்பாராமெ *edirpaaraame* is the negative AVP of an *intransitive*[5] form of the verb பாரு *paaru*, meaning 'unexpectedly, against all odds, unforeseen', etc.

6.5.5.1 Simultaneous Negative + இரு *iru*: Durative Negative

The negative adverbial participle (VB + ஆமெ *aame*) when followed by the verb இரு *iru* in its 'stative' meaning, is equivalent to the English 'to persist in not doing (something)' or 'to continue' or 'keep on not doing such-and-such':

- அவரு சாப்பிடாமெ இருக்குறாரு *avaru saappiḍaame irukkraaru*
  'He is fasting (he is going without eating'.)

- ஏன் பணம் அனுப்பாமெ இருக்குறீங்க *een paṇam anuppaame irukkriinga* 'Why do you continue to not send money?'

This semantic complex is the negative equivalent of positive verbs with கிட்டிரு *kiṭṭiru* 'durative':

பணம் அனுப்பிகிட்டிருக்குறீங்க *paṇam anuppi***kiṭṭiru***kkringa*
'You continue to send money.'

[5]Dictionaries list both a transitive and intransitive form of பார் *paar* but only the transitive form is common in ST; this form seems to have been lexicalized from the intransitive stem.

6.5.6 Obstinate Negative: VB + மாட்டேன்-ங்கது *maaṭṭeen-ngadu*

The future negative first person singular, when followed by the quotative verb என் *(e)n* in its finite form, i.e. ங்கது *-ngadu*, ங்குறான் *ngraan*, ண்ணாரு *ṇṇaaru*, etc., gives the meaning 'refuse to VB.'[6]

- துணி காயமாட்டேன்-ங்கது *tuṇi kaaya-maaṭṭeen-ngadu* 'The clothes refuse to dry.' (lit. 'The clothes say, "I won't dry."')
- கொழந்தெ சாப்பிடமாட்டேன்-ங்கது *kor̲ande saappiḍa-maaṭṭeen-ngadu* 'The child refuses to eat.' (lit. 'The child says, "I won't eat."')
- பையன் ஸ்கூலுக்கு போகமாட்டேன்-ங்குறான் *payyan skuulukku pooha-maaṭṭeen-ngraan* 'the boy refuses to go to school'

Since it is possible for inanimate objects to be the subject of these sentences, it is not feasible to call this a quotative form, i.e. the literal meaning, 'the x says it won't y' is not a possible semantic interpretation here. Rather, the metaphoric meaning 'x refuses to y' is to be preferred. Note that the PNG marker attached to *maaṭṭ-* is always first person singular in form, i.e. ஏன் *-een*. It never agrees with the subject—only the PNG of the 'quotative' verb agrees with the subject.

உப்பு வரமாட்டேன்-ங்கது *uppu varamaaṭṭeen-ngadu*
'The salt refuses to come out (of the shaker).'

Note that the tense of the verb என் *-n-* can be past or present (but future intent does not occur):

- அவன் போகமாட்டேன்-ண்ணான் *avan poohamaaṭṭeen-ṇṇaan*
  'He refused to go; he said he wouldn't go.'
- அவன் தூங்கமாட்டேன்-ங்குறான் *avan tuungamaaṭṭeen-ngraan*
  'He refuses to sleep.'

This tendency for the LT quotative verb என் *en* to function as a marker of various morphological and syntactic processes indicates that it is in the process of being *grammaticalized* in various ways, and is usually not to be treated as a lexical verb in ST.[7]

[6] Though we transliterate ங்கது as *-ngadu*, the first vowel is usually closer to [ʉ], i.e. *-ngadu* is phonetically [ŋgʉðʉ].

[7] The LT form is என் *en̲* and the AVP form is என்று *en̲r̲u*, so the change to retroflex ண் ண் *ṇṇ* is predictable. What is not predictable is the loss of the initial vowel எ *e*, which gives credence to the claim that this verb is being grammaticalized. Like aspectual verbs that have been grammaticalized from lexical verbs, the phonological rules governing their derivation has changed.

6.5.6.1 The Obstinate Negative Embedded

For a discussion of 'obstinate negative' forms embedded before other verbs, cf Chapter 7, ∮7.3.3.1.

6.5.7 The Archaic Tenseless Negative

ST retains in modern usage the relic of an archaic tenseless Old Tamil negative form where PNG markers are added directly to the stem with no tense marker intervening. This formation is preserved mainly in certain idiomatic expressions, e.g.:

(136) ஆளெயே காணோம்
aaḷeyed kaaṇoom
man-ACC-EMPH see-1-PL-PNG

'Where *is* everybody?' (lit. 'We do not see the man at all')

(137) யாரெயும் காணோம்
yaareyum kaaṇoom
whom-INCL see-1 PL PNG

'I don't see a soul.' (lit. 'everybody not-seen')

Here the PNG marker ஓம் *-oom* 'first person plural' is added directly to the stem of the verb காண் *kaaṇ* 'see', a verb not generally in use in ST. This expression is used idiomatically to mean something like 'I don't see a soul; there's nobody around, nobody in sight.' This negative cannot be generated indiscriminately, since it is unproductive.[8] Remnants of this process are preserved also in the future negative animate, where PNG markers are affixed directly to the stem மாட்ட் *maaṭṭ* (cf. ∮6.5.3).

6.6 Interrogation

Interrogatives, or question sentences, are formed in Tamil in a number of ways, the most common being by the addition of clitic suffixes or prefixes, rather than by subject–verb inversion as in some languages. (For a discussion of clitics, cf. ∮7.8.)

[8] The practice of affixing PNG markers directly to the stem is common in Old Tamil, where it was a productive negativizing process—the absence of a tense marker indicated negation, and complete negative paradigms of verbs could be generated.

6.6.1 The yes-no Question Marker Suffix ஆ *-aa*

The type of question where the speaker simply requests information (usually the 'truth value') about some event is formed by the addition of the suffix ஆ *aa* to the LAST element in the sentence. This kind of question is known as a YES-NO question. Questions of other sorts, such as WHICH of several alternatives are valid, are formed with a different prefix.[9]

ஆ *aa* is usually added to the last element in a sentence, but it can occur elsewhere, to focus attention on a particular element other than the general truth value of the sentence. When other clitics are present, such as ஆம் *aam* (∮6.7), interrogative ஆ *aa* may occur somewhere other than in sentence-final position.

- ராமன் வந்தாரு *raaman vandaaru* 'Raman came' + ஆ *a* ⟶ ராமன் வந்தாரா? *raaman vandaar-aa?* 'Did Raman **come**?
- அவருக்கு ஒரு மகளாம் *avarukku oru mahaḷaam* 'They say he had a daughter' + ஆ *aa* ⟶ அவருக்கு ஒரு மகளாமா? *avarukku oru mahaḷaam-aa*? 'Do they say he had a daughter? (is it true that he is supposed to have had a daughter?)'
- ராமன் வந்தாரு *raaman vandaaru* 'Raman came' + ஆ *a* ⟶ ராமனா வந்தாரு? *raaman**aa** vandaaru*? 'Did **Raman** come? (is it Raman that came?)'

The usual rules about retention and deletion of final vowels and consonants apply with the use of ஆ *-aa*. That is, final உ *-u* is deleted from all nouns (for exceptions, see the sections ∮1.3 and ∮2.1.) before the addition of ஆ *-aa*, as in the first sentence above. Other vowels are retained and glides ய் *y* and வ *v* are inserted according to the usual rules: ய் *y* after *i* and *e*; வ *v* after ஊ *uu*, ஒ *o* and ஆ *aa* (other vowel sequences do not occur).

- மழெ *mar̤e* 'rain' ⟶ மழெயா? *mar̤e-y-aa*? 'rain?'
- நரி *nari* 'fox' ⟶ நரியா? *nari-y-aa*? 'a fox?'
- பூ *puu* 'flower' ⟶ பூவா? *puu-v-aa*? 'a flower?'
- விழா *vir̤aa* 'festival' ⟶ விழாவா? *vir̤aa-v-aa*? 'a festival?'
- இளங்கோ *iḷangoo* '(a name)'⟶ இளங்கோவா? *iḷangoovaa*? 'Do you mean Ilango?'

[9] Cf. ∮5.2 and ∮6.3.

6.6.2 The Question Marker Prefix எ *e-*

Question markers similar to English 'wh-' question words ('which, when, why, where, who,' etc.) have their Tamil equivalent in words which begin usually with எ *-e*, e.g. எங்கெ *enge* 'where', எத்தனெ *ettane* 'how many', எவ்வளவு *evvaḷavu* 'how much.' For a detailed explanation of *-e* forms, see ∮∮4.4 and 5.2.

Note, however, that the question marker *-aa* and the question words can never occur in the same sentence, unless one of them is referring to something someone had said elsewhere:

- அவரு எங்கெ-ண்ணு சொன்னாரு *avaru* **enge**-*ṇṇu sonnaaru*?
  'He said "where?"'

- அவரு எங்கெ-ண்ணு சொன்னாரா? *avaru* **enge**-*ṇṇu sonnaaraa*?
  'Did he say "where"?'

6.7 The Reportive Marker ஆம் *-aam*

In Tamil a 'reportive' suffix ஆம் *aam* can be added to various constituents to indicate that the speaker does not claim responsibility for the veracity of the statement, but merely reports something. It translates into English as 'they say' or 'apparently' or 'allegedly' or 'it seems that' or 'supposedly', etc. It is usually added to the last constituent of the sentence (i.e. the verb), but will be followed by interrogative ஆ *-aa* if the sentence is a question:

> அவரு போறாராம் *avaru pooraar-aam* 'Apparently he'll go' + ஆ *aa* ⟶ அவரு போறாராமா? *avaru pooraaraamaa*? 'Do they say he'll go?'

But it can also occur somewhat idiomatically (or ironically) in other places in a sentence, e.g. with reduplicated noun phrases:

(138)	பெரிய	இவர்	ஆம்	இவரு
	periya	*ivar*	*aam*	*ivaru*
	big	this-man-HON	REPORT	this-man-HON

'Well la-de-da, get a load of **him**.' (i.e. 'he thinks he's hot stuff')

6.8 Quotative Sentences

In Tamil we find many sentences with an AVP form of the 'quotative' LT verb என் *en* following a quoted phrase or sentence: S ண்ணு *-ṇṇu* VB. They cannot all be considered to have the semantic value of direct quotation. Some instances of ண்ணு *-ṇṇu* are used to indicate indirect speech while others indicate direct quotations. Still other uses express intent while others indicate thought, hope, conjecture or other psychological states. When the verb is finite, as in ங்குறாங்க *-ngraanga*, the semantic value is equivalent to English 'they say' or 'people say' or 'it's rumored that ...' 'it's supposed to be true that ...', 'it's supposedly the case that ...'

6.8.1 Direct and Indirect Speech

To generate sentences such as English 'John said that he would come' or 'Harry asked what time it was' or 'Mary thinks the weather will be nice', one uses ண்ணு *ṇṇu* plus verbs such as சொல்லு *sollu* 'say', கேளு *keeḷu* 'ask, hear', நெனெ *nene* 'think.' One simply takes the sentence which is being indirectly quoted and embeds it in the matrix sentence 'NOUN ... ண்ணு *-ṇṇu* VERB.'

(139) ஜான் [வர்றார்] ண்ணு சொன்னாரு
jaan [varraar] ṇṇu sonnaaru
John will-come QT said
'John said he would come.'

(140) ராமசாமி [மணி என்னாச்சு] ண்ணு கேட்டாரு
raamasaami [maṇi ennaaccu] ṇṇu keeṭṭaaru
Ramasamy [time what] QT asked
'Ramasamy asked what time it was.'

(141) ரோஜாபூ [காலம் நல்லா இருக்கு] ண்ணு நெனெச்சாங்க
roojaapuu [kaalam nallaa irukkum] ṇṇu neneccaanga
Roojaapuu [weather nice will-be] QT thought
'Rojaapuu thought the weather would be nice.'

When this is done in some languages (such as English), the verb of the quoted sentence is changed to conform in tense to the other verb, i.e. WILL becomes WOULD; IS becomes WAS, etc. In Tamil, this does not happen. The embedded sentences have verbs with the same tense as they would have if directly quoted, e.g. in English, 'Rojaapuu said, "The weather WILL be nice."' What *does* change in Tamil is the pronoun, e.g. in the first sentence John is being indirectly quoted. If we were quoting him directly in Tamil, as in English, we would say ஜான் நான் வர்றேன்-ண்ணு சொன்னாரு *jaan [naan varreen]-ṇṇu sonnaaru* 'John said, "I will come."' Thus the only difference in Tamil between direct and indirect speech is in the pronoun concord.[10]

[10] See Asher 1982 for a further discussion of this.

Thus, in Tamil, surface structure is simpler for asking questions or quoting statements about other questions than it is in English. Suppose we have the following situation in English:

- Bob asks, 'Did the train come?'
- John, to Harry: 'Did Bob ask WHETHER the train HAD come?'

In English, two changes must be made in Bob's question by John. In Tamil the situation is simpler:

- Pillai asks: ரெயில் வந்தாச்சா? *reyil vandaaccaa?* 'Did the train come?'
- Raja asks Sundaram: பிள்ளெ ரெயில் வந்தாச்சாண்ணு கேட்டாங்களா? *pil̤l̤e reyil vandaaccaa-ṇu keeṭṭaangal̤aa?* 'Did Pillai ask whether the train had come?'

In Tamil, Raja is not obliged to change the form of Pillai's question, only to embed it in another sentence before the quotative verb.

6.8.2 Intent

Often, the semantic notion of INTENT, i.e. 'x intends to do y' is expressed in Tamil by a construction involving the verb (of the intended action) in the form of the modal லாம் *-laam*, followed by 'quotative' ண்ணு *-ṇṇu* and the verb இரு *iru* or நெனெ *nene* 'think' in a finite form with PNG agreeing with the subject.

> அவரு மலெ பக்கம் போகலாம்ண்ணு இருக்காரு or நெனெக்குறாரு
> *avaru male pakkam poohalaam-ṇṇu irukkaaru* or *nenekkraaru*
> 'He intends to go to the mountains.'

In some dialects, particularly western dialects (Coimbatore and Salem districts) near the Kannada-speaking area, as well as in the Tamil spoken in Karnataka State, the modal used is ணும் *-ṇum* 'must' instead of லாம் *-laam* 'may.' There is, however, no difference in meaning and furthermore, there is no notion of obligation intended. The meaning is still 'intend to do such-and-such.' The above sentence in these dialects would thus be:

> அவரு மலெ பக்கம் போகணும்ண்ணு இருக்காரு or நெனெக்குறாரு
> *avaru male pakkam poohaṇum-ṇṇu irukkaaru* or *nenekkraaru*
> 'He intends to go to the mountains.'

6.8.3 Adverbial Participles (AVP)

6.8.3.1 Consecutive Action, Positive

Two sentences, the action of one of which is subsequent to the action of the other, can be conjoined to produce one sentence of the English type, (1) 'After coming to India, (2) I studied Tamil. When two Tamil sentences are conjoined, the verb of the first is given past tense marking, and PNG is deleted. If there is no vowel following the past marker, உ *u* is added.

(142) நான் இந்த்யாவுக்கு வந்தேன் + தமிழ் படிச்சேன்
naan indyaavukku vandeen + tamiṟ̤ paḍicceen
I India-to came + Tamil studied

'I came to India' + 'I studied Tamil'

Since the tense of வந்தேன் *vandeen* is already past, PNG is deleted:

(143) நான் இந்த்யாவுக்கு வந்து தமிழ் படிச்சேன்
naan indyaavukku vandu tamiṟ̤ paḍicceen
I India-to having-come Tamil studied

'After coming to India, I studied Tamil.'

This form of the verb without PNG is often called the PAST ADVERBIAL PARTICIPLE, or AVP for short. With most verbs there is no problem in its formation, but verbs which have past markers இன் *-in-*, we find, instead of the expected participle, e.g. * வாங்கினு **vaanginu*, that they have the form வாங்கி *vaangi* 'having bought, after buying' without னு *nu*. Furthermore, a few verbs, namely ஆகு *aaku* 'become' and போ *poo* 'go' have the AVP forms ஆய் *aay* and போய்(இ) *pooy(i)*. These sentences translate as 'after VERB-ing' in English but there is no 'word' meaning 'after' in the Tamil sentences because this notion is given by the construction. The two actions are understood to be CONSECUTIVE.

6.8.3.2 Consecutive Action, Negative *-aame, aama(l)*

The negative ('past') participle is attached to the infinitive, and has the form *-aame* (LT *aamai*) or *-aama(l)*. Its meaning is 'not having VERB-ed' or 'without VERB-ing' or 'instead of VERB-ing' or 'rather than VERB-ing.' The negative adverbial participle of the copula *iru* is formed with the negative stem *ill-*:

- இல்லாமெ *illaame* 'not being', 'without (being)', 'instead of (being)'
- போகாமெ *pooh-aame* 'without going, instead of going'

- வராமெ *var-aame* 'without coming, rather than coming'
- சமெக்காமெ *samekk-aame* 'without cooking, instead of cooking'

When two clauses are conjoined and the first NP is not identical to the second, there is a RESULT implied between the two clauses.

(144) அவன் வராமெ நான் போய்ட்டேன்
avan varaame, naan pooyṭṭeen
he come-not-having, I go-DEF-PAST-PNG
'**Since** he didn't come, I left.'

For other NEGATIVE RESULT CLAUSES cf. §6.5.4.

6.8.4 Adjectival Participles

The subject of adjectival clauses in Tamil has been dealt with extensively in a recent work by Annamalai (1997).

6.8.4.1 Positive Adjectival Participles: Past or Present Tense Marker + அ *-a*

The adjectival participle (or AJP) is formed by deleting PNG from the past or present tense marker and replacing them with adjectival அ *-a*.

Embedded before a noun phrase only, the adjectival participle is used in relative clause constructions in situations where English often uses lexical adjectives.[11]

- நான் பாத்த பையன் *naan paa-tt-a payyan* 'the boy I saw'
- நேத்து கை மாத்து வாங்குன பணம் *neettu kay maattu vaangna paṇam* 'the money borrowed yesterday'
- எதுத்தாப்ப்லெ இருக்குற வீடு *eduttaaple irukkra viiḍu* 'the house which is opposite'

Note that the அ *-a* of the adjectival participle is syntactically equivalent to the RELATIVE PRONOUNS 'which, that' of the relative clause in languages that have postposed relative clauses, such as English. The அ *-a* in Tamil is always present, although the English equivalent may sometimes be deleted.

Adjectival participles can also be embedded before third person pronouns அது, அவன், அவ(ள்), அவங்க(ள்), அவரு *adu, avan, ava(ḷ), avanga(ḷ), avaru* with the meaning 's/he (etc.) who VERB-s/-ed'.

[11] See Chapter 5.

- நான் நேத்து பாத்தவன் *naan neettu paatt-avan*
  'he whom I saw yesterday' (lit. 'I yesterday saw-man')
- மரத்து மேலெ இருக்குறது *marattu meele irukkradu*
  'that-which is at-the-top of-the-tree'
- கணக்கு தீத்தவங்க கிட்டெ போயி *kaṇakku tiitt-avanga-kiṭṭe pooyi*
  'Going to the people (with) whom we paid-off the account'
  (lit. 'account cleared-people-to going')

Often these third person pronouns are best translated with phrases like 'the people who', 'the thing which', 'the man/woman who' rather than literally. Since they are noun phrases, they can take case and postpositions, other adjectives, and can be subjected to all the normal rules governing noun phrases.

Note that relative clauses formed with AJP's are embedded *before* other elements such as possessive pronouns, not after:

> நேத்து வந்த என் தம்பி *neettu vanda en tambi*
> 'My younger brother who came yesterday'

instead of *என் நேத்து வந்த தம்பி **en neettu vanda tambi.*

6.8.4.2 Negative Adjectival Participle: ஆத *-aada*

A negative adjectival participle (NAJP) can be formed by affixing ஆத *aada* to the infinitive of the verb. As with most other negative constructions, there are no tense distinctions in the negative adjectival participle.

- எப்பவும் இல்லாத திருநாளு *eppavum illaada tirunaaḷu*
  'a holiday not (being) like always' ('an unusual day')
- இண்ணெக்கி வராதவங்க *iṇṇekki varaadavanga* 'the people who didn't/ don't come today'
- கடவுள் இல்லாத எடத்தெ எனக்குக் காட்டு *kaḍavuḷ illaada eḍatte enakku kaaṭṭu* 'Show me the place where there is no God.'

As with the positive adjectival participle, the negative participle can be affixed with pronouns, as in the example above. The negative stem இல் *ill* is used instead of இரு *iru*. Just as இல்லாமெ *illaame* often translates in English as 'without (VERB)ing' இல்லாத *illaada* often translates as 'that which lacks (s.t.), (that which is) without (s.t.) (s.t.)-**less**', e.g. கடவுள் இல்லாத எடம் *kaḍavuḷ illaada eḍam* 'a godless place.'

6.8.4.3 Verbal Nouns

Verbal nouns (also called participial nouns) can be formed by suffixing third person pronouns அது, அவன், அவ(ள்), அவங்க(ள்), அவரு *adu, avan, ava(ḷ), avanga(ḷ), avaru* to adjectival participles.

- பாத்த+ அது *paatta + adu* ⟶ பாத்தது *paattadu*
  'that which saw, was seen; the act of seeing'
- வந்த+ அவங்க *vanda + avanga* ⟶ வந்தவங்க *vandavanga*
  'the people who came'
- போகாத+அது *poohaada + adu* போகாதது ⟶ *poohaadadu*
  'that which did not go; the act of not going'
- இல்லாத+அவன் *illaada + avan* ⟶ இல்லாதவன் *illaadavan*
  'he who is/was not'

Verbal nouns can thus be either past or present, if positive, or they can be negative, but without tense. Since they are nouns, they can also take case.

(145) இல்லாததனாலெ
illaad-ad-anaale

'as a result of not being, since it was not'

(146) கணக்கு தீத்தவங்ககிட்டெ போயி
kaṇakku tiittavanga-kiṭṭe pooyi

going to the people (with) whom we cleared the account'

Note that when அது *adu* is affixed, the meaning can be either relative or factive. That is, இருக்குறது *irukkradu* can either mean 'that which is' or 'the act of being'. The verbal noun of the quotative verb ண் *-ṇ* (see ∮7.3.3.) is regularly used in factive constructions.

(147) அவருக்கு தமிழ் தெரியாது ங்க்றதெ பத்தி மறந்துட்டேன்
avarukku tamir̤ teriyaadu -ngrade patti maranduṭṭeen
him-to Tamil not-known FACTIVE, about I-forgot-COMPL

'I completely forgot about the fact that he doesn't know Tamil.'

6.9 WH-Interrogatives and Clitic Suffixes

Wh-interrogatives can combine with various clitic suffixes such as உம் *-um*, ஓ *-oo*, ஆவது *aavadu*, and with negatives and conditionals, with interesting semantic results.

6.9.1 WH-INTERROGATIVES + உம் *-um*

The clitic உம் when affixed to noun phrases generally means 'and, even, too.' When affixed to WH-interrogatives, the meaning is all-inclusive, or universal.

- எப்ப *eppa* 'when' + உம் *um* ⟶ எப்பவும் *eppa-v-um*
  'always, every time, all the time'
- யாரு *yaaru* 'who' + உம் *um* ⟶ யாரும் *yaar-um* 'everyone, everybody'
- எங்கெ *enge* 'where' + உம் *um* ⟶ எங்கெயும் *enge-y-um* 'everywhere'

Not all எ *-e* words can be combined with உம் *um*, however. * எந்த *enda* + *um* 'which' and * *edum* 'which thing' do not occur. Instead, where one would expect எது *edu* + உம் *um*, we get எதுவும் *eduvum* or எல்லாம் *ellaam* 'all, everything.' Since எந்த *enda* has to be followed by a noun, the expected *enda* + NOUN + *um* is replaced by எல்லா *ellaa* + NOUN + உம் *um*. E.g.:

எல்லா விட்டுலெயும் *ellaa viiṭṭ-le-y-um* 'in all houses'

When எல்லா ... உம் *ellaa ... um* modifies a 'count' noun, that noun must be in the plural (or at least be an unmarked plural, as above), as in English. When எல்லா ... உம் *ellaa ... um* modifies a mass noun, it follows the noun and is then realized as எல்லாம் *ellaam*, e.g. *paal-ellaam* 'all the milk', ஊரெல் லாம் *uur-ellaam* 'the whole town.' எல்லா ஊரும் *ellaa uur-um* also occurs, but means 'all the towns.' எல்லாரும் *ellaarum* is used with animates and means 'all people.' 'Every' as an adjective is otherwise realised as ஒவ்வொரு *ovvoru* 'each, every', e.g. ஒவ்வொரு சமயமும் *ovvoru samayamum* 'every time, sometimes.' 'Everyday' தெனம் *denam* or ஒவ்வொரு நாளும் *ovvoru naaḷum*.

Some of the other எ *-e* + உம் *um* types do not occur at all, e.g. **eppaḍiyum* and **evvaḷavum*.

6.9.2 WH-INTERROGATIVES + ஓ *-oo*

The clitic suffix ஓ *oo* when added to verbs expresses doubt about the likelihood of an occurrence. When this suffix is added to WH-interrogatives, we get what have been referred to as 'indeterminate' pro-forms.

- எங்கெயோ *enge-y-oo* 'somewhere (I don't know where)'
- எப்படியோ *eppaḍiyoo* 'somehow (I don't know how)'

- எப்பவோ *eppavoo* 'sometime, at some point; whenever'
- யாரோ *yaaroo* 'somebody'
- எதோ *edoo* 'some, something'
- எத்தனெயோ *ettaneyoo* 'several (I don't know how many)'
- எவ்வளவோ *evvaḷavoo* 'a lot (I don't know how much)'

Sometimes எத்தனெயோ *ettaneyoo* is reduplicated எத்தனெயெத்தனெயோ *ettaneyettaneyoo* to mean 'unbelievable amounts; unfathomable quantities; lots and lots.' எதோ *edoo* may be used adjectivally to mean 'some(thing).'

> எதோ கொஞ்சம் பணம் குடுத்தா *edoo konjam paṇam kuḍuttaa...*
> 'If you give (me) a little something ...'

We do not find எந்தவோ **endavoo* of course, since எந்த *enda* must be followed by a noun, which then could be affixed with ஓ *oo*, as in எந்தப் பணமோ *enda paṇamoo* 'whatever money.'

6.9.3 WH-INTERROGATIVES + ஆவது *aavadu*

This suffix makes things less doubtful than ஓ *oo*; it implies that whatever it is that is not clear will eventually be clear, or that specificity is not required at this point—the details are known but not relevant, or not important, but are retrievable.

- எங்கெயாவது *engeyaavadu* 'somewhere or other (I don't know right now, or don't care, but it is somewhere)'
- யாராவது *yaaraavadu* 'somebody or other (I don't know who but we could find out)'
- எதாவது *edaavadu* 'some kind or other (it doesn't matter what)'
- எப்படியாவது *eppaḍiyaavadu* 'somehow or other (we'll find a way)'

எதாவது *edaavadu* also can function as a kind of indeterminate adjective: எதாவது ஒரு ஆளு *edaavadu oru aaḷu* 'some guy or other (it doesn't matter who).' This contrasts with யாரோ ஒரு ஆளு *yaaroo oru aaḷu* 'some guy, I don't know anything about him'.

6.9.4 WH-INTERROGATIVES + உம் *um* + NEGATIVE

If உம் *um* + negative is added to எ *-e* forms, we get 'no-WH' type expressions. The same construction, involving a negative verb, can also occur:

- எங்கெயும் இல்லெ *engeyum ille* 'nowhere'
- எப்பவும் இல்லெ *eppavum ille* 'never'
- யாரும் போகல்லெ *yaarum poohalle* 'nobody went'
- ஒண்ணும் இருக்காது *oṇṇum irukkaadu* 'there won't be anything'
- யாரெயும் காணோம் *yaareyum kaaṇoom* 'I don't see anybody'
- அவரு எங்கெயும் போகல்லெ *avaru engeyum poohalle* 'he didn't go anywhere'
- ஒண்ணும் குடுக்கல்லெ *oṇṇum kuḍukkalle* '(he) didn't give a thing'
- எனக்கு அங்கெ யாரெயும் தெரியல்லெ *enakku ange yaarum teriyalle* 'I don't know anyone there'
- எதுவும் இல்லெ *eduvum ille* means something different from ஒண்ணும் இல்லெ but I can't put my finger on it.

Note that for 'nothing' we get ஒண்ணும் இல்லெ *oṇṇum ille* 'nothing' ('not even one thing'). The literal meaning of உம் இல்லெ *-um ille* is 'not even' and used with NOUNS instead of எ *e-* forms, it has this meaning:

- ஒரு பைசாவும் இல்லெ *oru paysaav-um ille* 'not even a paysaa'
- ஒரு கப் காப்பியும் போடலெ *oru kap kaappi-y-um pooḍalle*
  '(They) didn't even offer (me) a cup of coffee'

6.10 Conditional

Conditional sentences ('If'-type sentences in English) are formed by adding, in the place where PNG would normally occur, the suffix ஆ(ல்) *-aa(l)*. This is added to the PAST stem of the verb only, and thus tense and PNG are neutralized, i.e. the conditional of a verb gives us no information about tense or PNG.

- பாத்தா *paattaa* ... 'if (some)one sees ...'
- அவரு வந்தா *avaru vandaa* 'if he/she came/comes'

- நீ சாப்பிட்டா *nii saappiṭṭaa* 'if you eat/ate'

If the verb is aspectually marked, such as with இரு *iru* or (வி)டு *(v)iḍu*, the suffix ஆ *-aa* is added to the AM in the past:

- அவன் வந்திருந்தா *avan vandirundaa* 'if he had come...'
- போஸ்ட் வந்திட்டா *poosṭ vandiṭṭaa* 'if the mail definitely came...'
- நீ போயிருந்தா அதெ பாத்திருப்பே *nii pooyirundaa ade paattiruppee* 'if you had gone, you would have seen that.'

In some dialects, a variant ஆக்கா *-aakkaa* occurs instead of ஆ(ல்) *-aa(l)*:

அவரு வந்தாக்கா *avaru vandaakka* 'If he comes...'

Since tense is neutralized in the conditional, the tense of the verb in conditional clauses is determined (interpreted semantically) by the tense of the verb in the larger context, usually the verb in the next clause:

(148) அவரு வந்தா நான் போறேன்
avaru vandaa, naan pooreen
'If he/she COMES, I'll go'

(149) எதோ கொஞ்சம் பணம் குடுத்தா ஊரெல்லாம் சுத்தி காட்டுறேன்
edoo konjam paṇam kuḍuttaa, uur-ellaam sutti kaaṭṭreen
some little money give-COND town-all around show
'If you GIVE me a little money, I'll show you the whole town' (or 'If you GAVE me a little money, I'd show you the whole town')

(150) தந்தி வந்திருந்தா நான் போயிருப்பேன்
tandi vand-irundaa, naan pooy-iruppeen
'If a telegram HAD COME, I would have gone'

Since the conditional marker is added to the past of the verb it is also not possible to have conditionals of certain modals and other categories, except by periphrastic constructions (cf. §6.10.1 below). Note that the conditional suffix contains a final ல் *-l* which does not appear unless something is suffixed to it (cf. the Concessive §6.10.4 below).

6.10.1 Syntactic Conditional: ண்ணு *-ṇṇu* + ஆல் *aa(l)*

The quotative verb (எ)ன் *(e)n* may be conditionalized; the form is then ண்ணா *ṇṇaa*. When a sentence precedes ண்ணா *-ṇaa* we can get a kind of sentence-conditional meaning 'if it is the case (that x)' Nouns alone may be followed by ண்ணா *ṇṇaa*, which then functions as a kind of TOPICALIZER or a marker of FOCUS. Its meaning is somewhat difficult to translate idiomatically in English; (lit. 'if one SAYS X ...'), but the loose translation is generally something like, 'as far as X is concerned' or 'regarding X ...' or 'since you mentioned X ...' or 'speaking of X ...'

- சினிமாண்ணா அவனுக்கு பயித்தியம் *sinimaa-ṇṇaa, avanukku payttyam* 'AS FAR AS movies are CONCERNED, he's just crazy (about them).'
- மீன் கறிண்ணா எனக்கு ரொம்ப இஷ்டம் *miin kari-ṇṇaa, enakku rompa iṣṭam* 'Now fish curries, that's something I really like.'

When a sentence precedes the ண்ணா *-ṇṇaa*, the construction is equivalent to the ordinary conditional, semantically. That is, the following sentence pairs mean the same thing:

- அவன் வந்தான்-ண்ணா *avan vandaan-ṇṇaa* 'if he comes ...'
- அவன் வந்தா *avan vandaa* 'if he comes ...'

The *-ṇṇaa* type of conditional is somewhat more common in ST than in LT; it is however REQUIRED when the verb that precedes it cannot be conditionalized the ordinary way, i.e. it has no past stem. Modals or habitual negatives are of this type:

> அது வேணும்ண்ணா நான் வர்றேன் *adu veeṇumṇṇaa, naan varreen* 'If that is needed, I'll come.'

The meaning of ண்ணா *-ṇṇaa* is often epistemic, i.e. it can often be translated 'if it is true that ...' or 'if it is such that ...' or 'If it turns out that ...', etc.

6.10.2 Negative Conditional ஆட்டா *-aaṭṭaa*

The negatives of the conditional are formed by the addition of a negative morpheme ஆட்ட் *-aaṭṭ-* to the INFINITIVE (the usual rule) followed by the conditional morpheme ஆ(ல்)*-aa(l)*. In some dialects, the form is ஆட்டி *aaṭṭi* instead of ஆட்டா *-aaṭṭaa*

- வராட்டா *vara-aaṭṭ-aa* 'if (s.o.) doesn't come.'
- சாப்பிடாட்டா *saappiḍaaṭṭaa* 'if (s.o.) doesn't eat'
- நீ சொல்லாட்டி நான் சொல்லுறேன் *nii sollaaṭṭi naan solreen* 'If *you're* not going to say it, *I'll* say it.'

A morphophonemic rule reduces vowel sequences *-aa* to *a*, i.e. வர + ஆட்டா *vara* + *aaṭṭaa* becomes *varaaṭṭaa*. Modals and defective verbs can also have negative conditionals.

போகமுடியாட்டா *pooha-muḍiyaaṭṭaa* 'if (one) can not go'

The syntactic version of the negative conditional is more common in ST than the morphological, however. This consists of embedding a negatively marked verb before ண்ணா *ṇṇaa*, rather than 'negativizing' ண்ணு *ṇṇu*:

- நீ போகமுடியல்லெண்ணா நான் போறேன் *nii poohamuḍiyalleṇṇaa naan pooreen* 'If you can't go, I'll go.'
- வேண்டாம்ண்ணா சரி *veeṇḍaamṇṇaa sari*
  'If you don't want (s.t.) it's okay.'

6.10.2.1 Negative Conditional of இரு *iru*

The verb 'be' இரு *iru*, which is irregular in its negative (இல்லெ *ille* instead of the expected இருக்கல்லெ *irukkalle*), also has a negative conditional which uses the இல்ல் *ill-* morph as the verb stem to which the negative and conditional morphemes are added:

இல்லாட்டா *illaaṭṭaa* 'if it is not...'

This often is equivalent semantically to English 'otherwise' as in:

அலமாரியிலெ போடு இல்லாட்டா காஞ்சு போகும் *alamaariyle pooḍu illaaṭṭaa kaanju poohum* 'Put it in the cupboard. Otherwise, it'll get dried out.'

இல்லாட்டா *illaatṭṭaa* may also function as a marker of 'disjunction', i.e. '(either) this **or** that' or to mean 'or if not' or 'otherwise.'

நீ நாளெக்கி போகலாம்; இல்லாட்டா நாநாளெக்கி போகணும் *nii naaḷekki poohalaam; illaaṭṭaa naanaaḷekki poohaṇum* 'You may go tomorrow; **or**, you will have to go the next day.'

6.10.3 The Conditional + தானே *-taanee*

The conditional plus தானே *-taanee* 'emphatic' often occurs without a result clause, meaning 'if you'd only VERB-ed' (with the illocutionary force of 'I told you so!').

கேட்டா தானே *...keeṭṭaa-taanee* ...'If you (had/would) only ask(ed) (me, I would have told you].'

6.10.4 Concessive

By the addition of the clitic உம் *-um* to the ஆல் *aal-* suffix, we get a construction known as 'concessive', i.e. 'even if ...', 'it doesn't matter if ....' 'Even conceding (x)...'

- அவரு பணம் குடுத்தாலும் நான் போகமாட்டேன்
  avaru paṇam kuḍuttaalum naan pookamaaṭṭeen
  'Even if he pays (me) money, I won't go.'

- பணம் வந்திருந்தாலும் நேரம் இருந்திருக்காது
  paṇam vandirundaalum neeram irundirukkaadu
  'Even if the money had come there wouldn't be enough time.'

- நீங்க போகலாம்ண்ணு இருந்தாலும் *niinga poohalaam-ṇu irundaalum*
  ...'Even if you intend(ed) to go ...'

6.10.5 Concessive + எ *e*-words

If a எ *e*-word (WH-interrogative) is followed by a verb in the concessive, we get clauses which translate in English as 'no matter wh-' or 'wh-ever' or 'any old wh-':

> எப்ப பாத்தாலும் ஜன்னல் பக்கம் நாலு பேரு கூடி நிண்ண மயமா தானே இருக்குறாங்க *eppa paattaalum jannal pakkam naalu peeru kuuḍi niṇṇa mayamaa-taanee irukkraanga.* 'Whenever you look, a bunch of people are crowded around the window, gawking.'

The phrase எப்ப பாத்தாலும் *eppa paattaalum*, though it can be interpreted lit. ('whenever seen') has assumed the illocutionary force of 'always' or 'every time you look' or 'every time you turn around' or simply 'often.'

- யாரு வந்தாலும் சரி *yaaru vandaalum, sari* 'Whoever comes, it's okay' ('It doesn't matter/doesn't make any difference who comes', etc.)

- எங்கெ போனாலும் அதெ வாங்கலாம் *enge poonaalum ade vaangalaam*
  'Wherever you go, you can buy it.'

- எவ்வளவு கேட்டாலும் அவன் குடுப்பான் *evvaḷavu keeṭṭaalum avan kuḍuppaan* 'He'll pay whatever (they) ask.'

- எத்தனெ தடவெ சொன்னாலும் அவன் கேக்கமாட்டான்
  ettane taḍave sonnaalum avan keekkamaaṭṭaan
  'No matter how many times (you) say (it), he won't get it.'

6.10.6 Syntactic Concessive

In addition to the 'morphological' concessive form discussed in ∮6.10.4. above, there is another form called the syntactic concessive, formed by the use of the quotative verb ண்ணு *ṇṇu* in its conditional form ண்ணா(ல்) -*ṇṇaa(l)*. By the addition of உம் *um* or கூட *kuuḍa* to ண்ணா(ல்) -*ṇṇaa(l)*, we get the syntactic concessive. What is embedded before ண்ணு *ṇṇu* is, of course, a complete sentence with a finite verb (if there is any verb), in contrast to the morphological concessive, where ஆலும் -*aalum* or ஆ *aa* + கூட *kuuḍa* is added to the past stem of the verb. Thus we get sentences like:

- வேணும்ண்ணாலும் நான் போகமாட்டேன்
  veeṇum-ṇṇaalum, naan poohamaaṭṭeen
  'Even if required to, I won't go.'
- ஒங்களுக்குத் தமிழ் புரியும்ண்ணாலும் அவன் ஆங்கிலம் பேசுவான்
  ongaḷukku tamiṟ puriyum-ṇṇaalum avan aangilam peesuvaan
  'Even if (you) understand Tamil, he'll speak English.'

6.10.7 Negative Concessives

The negative concessive forms are formed by the addition of the negative (conditional) morpheme ஆட்ட் -*aaṭṭ*- to the INFINITIVE followed by the conditional morpheme ஆ(ல்) -*aa(l)* and the concessive உம் -*um* or கூட *kuuḍa*.

போகாட்டாலும் *pooha-aaṭṭ-aalum* 'Even-if (one) doesn't go...'

A morphophonemic rule reduces vowel sequence -*aaa* to ஆ *aa*, i.e. *varaaaṭṭaa* becomes *varaaṭṭaa*.[12]

A negative syntactic concessive can be formed by embedding a negative sentence before the ordinary -*ṇṇaalum* of the syntactic concessive.

புரியல்லெண்ணாலும் சரி *puriyalle-ṇṇaalum, sari*
'Even if (you) don't understand, it's okay.'

6.10.8 WH-Interrogatives + Dubitative ஓ *oo*

WH- interrogatives plus a verb plus dubitative ஓ *oo* gives a structure which means 'it doesn't matter wh-' or 'no matter wh-' or 'wh-ever (VERB)'.

[12] The LT form of ஆட்டா -*aaṭṭaa* is formed by suffixing an archaic negative ஆ *aa* to the infinitive, followed by the conditional of the verb விடு *viḍu*: போகாவிட்டால் *poohaaviṭṭaal*, followed by உம் *um* for concessive, etc. The intervocalic வ *v* is deleted by a process that is complicated but fairly regular in ST. Cf. ∮1.3, Sandhi.

மீட்டர் எவ்வளவு காட்டுறதோ அவ்வளவு தான் குடுப்பேன்
miiṭṭar evvaḷavu kaaṭṭradoo avvaḷavu taan kuḍuppeen
'I will pay whatever amount the meter shows and no more ('No
matter what amount the meter shows, I will pay that amount
only').'

This differs in meaning from wh-words plus concessive, e.g. மீட்டர்
எவ்வளவு காட்டினாலும் அவ்வளவு குடுப்பேன் *meeṭar evvaḷavu kaaṭṭnaalum
avvaḷavu kuḍuppeen* would mean 'I will pay whatever the meter indicates,
no matter how high it goes' whereas with ஓ *oo* it means 'whatever the
correct amount is, as indicated by what the meter shows'. (This might be
in the context of a taxi driver demanding supplements and extras ('night-
rate') in excess of charges registered on the meter.)

6.11   Consecutive Action

Tamil has a number of ways to express one action following another. Most
of these constructions differ slightly in how they express the IMMEDIACY
of the action that follows. That is, one can express whether the action
is almost simultaneous, follows on the heels of another action, or merely
follows it some time afterward.

6.11.1   Simultaneity

When simultaneity or co-occurrence of two actions is what is expressed,
especially if the subjects of the two verb phrases are different, AJP + அப்ப
appa 'time-when' usually occurs.

நான் வர்றப்ப அவரு கோயிலுக்கு போனாரு *naan varrappa, avaru
kooyilukku poonaaru* 'When I came, he went to the temple.'

The phrase வர்றப்ப *varrappa* is formed by the addition of *ppa* 'when'
to the ADJECTIVAL PARTICIPLE.[13] This expresses the notion that the two
actions described are, for all practical purposes, simultaneous, or the first
is triggered by the onset of the other action: 'When I came, he went to the
temple.'

The structure of the syntax of these phrases is basically:

VERB[1]-sc AJP அப்ப *appa*, ...VERB[2]

[13]See §5.2.1. for a discussion of different ways to form this expression. ப்ப *ppa* is a
reduced form of LT போது *poodu* 'time.'

The AJP form can be either past or present. For future, many speakers use a more LT-like phrase வரும் போது *varum poodu* which uses the future neuter as an AJP before the LT போது *poodu* 'time.'

6.11.2 Immediate Consecutive Action

Immediate consecutive action may be expressed by suffixing உம் -*um* (or ஒடனெ *oḍane* 'immediately') to the PAST VERBAL NOUN, as in:

- சினிமா விட்டதும் சாப்பிட போகலாமா *sinimaa viṭṭadum, saappiḍa poohalaamaa?* 'Shall we go somewhere to eat after the movie (lets out)?'

- நான் அதெ சொன்னதும் அவருக்கு கோபம் வந்தது *naan ade sonnadum avarukku koobam vandadu* 'As soon as I said that he got mad.'

- அவரு சாப்பிட்டதும் டவுனுக்கு போனாரு *avaru saappiṭṭadum, ṭavunukku poonaaru* 'As soon as he had eaten, he went to town.'

For an explanation of formation of verbal nouns, see ∮6.8.4.3.

6.11.3 Immediate Consecutive with ஒடனெ *oḍane*

Another way of forming the immediate consecutive is by adding the postposition ஒடனெ *oṭane* 'immediately' to the PAST ADJECTIVAL PARTICIPLE (AJP).

நான் மதுரைக்கி போன ஒடனெ அவரெ பாத்தேன்
naan madureykki poona-oḍane, avare paatteen.
'I saw him right after I got to Madurai.'

6.11.4 Verbal Noun and Dative

Relative consecutive action can also be expressed with verbal nouns (in the dative) followed by postpositions that mean 'before' or 'after.' (Cf. ∮2.4.3 on postpositions with the dative.)

The VERBAL NOUN is in the PRESENT and marked for the DATIVE CASE, followed by பின்னாலெ *pinnaale* or அப்புறம் *appram*; both mean 'after.'[14]

- சாப்பிடுறதுக்கு பின்னாலெ *saappiḍradukku pinnaale* 'after eating'

- போறதுக்கு அப்புறம் *pooradukk-appram* 'after going'

---

[14] The ST reflexes of LT பின் *pin* and முன் *mun* vary tremendously from dialect to dialect; cf. ∮2.4.3.9.

- போனதுக்கு அப்புறம் *poonadukk-appram* ‘after (s.o.) went’

If the intention is to state an action that followed another action in the past, the past verbal noun is needed; the present may be used to describe actions that have not happened yet, but will be in a certain sequence when they happen. No immediacy is expressed with these forms.

6.11.5 Infinitive for Simultaneity

In some cases, the infinitive can be used to express simultaneity. This is very common in LT and less so in spoken.

- அவன் வர நான் சாப்பிட்ட்கிட்டிருந்தேன்
  avan vara, naan saappiṭṭukiṭṭirundeen
  ‘I was eating *as* he came.’

- நாம ஒண்ணு நெனெக்க நடந்தது வேறெ ஒண்ணா போச்சு
  naama oṇṇu nenekka, naḍandadu veere oṇṇaa poocc̣u
  ‘All the time (that) we were thinking one thing, something completely different (and unexpected) was happening.’

This use of the infinitive can be replaced by adjectival participle plus அப்ப *-appa* in most cases:

- அவன் வர்றப்ப நான் சாப்பிட்டுகிட்டிருந்தேன்
  avan varrappa, naan saappiṭṭukiṭṭirundeen.
  ‘When he came, I was eating.’

Chapter 7

Complex Syntax and Related Topics

7.1 Syntactic Modality: Probability, Possibility and Chance

7.1.1 Syntactic Possibility

In addition to the 'morphological' modals லாம் *laam* 'may', ணும் *-Num* 'must' and முடி *muḍi* 'can', there are syntactic constructions which give various degrees of probability and/or possibility. One of these, a form which generally can be translated '(it) might just be possible that (x)' or perhaps (x) will (y)', takes the form of a verb appearing in the concessive (cf. ∮6.10.4) followed by the same verb with the modal *laam* affixed to it. Examples:

- மழெ வந்தாலும் வரலாம் *mar̤e vandaalum varalaam*
  'Rain might just possibly come.'

- அங்கெய்ருந்து திரும்பி வரவேண்டியிருந்தாலும் இருக்கலாம்
  angeyrundu tirumbi varaveeṇḍiyirundaalum irukkalaam
  'It might just turn out to be necessary to come back from there.'

In terms of chance and probability, the degree of certainty underlying the semantics of this form could be said to be approximately 40%, i.e. the chances are LESS THAN EVEN that the event in question will occur.

7.1.2 60% or more Certainty

When the degree of certainty or probability that an event will occur is greater than chance, i.e. more than 50%, a different construction from that in ∮7.1.1 is used, namely, one where the verb in the concessive is followed by the same verb in the future/indefinite, instead of with the modal லாம் *laam*.

- இருந்தாலும் இருப்பான் *irundaalum iruppaan*
  'He will probably be (there).'

- நாம முன்னாலேயெ சாப்பிட்டாலும் சாப்பிடுவோம் *naama munnaaleeye saappiṭṭaalum saappiṭuvoom* 'We'll probably eat beforehand.'

Note that the reduplicated verbs with concessive and either *laam* or future indefinite can be affixed to other verbs to get more complex constructions, as in ∮7.1.1 above.

7.1.3 Negative Probability

The negative of the forms in ∮7.1.1 is formed by affixing the 'negative participle' ஆமெ *aame* to the verb in question and following it by இருந் தாலும் இருக்கலாம் *irundaalum irukkalaam*, e.g.

அவன் வரமாட்டேன்-ண்ணு சொன்னாலும் சொல்லலாம்
avan varamaaṭṭeenṇṇu sonnaalum sollalaam
'He might say that he won't come.'

Similarly, the negative of ∮7.1.2 is formed by affixing ஆமெ *-aame* to the verb, and following it by இருந்தாலும் இருப்பான் *irundaalum iruppaan*, e.g.

அவர் விட்டுலே சமெக்காமெ இருந்தாலும் இருப்பான்
avar viiṭṭle samekkaame irundaalum iruppaan
'He probably won't be (doing his own) cooking at home.'

The 'expected' negative forms, i.e. something like **poohaaṭṭaalum poohamaaṭṭaan*, while perhaps acceptable grammatically to a native speaker, would not be assigned the meaning a speaker of English would expect and would not be used by a native speaker.

7.2 Reduplication

7.2.1 Reduplication, Positive-Negative: VB[1] POS-AVP + VB[1] NEG-AVP

Tamil has various ways of indicating that two actions are almost simultaneous, or so immediate that absolutely no time elapsed between them. Essentially this involves taking a positive form of a verb and reduplicating it in the negative. One way is to reduplicate a verb where the first term is in the form of the positive past participle (AVP) plus optional உம் *-um* followed by the same verb stem in the form of the negative past participle (AVP) means 'before (even) VERB-ing.' Another way is to take a verbal noun and follow it by the negative form of the verbal noun; both are suffixed with உம் *um* as a kind of conjunction. Sometimes the immediacy is perceived as so quick that the one following almost *precedes* the other.

- வந்தும் வராமெ *vandum varaame* 'before even coming; (or) as soon as (he) arrived'
- சாப்பிட்டும் சாப்பிடாமெ *saappiṭṭum saappiḍaame* 'before eating; before even getting a chance to eat; as soon as (s.o.) ate'
- வந்தும் வராததுமா *vandum varaadadumaa* 'before coming, even before coming; (or) the minute (he) walked in'
- ஏந்திருச்சதும் ஏந்திருக்காததுமா *eendiruccadum eendirukkaadadumaa* 'before (I) even had a chance to get out of bed'
- பாத்தும் பாக்காததுமா *paattum paakkaadadumaa* 'without seeing, before seeing, pretending not to see (i.e. blindly, ignorantly)'
- தெரிஞ்சும் தெரியாமெ *terinjum teriyaame* 'without knowing, unwittingly, whether knowingly or not, i.e. ignorantly'
- குளிச்சதும் குளிக்காததுமா *kuḷiccadum kuḷikkaadadumaa* 'before bathing was finished; before (I) could do anything else, i.e. (very) early in the morning'

While the first instance of the verb is usually the simple past participle (positive) plus உம் *-um*, the second member can be various forms of the negative participle, either adjectival or adverbial, and often with an adverbial ஆ(ய்) *-aa(y)* attached, as in பாத்தும் பாக்காததுமா *paattum paakkaadadumaa* 'unseeingly, blindly, ignorantly (lit. 'seeing and yet not seeing') which of course translates best as an English adverb.[1]

[1]Note that ஏந்திரு *eendiru* 'to arise, get out of bed' is derived from LT எழுந்திரு *eruntiru* by deletion of intervocalic ழ் *ṟ* and compensatory lengthening of the vowel.

7.2.2 'Echo-word' Reduplication

In Tamil, as in other South Asian languages, there is a kind of reduplication process which consists of taking a lexical item, e.g. *puli* 'tiger' and following it with the same item reduplicated, except that the first CONSONANT AND VOWEL are replaced by the CV sequence கி *ki-*, e.g. புலி கிலி *puli ki-li*. The meaning of this construction is '(Item) and other things like it.'

- புலி கிலி *puli kili* 'tigers and other beasts'
- பரட்டெ கிரட்டெ *paraṭṭe kiraṭṭe* '(a) disheveled and unkempt (person)'
- காப்பி கீப்பி *kaappi kiippi* 'coffee and other beverages'
- போய்ட்டு கீட்டு *pooyṭṭu kiiṭṭu* 'going, and other activities'
- பாம்பு கீம்பு *paambu kiimbu* 'snakes and other reptiles/pests'
- மரம் கிரம் *maram kiram* 'trees and other growing things'
- தும்மி கிம்மி *tummi kimmi* 'sneezing and other inauspicious noises'

Note that if the vowel of the first item is long, the vowel in கி *ki* becomes கீ *kii*; note also that *verbs* can also be the 'item' involved in the process, as in போய்ட்டு கீட்டு *pooyṭṭu kiiṭṭu* and தும்மி கிம்மி *tummi kimmi* above.

7.2.3 Emphatic Reduplication of Infinitive and Finite Verb

The last verb of an utterance (usually a modal verb) can be reduplicated for emphasis by taking the infinitive of the finite verb and adding emphatic ஏ *-ee* to it while placing it before the finite verb, i.e. VB^1 + INF + *ee* + VB^1 FINITE. There can be various possible configurations: reduplicate the infinitive of the main verb (plus ஏ *ee*), reduplicate the auxiliary verb, etc.

- வாங்க மாட்டவே மாட்டேன் *vaanga maaṭṭa-v-ee maaṭṭeen*
  'I just won't buy (it), that's all.'
- போகவே போகமாட்டேன் *poohavee poohamaaṭṭeen* 'I won't go at all.'
- முடியவே முடியாது *muḍiya-v-ee muḍiyaadu*
  '(I) just can't possibly (do it).'
- இருக்கவே இருக்கு *irukka-v-ee irukku* ...
  'It's there, no doubt about it ...'

Asher (1982:168) gives examples of many combinations of this pattern.

7.2.4 Distributive Reduplication

Reduplication of interrogative pronouns (and some non-interrogative pronouns) has a DISTRIBUTIVE function, i.e. it specifies different kinds of things, or links different things in a certain relationship, or distributes qualities among various members of a set of things.

- என்ன + என்ன *enna* + *enna* ⟶ என்னென்ன *enn-enna*
  'what (all) kinds of (things are there)?'
- எங்கெ + எங்கெ *enge* + *enge* ⟶ எங்கெங்கெ *engenge*
  'where-all; in what different places?'
- யாரு + யாரு *yaaryaaru* 'who-all?'
- அவங்கவங்க *avangavanga* 'all kinds of different people'
- எத்தனெயெத்தனெயோ *ettaneyettaneyoo* '(I) don't know how many (different things)'
- அது + அது *adu* + *adu* ⟶ அதது *adadu* 'each and every thing'

(151) எங்கெங்கெ போயிருக்கீங்க?
engenge pooyirukkiinga
where-where go-PERFECT
'Where-all did you go?'

(152) என்னென்ன பழம் வாங்கணும்
enn-enna par̤am vaanganṇum?
what-what fruit buy-MUST
'What-all kinds of fruit should (I) buy?'

(153) அவங்கவங்க கொழந்தெங்க அவங்கவங்களுக்கு அழகாதான் தெரியும்
avang-avanga kor̤andenga avang-avangaḷukku ar̤akaa-taan teriyum
different-people's children different-people-DAT, beauty-only appears
'To each (different) person, their own children are beautiful.'

(154) அததுக்கு நேரம் காலம் வரணும்
ad-adukku neeram kaalam varaṇum
it-it-DAT time season come-MUST
'For each and every thing there is a time and place.'

7.2.5 Reduplicated Onomatopoeic Expressions

For a discussion of onomatopoeic expressions, cf. ∮7.5.

7.3 The Quotative Verb ண்ணு *-ṇṇu* in Complex Sentences

(Cf. ∮6.4 for a discussion of ண்ணு *-ṇṇu* in simple sentences.)

7.3.1 ண்ணு *-ṇṇu*: Relative Clause/Embedded Sentence Marker

In LT there is a verb என் *en-* which historically meant 'say, think, mean' and occurred in all finite and non-finite forms. In ST the stem of this verb has the form ன் *-n-* but not all the finite forms occur. Furthermore, it is not clear that syntactically it is a lexical verb in all of these structures, though it is usual in Tamil grammatical tradition always to treat it thus. The most frequent form of it is the 'past participle' which in spoken BT is னு *-nnu* and in NBT ண்ணு *-ṇṇu*. If we take this item to be a lexical verb, it would mean literally, 'having said, thought, meant'; but since it is used in many different ways, not all of which can be assumed to overtly represent explicit oral or mental activity, it is more convenient to consider ண்ணு *-ṇṇu* and its finite forms to represent a number of different things in Tamil grammar. Primarily, we see it as a form that is being GRAMMATICALIZED to function as a syntactic marker of various sorts, not as a lexical verb.[2]

The commonest use of ண்ணு *-ṇṇu* is as a marker of relative or complement clauses, which in English are usually marked with THAT, as in:

> நான் வருவேன்ண்ணு சொன்னேன் *naan varuveen-ṇṇu sonneen*
> 'I said **that** I would come.'

The English relative/complement clause marker, THAT, is often deleted, as in 'I said (that) I would come' but in Tamil the ண்ணு *-ṇṇu* is always present in surface structure. Many kinds of other embedded sentences and clauses are followed by ண்ணு *-ṇṇu* in Tamil, and we will consider ண்ணு *-ṇṇu* in these to be simply a marker that something is embedded, i.e. originates in another clause or sentence but is brought into the MATRIX sentence by some process. Usually what precedes ண்ணு *-ṇṇu* is a complete sentence, i.e. it could stand alone without that which follows ண்ணு *-ṇṇu*. When

[2] This is evident also from its reduced phonological form, i.e. lacking the original initial vowel.

non-sentences precede it, ண்ணு *ṇṇu* it must take a different form; these are discussed in ∮7.4 and ∮7.5 below.

7.3.2 ண்ணு *ṇṇu* in Intent Constructions

In addition to the 'intent' constructions described in ∮6.8.2, there are some alternative constructions and other problems connected with INTENT.

7.3.2.1 Intent

The commonest intent construction has the structure VB-லாம் *laam*-ண்ணு *ṇṇu* + இரு *iru*.

> நான் போகலாம்ண்ணு இருக்குறேன் *naan poohalaamṇṇu irukkreen*
> 'I intend to go; I'm planning to go; I'm thinking of going.'

In most of these constructions the copula இரு *iru* can be replaced by the verb நெனெ *nene* 'think, hope' without semantic change, except that the constructions with நெனெ *nene* seem to be somewhat more DEFINITE in intent.

It should be also noted that the semantic range of these constructions in English involves not only intent, but DECISION, FEELING LIKE, WANTING TO, as in:

- நான் மலெ பக்கம் போகலாம்ண்ணு இருந்தேன்

  naan male pakkam pookalaam-ṇṇu irundeen

  'I was thinking of going/decided to go to the mountains.'

- கமலா சினிமாவுக்கு போகலாம்ண்ணு இருக்கா

  Kamala sinimaavukku poohalaam-ṇṇu irukkaa

  'Kamala feels like going to the movies.'

7.3.2.2 Tense

The tense of இரு *iru* 'be (located)' and நெனெ *nene* 'think' can only be past or present; future cannot occur.[3]

[3] Just as in English, '*I will intend to go' is unacceptable for some speakers and strange for most others.

7.3.2.3 Variants

As mentioned in ∮6.8.2, there is a form with the modal ணும் *ṇum* instead of the modal *laam*. This form occurs mostly in western dialects and means the same as the common *laam* form. Both இரு *iru* and நெனெ *nene* occur with the ணும் *ṇum* modal with meanings as described in ∮7.3.2.1.

7.3.2.4 Intent Constructions with Nouns

Another form of intent construction also occurs, where the verbs இரு *iru* 'be (located)' and நெனெ *nene* 'think' are replaced by nouns நெனெப்பு *neneppu* and எண்ணம் *eṇṇam* 'thought' and உத்தேசம் *utteesam* 'intent.'[4]

- நான்/எனக்கு போகலாம்ண்ணு உத்தேசம் ~ நெனெப்பு

  naan/enakku poohalaam-ṇṇu utteesam ~ neneppu

  'I'm leaning towards going (I intend to go; my intent is to go).'

- எனக்கு அங்கெ ரெண்டு மாசம் இருக்கலாம்ண்ணு நெனெப்பு

  enakku ange reṇḍu maasam irukkalaam-ṇṇu neneppu

  'I plan (my thought is) to stay there two months (but it's negotiable).'

The noun உத்தேசம் *utteesam* replaces இரு *iru* and நெனெப்பு *neneppu* replaces the verb நெனெ *nene*.

7.3.2.5 Verbal Noun + Adverbial *-aa(y)* + இரு/நெனெ/சொல்லு *iru/nene/sollu*

Another kind of intent construction involves the use of the verbal noun (cf. ∮6.5) plus the adverbial marker ஆ(ய்) *-aa(y)* plus the verbs இரு/நெனெ/சொல்லு *iru/nene/sollu*, and some others. There is no quotative ண்ணு *-ṇṇu* in these constructions. This type of intent construction, it should be noted, is more definite than those in ∮7.3.2.4.

- நான் போறதா இருக்குறேன்

  naan pooradaa irukkreen

  'I intend to go (I'm all set to go).'

[4] For some speakers, உத்தேசம் *utteesam* is more definite than நெனெப்பு *neneppu*. It should also be noted that in Tamil linguistic culture it may be inauspicious to make firm declarations of intent to do various things, especially if it involves travel; travel in certain directions is inauspicious on certain days, so the degree of intent, feeling, decision, etc. here must be taken with many grains of salt.

- பணம் தர்றதா சொன்னீங்களே

  paṇam tarradaa sonniingaḷee

  'But you said you would give the money!'

Since this construction is equivalent syntactically to the SENTENCE + ண்ணு *ṇṇu* constructions, sometimes the meaning of VERBAL NOUN + *aa* + VERB is not INTENT but simply an embedding construction, such as the following, where பொய்யெ தூக்கி போடு *poyye tuukki pooḍu* means 'fabricate a lie (that S)' followed by the phrase that represents the falsehood.

(155) அதுலெ வெஷம் கலந்திருக்குறதா ஒரு பெரிய பொய்யெ
adule veṣam kalandirukkradaa oru periya poyye
in-it poison having-mixed-ADV one big lie
பிரமாதமா தூக்கி போட்டு
pramaadamaa tuukki pooṭṭu
splendidly having-lifted having-put
'Having fabricated a magnificent lie **that** poison had been mixed in it ...'

7.3.2.6 Noun + Dative + ண்ணு *ṇṇu*: 'intended for'

A noun in the dative followed by ண்ணு *ṇṇu* means 'for the special use of NOUN', 'intended especially for NOUN'.

(156) அவருக்குண்ணு ஒரு தனி காரு இருக்கு அவங்க வீட்டுலெ
avarukkuṇṇu oru tani kaaru irukku avanga viiṭṭle
him-DAT-QTV a separate car is their house-in
'In their house there is a separate car intended for his exclusive use.'

It should be noted that the உ *u* vowel immediately preceding ண்ணு *ṇṇu* in அவருக்குண்ணு *avar-ukkuṇṇu* is phonetically longer ([ʉː]) than the usual fleeting vowel, i.e. [avərʉkʉːṇṇʉ].

7.3.3 Quotative ண்ணு -*ṇṇu* Embedded

A sentence containing the embedding marker ண்ணு -*ṇṇu* and a finite verb cannot be embedded with ண்ணு -*ṇṇu* before another finite verb, if the subjects of the two verbs is the same. That is, the Tamil equivalent of an English sentence like 'I said THAT I said THAT I would go' cannot have two ண்ணு's -*ṇṇu*'s because the subject of the two verbs is identical. If the subject is different, as in 'I said that *he* said he would go', two instances of ண்ணு -*ṇṇu*'s occur. That is, the first of the following examples is ungrammatical; the second is grammatical.

(157)

*நான்	வருவேன்	ண்ணு	சொன்னேன்	ண்ணு	சொன்னேன்
naan	*varuveen*	*ṇṇu*	*sonneen*	*ṇṇu*	*sonneen.*
I	will-come	QTV	said-I	QTV	said-I

'I said that I said that I would come.'

(158)

நான்	வருவேன்	ண்ணு	சொன்னான்	ண்ணு	சொன்னேன்
naan	*varuveen*	*ṇṇu*	*sonnaan*	*ṇṇu*	*sonneen.*
I	will-come	QTV	said-he	QTV	said-he

'I said that he said "I will come."'

For sentence (157) above to be grammatical, one verb phrase with ண்ணு சொன்னேன் *ṇṇu sonneen* must be deleted or the verb changed to perfect tense:

(159)

நான்	வருவேன்	ண்ணு	சொல்லியிருக்கேன்	*or*	சொல்லியிருந்தேன்
naan	*varuveen*	*ṇṇu*	*solli-yirukkeen*	or	*solli-yirundeen*
I	will-come	QTV	I-have-said	~	I-had-said

'I have/had told someone that I would come'

7.3.3.1 Obstinate Negative Embedded

Since the obstinate negative (∮6.5.6) has the structure of an embedded sentence before the 'quotative verb', it is not possible to embed it before another ண்ணு *ṇṇu* + VERB when the subject of the second verb is first person, which would make the subjects the same and would violate the requirement of non-identity of subject NP's discussed in the previous section. Thus, an obstinate negative sentence like:

> நான் வரமாட்டேன் ண்ணேன் *naan varamaaṭṭeen-ṇṇeen*
> 'I refused to come.'

cannot be embedded before ண்ணு சொன்னேன் *-ṇṇu sonneen* 'I said that', i.e. quotations cannot be infinitely embedded if their subjects are the same. However, the previous example sentence can be embedded before ண்ணு சொன்னான் *-ṇṇu sonnaan* 'he said' because the subjects of the two verbs are different:

> நான் வரமாட்டேன் ண்ணு சொன்னான் *naan varamaaṭṭeen-ṇṇu sonnaan* 'He said that I refused to come.'[5]

One can have embeddings of obstinate negative constructions before other quotative verbs, however, but in order to be grammatical, the first ண்ணேன் *ṇṇeen* must be deleted, as in:

[5] This sentence can also be glossed as 'He said that he refused to come.'

நான் வரமாட்டேன் ண்ணு சொன்னேன்
naan varamaaṭṭeen-ṇṇu sonneen
'I said that I refused to come.'

Since Tamil direct and indirect quotations are structurally the same, the above sentence could also be glossed as a direct quote: 'I said, "I will not come."' Note that Tamil future-negatives sometimes have the illocutionary force of an obstinate negative, i.e. the sentence

நான் இண்ணெக்கி சாயங்காலம் இங்கெ சாப்பிடமாட்டேன்
naan iṇṇekki saayangaalam inge saappiḍamaaṭṭeen

'I will not eat here this evening.'

could have the illocutionary force of 'I **refuse** to eat here this evening'; the obstinacy can be attenuated by changing the verb to சாப்பிட வரமாட்டேன் *saappiḍa varamaaṭṭeen* 'I won't be coming to eat here ...'

7.4 Factive Constructions

Tamil does not use lexical equivalents of English 'fact' to make factive sentences of the sort 'The fact that X=Y' etc. Instead, the quotative verb in its adjectival participle (AJP) form ன்குற (*ngra*) or as a verbal noun ன் குரது *ngradu* or as a participial noun ன்குறவரு *ngravaru* are used. The participial noun is marked for PNG and means 'the person X' or 'the person named/referred to/called X.'

வெங்கடாசலம்-ங்குறவரு *venkaḍaacalam-ngravaru*
'a/the person named Venkatacalam'

7.4.1 Factive Complement Clauses

In English, factive clauses are introduced by 'the fact that' preceded by verbs like 'know, forget, remember', etc.

- I forgot about the fact that Ram doesn't speak Tamil.
- The fact that he doesn't speak English surprises me.
- The fact that he failed his B.A. is not known to many.

These contrast with non-factive sentences such as:

- I forgot about Ram's not speaking Tamil.

- His not speaking English surprises me.

- His failing his B.A. is not known to many.

The latter examples sentences contrast with the previous three in that they refer to *specific* instances of some event, rather than general facts about someone or something; it is possible that Ram in the second example actually speaks Tamil, but didn't happen to speak it during the incident referred to, while in the factive sentence it is clear that the speaker thinks that it is a fact that Ram doesn't know Tamil. The second set, in other words, refer to specific events or **acts**, rather than what are (at least thought to be) facts, i.e. 'true knowledge.'

In Tamil, factive sentences consist of a sentence followed by ன்குற *ngra* + NP or ன்குறது *-ngradu* (nominalizations of the quotative verb) plus psychological verbs like தெரி *teri* 'know', மற *mara* 'forget', பொய் சொல்லு *poy sollu* 'lie', etc. That is, in Tamil, lies are also dealt with in factive constructions.

(160)

ராமுக்கு	தமிழ்	வராது	ங்குறதெ	பத்தி	மறந்திட்டேன்
raam-ukku	*tamir̤*	*varaadu*	*ngrade*	*patti*	*maranditteen*
Ram-to	Tamil	not-come	FACTIVE-ACC	about	forgot-COMPL-I

'I totally forgot about the fact that Ram doesn't know Tamil.'

(161)

ராம்	தமிழ்	பேசாததெ	பத்தி	மறந்திட்டேன்
raam	*tamir̤*	*peesaadade*	*patti*	*maranditteen*
Ram	Tamil	speaking-not	about	forgot-COMPL-I

'I totally forgot about (this particular incident of) Ram's not speaking Tamil.'

(162)

மந்திரி	லஞ்சம்	வாங்குறாரு	ங்குற	பொய்யெ	பத்தி
mandiri	*lanjam*	*vaangraaru*	*ngra*	*poyye*	*patti*
minister	bribe	takes	FACTIVE	lie	about

மறந்திட்டேன்
maranditteen
forgot-I

'I forgot about the lie (which is masquerading as a fact) that the minister takes bribes.'

(163) டாலருக்கு முப்பது ரூபா ங்குற ரேட்டு பொய்யா போச்சு
ḍaalarukku muppadu ruupaa ngra reeṭṭu poyyaa poocсu
to-the-dollar thirty rupee saying rate lie-like went

'The rate of thirty rupees to the dollar is deceptive.'[6]

Often, as in the last sentence above, the factive ங்குற *ngra* is used more as a verbalizer than as a fact-establishing construction due to the lack of any other verb in the construction *ḍaalarukku muppadu ruupaa* '(There are) thirty rupees to the dollar.' Often ங்குற *ngra* corresponds in English to prepositions or prepositional phrases like 'of, as, which is, according to which, as in', i.e. 'the rate OF eight rupees to the dollar.'

In sentence (163) above there is a translation problem, i.e. literally (163) says 'I forgot about the lie that it is a fact that the minister takes bribes' which may seem strange to some English speakers. However, perhaps 'contend falsely that it is a fact' as a translation for 'X *ngra poy sollu*' might help overcome this problem in English.[7]

7.4.1.1 X ங்குறவரு *ngravaru*: '(someone) called X'

The present animate verbal noun of the quotative verb ன் *n*, which has the form ங்குறவரு *ngravaru*, is translated in English as 'someone called X' or 'X by name', 'known as X.'

> வெங்கடாசலம்-ங்குறவரு வீடு இது தான்-ங்களேன்? *venkaḍaacalam ngravaru viiḍu idu-taan-ngaḷ-een?* Might this be the house of the man called Venkadacalam (if you don't mind my asking)?

Note that this sentence uses deferential ஏன் *een* (which we translate as 'if you don't mind my asking') instead of interrogative ஆ *aa*. Cf. ∮7.8.1.2.

7.5 Onomatopoeic Expressions with ண்ணு *ṇṇu*

Onomatopoeic expressions, similar to words in English like 'bang, crash, thud, whiz, zap, zonk, crunch', etc., are formed in Tamil by prefixing the onomatopoeic item before ண்ணு *-ṇṇu*. The structure of these emulates a 'quotative' construction, i.e. it is as if there is a sound of some sort being quoted.

[6] Or, is no longer true, owing to inflation and constant fluctuation of currency exchange rates.

[7] I am indebted to E. Annamalai for this example. One might also note that there has recently appeared a movie with the title 'True Lies'. This may seem a contradiction in terms unless the emphasis is on the notion that 'it is true that it is a lie.'

- தொணெதொணெண்ணு *toṇe toṇe-ṇṇu* ‘natter, nag, bitch at’
- குப்ண்ணு *kup-ṇṇu* ‘sound of sucking’
- திடீர்ண்ணு *tiḍiir-ṇṇu* ‘suddenly’
- சதக்சதக்ண்ணு *sadak-sadak-ṇṇu* ‘chopping sound’
- டக்குண்ணு *ṭakku-ṇṇu* ‘knocking sound; regularity’
- வளவளண்ணு *vaḷa-vaḷa-ṇṇu* ‘chattering, babbling’
- சொடெசொடெண்ணு *soṭṭe-soṭṭe-ṇṇu* ‘dripping wet’
- சலசலண்ணு *sala-sala-ṇṇu* ‘chattering, babbling’
- ஜில்லுண்ணு *jill-ṇṇu* ‘chilly’
- டமார் டமார்ண்ணு *ḍamaar-ḍamaar-ṇṇu* ‘bumping, thumping’
- படார் படார்ண்ணு *paḍaar-ṇṇu* ‘crashing’
- மடமடண்ணு *maḍa-maḍa-ṇṇu* ‘gushing’
- மடார்ண்ணு *maḍaar-ṇṇu* ‘thump, bonk’
- கடகடண்ணு *kaḍa-kaḍa-ṇṇu* ‘clickety-clack; rattling’
- உம்முண்ணு *umm-ṇṇu* ‘seriously; like a bump on a log’
- புஸ்ஸுண்ணு *bussu-ṇṇu* ‘woosh; puffed up arrogantly’
- டகார்ண்ணு *ṭahaar-ṇṇu* ‘suddenly’
- சுருக்கண்ணு *surukka-ṇṇu* ‘quickly (anger)’
- கிடுகிடுண்ணு *giḍu-giḍu-ṇṇu* ‘running quickly’
- சடக்ண்ணு *saḍak-ṇṇu* ‘spontaneously’
- சடசடண்ணு *saḍa-saḍa-ṇṇu* ‘rain drumming’

Many more examples of such expressions can be found; what is interesting about these expressions is that they are often phonologically aberrant. That is, the phonological structure of some of these expressions violates the usual rules about morpheme structure in Tamil—retroflex consonants can occur in initial position, some consonants are voiced initially, consonants occur finally without automatic vowels, and in general, the usual phonological constraints about what are possible words in Tamil are suspended.

Often these expressions are used where adverbs would be more common in English, as in ஜில்லுண்ணு இருக்கு *jill-ṇṇu irukku* for 'it's chilly' or உம்முண்ணு *umm-ṇṇu* for 'seriously, quietly, like a bump on a log.'

அவரு சும்மா உம்முண்ணு ஒக்காந்துகிட்டிருந்தாரு
avaru summaa umm-ṇṇu okkaandukiṭṭrundaaru
'He just sat there with his mouth clamped shut (not saying anything).'

Some expressions, when reduplicated, have slightly different meaning, i.e. டக்குண்ணு *ṭakku-ṇṇu* can mean 'knock, knock' but டக்குடக்குண்ணு *ṭakku-ṭakku-ṇṇu* means 'regularly, like clockwork, with mechanical efficiency.'[8]

7.6 போல *poola* and மாதிரி *maadiri*

7.6.1 Sentence + போல இருக்கு *poola irukku*

As a postposition meaning 'like', போல *poola* follows the accusative case. When a sentence precedes and இரு *iru* follows, the construction has the meaning 'it seems as if X' or 'it seems to be the case that X', or 'it's like X.'

(164) கொழந்தெ தூங்குறது போல இருக்கு
koṛande tuungradu poola irukku
Child sleeps like is

'The child seems to be sleeping.'

(165) அவரெ எங்கெயோ பாத்தது போல இருந்தது
avare engeyoo paattadu poola irundadu
him somewhere saw-I like it-was

'It was as if (like) I had seen him somewhere before; (I had the feeling I'd seen him somewhere before).'

7.6.2 போல *poola* Contracted: Counterfactual?

போல *poola* also has a contracted form ப்லெ *ple* or ப்ல *pla*. This is added to what seems to be a conditional ending ஆல் *-aal* attached to the present stem; or, it is an ambiguously-marked PNG ending, but the net result is that what precedes ப்லெ *ple* is ஆ *aa*:

[8] There is one published work on reduplication in LT, Malten 1989; Kausalya Hart (ms.) also has hundreds of examples of these in ST.

அவரு தூங்குறார்(?) *avaru tuungraar* + போல தெரியுது *p(oo)la teriyadu* ⟶ அவரு தூங்க்றாப்ல தெரியுது *avaru tuungraapla teriyadu*
'He seems to be sleeping (but it's not clear).'

The verb இரு *iru* after contracted ப்ல *p(oo)la* agrees in PNG with the noun phrase subject rather than being neuter to agree with a sentential subject. For some speakers, the meaning of this contracted construction is slightly different from S + போல இருக்கு *poola irukku* constructions, i.e. it is COUNTERFACTUAL or at least more vague than the uncontracted form.

அவரு படிக்குறாப்ல இருக்குறாரு *avaru padikkraapla irukkraaru*
'It appears as if he's reading (but it's not clear).'

When contracted ப்ல *pla* follows சொல்லு *sollu*, 'say' the meaning is '(just) as, like (s.o.) says' as in

அங்கம்மா சொல்லுறாப்ல அசிங்கமா இருக்கு *angammaa solraapla, asingamaa irukku* 'As Angamma says, the place is filthy.'

7.6.2.1 Contracted ப்ல *pla* in Other Expressions

Contracted ப்ல *pla* also occurs in some other constructions, most particularly in the expression எதித்தாப்ல *eduttaaple* 'right opposite, right in front.' This apparently derives from the LT form எதிர் *etir* 'opposite' + தான் *taan* 'emphatic' + போல *poola* 'as if.'[9]

7.6.3 மாதிரி *maadiri*

மாதிரி *maadiri* is a noun meaning 'way, fashion, manner, likeness.' It can therefore be preceded by adjectival forms, and if sentences are embedded before it, the verbs in the sentences are in the form of adjectival participles (AJP's).

எனக்கு ஒங்களெ எங்கெயோ பாத்தேன் + மாதிரி இருக்கு
enakku ongaḷe engeyoo paatteen + maadiri irukku ⟶
எனக்கு ஒங்களெ எங்கெயோ பாத்த + மாதிரி இருக்கு
enakku ongaḷe engeyoo paatta + maadiri irukku
'It's like I saw you somewhere or other (I have the feeling I've seen you somewhere before).'

[9] The fact that this form loses a long vowel ஓ *oo*, which is otherwise not to be expected in changes from LT to ST is evidence for the grammaticalization of this form from a postposition to another grammatical category.

Table 7.1: CLEFT SENTENCES

Non-cleft sentences	Cleft sentences
Is he going to the market?	Is it that he is *going* to the market? Is it the *market* that he is going to? Is *he* going to the market?
What is he doing?	What is it that he's doing?
Raman is going to the market.	What Raman is doing is going to the market. Where Raman is going is to the market. It's the market Raman's going to.
I am calling you	It's I who am calling you. I'm the one calling you.
What shall I do?	What is it that I should do? What's to be done?

In LT படி *paḍi* would also be used in such sentences where மாதிரி *maadiri* occurs, but is rare in SST. மாதிரி *maadiri* may be shortened to மாரி *maari* in rapid speech.

> அந்த மாரி செய்யாதே *anda maari seyyaadee!*
> 'Don't do (it) like that!

7.7 Cleft Sentences

In Tamil, as in other languages, there exists a kind of sentence called the 'cleft sentence.'[10] They differ slightly in form and meaning from ordinary declarative sentences in that the 'focus' or 'emphasis' is on a special part of the sentence not ordinarily emphasized. Their form is different in that the subject of the sentence does not seem to agree with the verb, whereas actually the subject of the verb is sentential or clausal, so the verb is marked for neuter PNG. The difference (in English cleft sentences) is illustrated by Table 7.1.

In the English examples of Table 7.1, the cleft and pseudo-cleft sentences have 'it', 'what' or other WH-interrogatives as part of the surface output, while the non-cleft sentences have 'he' or 'Raman' as the subjects. In English as in Tamil, the subject of the cleft sentence seems to be a whole

[10] The distinction some linguists make between cleft and pseudo-cleft sentences does not seem to be salient in Tamil.

Table 7.2: NON-CLEFT SENTENCES - CLEFT SENTENCES

NON-CLEFT SENTENCES	CLEFT SENTENCES
நான் மார்கெட்டுக்கு போறேனா? *naan maarkeṭṭukku pooreenaa?* 'Am I going to the market?'	நான் மார்கெட்டுக்கு போறதா? *naan markeṭṭukku pooradaa?* 'Is it that I am going to the market?' 'Am I supposed to go to the market?'
துணியெ கொண்டுவந்தெயா? *tuṇiye koṇḍuvandeyaa?* 'Did you bring the laundry?'	துணியெ கொண்டுவர்றதா? *tuṇiye koṇḍuvarradaa?* 'Is it that you have brought the laundry?' 'Is it the laundry you've brought?'
நான் எதெ செய்றேன்? *naan ede ceyreen?* ' What will I do?'	நான் எதெ செய்றது? *naan ede seyradu?* ' What is it that I will do?' ' What am I supposed to do?' 'What's to be done?'
மாதவி பாடுறா *maadavi paaḍraa* 'Madavi is singing'	இப்ப பாடுறது மாதவி *ippa paaḍradu maadavi* 'The person who's singing now is Madavi'
நான் பேசுறேன் *naan peesureen* 'I am speaking'	இப்ப பேசுறது வேலு *ippa peesuradu veelu* 'Now (it's) Veelu (who) is speaking'

clause or phrase, i.e. the subject of 'what Raman is doing is going to the market' is 'what Raman is doing.'

In Tamil, the cleft sentences differ from the non-cleft in that the verb is conspicuously marked only for neuter PNG; this can also be analyzed as an occurrence of the verbal noun in predicate position, as in Table 7.2.

In Tamil the illocutionary force of the cleft sentence, especially in questions, is often similar to that of modals, i.e. 'supposed to' instead of 'will', as in the third example in Table 7.2. That is, pragmatically, cleft constructions are used instead of modal constructions when asking about who needs to do what, etc. Otherwise, the cleft sentence is used to focus on or emphasize a particular element not otherwise emphasized. Asher (1982:96) gives more examples of these constructions.

7.8 Clitics ஓ, ஏ, ஆ, உம், ஏன் *oo, ee, aa, um, een*

In Tamil there is a class of constituents known as clitics, so-called because they can be suffixed to many different kinds of constituents but can never occur alone. They are therefore neither verbal nor nominal suffixes exclusively.[11]

7.8.1 Doubt Markers ஓ *oo* and ஏன் *-een*

7.8.1.1 Clitic ஓ *-oo* plus Varia

The clitic ஓ *-oo* is added to different kinds of constituents to indicate vagueness, ambiguity or doubt in the speaker's mind about the certainty, veracity or truth value of some event or circumstance. Sometimes ஓ *oo* substitutes for an interrogative ஆ *aa*, but with an expression of 'doubt' or uncertainty. Sometimes, also, ஓ *oo* is pragmatically 'softer' than an outright interrogative.

Since a sequence of two noun phrases or whole sentences, both marked with ஆ *aa* is one way Tamil makes disjunctive phrases ('either X or Y'), a sequence of noun phrases or whole sentences, both marked instead with ஓ *oo*, gives a disjunctive pair with extra doubt, as in the last example in Table 7.3. This can often be translated 'whether or not' or, if both verbs are negative, 'neither ... nor':

- சாப்பிடாமலோ தூங்காமலோ இருக்காதீங்க
  saappiḍaamaloo tuungaamaloo irukkaadiinga

[11] The best study of Tamil clitics can be found in Arokianathan 1981.

Table 7.3: Ordinary and Doubt-Marked Sentences

ORDINARY SENTENCES	DOUBT-MARKED SENTENCES
அம்மா இருக்காங்களா? *ammaa irukkaangaḷaa?* 'Is (your) Mother there?'	அம்மா இருக்காங்களோ? *ammaa irukkangaḷoo?* 'I wonder if maybe (your) Mother is there?'
துணியெ கொண்டுவந்தெயா? *tuṇiye koṇḍuvandeyaa?* 'Did you bring the laundry?'	துணியெ கொண்டுவந்தெயோ? *tuṇiye koṇḍuvandeyoo?* 'Have you perhaps brought the laundry?'
வருவாரா வரமாட்டாரா? *varuvaaraa varamaaṭṭaaraa* 'He'll either come or he won't.' ('Will he come or won't he?')	வருவாரோ வரமாட்டாரோ (தெரியாது) *varuvaaroo varamaaṭṭaaroo (teriyaadu)* 'He might come, or he might not.; ('I don't know.)'

'Don't go without eating or sleeping.'

- அவனுக்கு பாஷெ புரியதோ புரியல்லெயோ அவன் சினிமாவுக்கு போவான் *avanukku baaṣe puriyadoo, puriyalleyoo avan sinimaavukku poovaan* 'Whether or not he knows the language, he'll go to the movies.'

When ஓ *oo* is added to WH-interrogatives, the meaning is as in ∮6.10.8.

- எங்கெ *enge* 'where' ⟶ எங்கெயோ *engeyoo* 'somewhere (or other)'
- யாரு *yaaru* 'who' ⟶ யாரோ *yaaroo* 'someone (or other)'
- எத்தனெத்தனெ *ettaneyettane* 'however many' ⟶ எத்தனெயெத்தனெயோ *ettaneyettaneyoo* 'I don't know how many.'

7.8.1.2 The Ultra-Polite/Deferential Doubt Marker ஏன் *-een*

When ஏன் *-een* (lit. 'why') is suffixed to a sentence in final position, the meaning is politeness with doubt and deference, and perhaps with a nuance of servility and/or obsequiousness. This is, of course, often used with caution or when great respect is being attempted. Compare:

வெங்கடாசலம்-ங்குறவரு வீடு இது தான்-ங்களா?
venkaḍaacalam-ngravaru viiḍu idu-taan-ngaḷ-aa?
'Is this the house of the man called Venkadacalam, please?'

வெங்கடாசலம்-ங்குறவரு வீடு இது தான்-ங்களேன்?

venkaḍaacalam-ngravaru viiḍu idu-taan-ngaḷ-een?

'Might this be the house of the man called Venkadacalam, if you don't mind my asking?'

Note that ஏன் *-een* occupies the place of the clitics so if the question is interrogative, it replaces the normal clitic ஆ *-aa*.

(166) கட்டாயமா   குடுத்திடுறிங்களேன்
       kaṭṭaayamaa kuḍuttiḍringaḷeen?
       certainly   give-COMPL-PNG-DEFER

'I trust you'll be so kind as to give it to him?'

(167) அய்யாகிட்டே ஒரு கொறச்சலான வாடகெய்லெ ஒரு வீடு   பாக்க
       ayyaa-kiṭṭee oru koraccalaana vaaḍaheyle oru viiḍu paakka
       master-LOC a   cheap   rent-LOC   a   house to-find
       சொல்லுங்களேன்
       sollungaḷ-een
       say-IMP-DEFER

'Would you be so kind as to ask the master to please find me a cheap place to live?'

7.8.1.3 'Whether-or-not' in Interrogative Constructions

When an English yes-no interrogative sentence containing 'whether or not' is translated into Tamil, ஒ *-oo* …ஒ *-oo* is not used. Rather, ஆ *-a* …ஆ *-aa* is required. These usually are simply requests for information, not expressions of doubt.

(168) அவரு வர்றாரா   வரல்லெயா ண்ணு கேட்டேன்
       avaru varraaraa   varalleyaa ṇṇu keeṭṭeen
       he   come-FUT Q comeNEG-Q QTV ask-I

'I asked whether he was coming or not.'

(169) துணியெ தர்றானா   இல்லெ போறானா ண்ணு கேளு
       tuṇiye tarraanaa ille pooraanaa ṇṇu keeḷu
       clothing give-FUT-Q not go-FUT-Q QT ask

'Ask whether he's going to deliver the clothes or just go away.'

7.8.2 Wh-interrogative + VB + ஒ *oo*, அ *a*-word VB

When a WH-interrogative word (beginning with எ *e*) is followed by a verb + *oo*, followed by the equivalent அ *a*-word plus a verb, the meaning is 'A is equal to B' or 'B is neither more nor less than A.' It therefore functions as a COMPARATIVE system between two sentences or phrases.

- அவன் எங்கெ போனானோ, அங்கெயும் நான் போனேன்
  avan enge poonaanoo, angeyum naan pooneen
  'Wherever he went, I also went (I went wherever he went).'

- அவ எவ்வளவு குடுத்தாளோ, நானும் அவ்வளவு குடுப்பேன்
  ava evvaḷavu kuḍuttaaḷoo, naan avvaḷavu kuḍuppeen
  'I will give as much as she gave (whatever amount she gave, I also will give).'

- மீட்டர் எவ்வளவு காட்டுறதோ அவ்வளவு தான் குடுப்பேன்
  miiṭṭar evvaḷavu kaaṭṭradoo avvaḷavu taan kuḍuppeen
  'I will pay whatever amount the meter shows and no more.' ('No matter what amount the meter shows, I will pay that amount only.')

7.8.3 The Clitic உம் *-um*

The clitic உம் *-um* has many functions in Tamil. When one உம் *-um* is added to a noun or noun phrase, the meaning is 'also, too' or 'even.'

> நானும் தமிழ் ஆசிரியரு தான் *naanum tamir̤ aasiriyaru taan*
> '*I'm* a Tamil teacher, *too*!'

When உம் *um* follows a noun phrase that includes a quantifier (cf. ∮5.5.1) the meaning is 'all-inclusive', i.e. 'all (of); both (of them)'. Compare the two following examples, one of which contains உம் *um* and the other which doesn't:

- With: ரெண்டு பேருக்கும் தமிழ் தெரியும் *reṇḍu peerukkum tamir̤ teriyum*
  'Both of them know Tamil.'

- Without: ரெண்டு பேருக்கு தமிழ் தெரியும் *reṇḍu peerukku tamir̤ teriyum*
  'Two persons know Tamil.'

உம் *um* is also suffixed to various verbal forms, such as the concessive (∮6.10.4), in positive negative reduplication (∮7.2.1), expressions of possibility (∮7.1.1) and in other cases discussed below. In some of these cases, it has the meaning 'even' which it can also have with nouns.

7.8.4 Conjunctions உம் ... உம் *-um ... -um*, ஆ ... ஆ *-aa ... -aa*

7.8.4.1 உம் ... உம் *um ... um*: 'X and Y'

When two similar constituents in a sentence are affixed with உம் ... உம் *um ... um* , the meaning is X 'and' Y.

- நானும் அவரும் போறோம் *naan-um avar-um pooroom*
  'He AND I are going.'

- நான் ரெண்டு நாளா சாப்பிடவும் இல்லெ தூங்கவும் இல்லெ
  naan reṇḍu naaḷaa saappiḍavum ille tuungavum ille
  'I didn't eat or sleep for two days.'

For some speakers, this sentence would be preferable with ஓ *oo* ... ஓ *oo* because of the negative verbs:

- நான் ரெண்டு நாளா சாப்பிடவோ தூங்கவோ இல்லெ
  naan reṇḍu naaḷaa saappiḍavoo tuungavoo ille
  'I didn't eat or sleep for two days.'

The constituents must be of the same type in order for them to be conjoined, i.e. two nouns, two verbs (infinitives, or AVP's), two adverbs, etc. can be conjoined, but not one noun and one adjective, for example. Sentences cannot be conjoined with உம் ... உம்; another method, discussed in ∮6.8.3.1, must be used.

7.8.4.2 ஆ ... ஆ *aa ... aa*: Disjunction

When two similar constituents have affixes ஆ ... ஆ *-aa ... -aa* , the meaning is disjunctive 'either ... or' but in an interrogative sense: 'Which alternative is correct?'

- அவன் வர்றானா போறானா தெரியல்லெ *avan varraanaa pooraanaa teriyalle?*
  'I don't know if he's coming or going.'

- இதா அதா? *idaa adaa*? '(Do you mean) this or that?'

- யாரு, நானா நீங்களா *yaaru, naanaa niingaḷaa*? 'Who, me or you?'

7.8.4.3 ஆவது ... ஆவது *aavadu ... aavadu* 'either, or'

When two noun phrases are conjoined by suffixes *aavadu ... aavadu*, the meaning is declarative 'either ... or' (but only one alternative is possible).

- நானாவது நீயாவது பேசலாம் *naanaavadu niiyaavadu peesalaam*
  'Either you or I may speak (but not both)'

7.8.4.4 ஆவது *aavadu* in Isolation

When only one ஆவது *-aavadu* appears, its meaning, if attached to a numeral, is ORDINAL, i.e. equivalent to English '-th': நாலாவது *naalaavadu* 'fourth.' If attached to a single noun (phrase) the meaning is 'at least': நீயாவது போயிருக்கலாம் *niiyaavadu pooyirukkalaam* 'you, at least, may go.' ஆவது *aavadu* may be attached to எத்தனெ *ettane* to mean 'how many-eth':

> இது எத்தனாவது தடவெ *idu ettanaavadu tadave?*
> 'This is the how-many-eth time?'

ஆவது *aavadu* and an alternative form ஆம் *aam* are used as ordinal markers of numerals, and thus for dates: இது அஞ்சாம் (அஞ்சாவது) தேதி *idu anjaam (anjaavadu) teedi* 'This is the fifth (day) of the month'.

7.8.5 'Emphatic' ஏ, தான், தானே, மட்டும் *-ee, taan, taanee, mattum*

There are a number of so-called emphatic particles in Tamil, such as ஏ *-ee*, மட்டும் *mattum* and தான் *taan*. They are used in Tamil to emphasize or focus attention on particular elements of the sentence, as well as to handle other discourse phenomena such as whether information is new, old but related to new, presupposed, and for other pragmatic functions. Many western languages (such as English) use emphatic word stress for these purposes.[12] Tamil does not have emphatic word stress, but uses 'emphatic particles' instead. Often they cannot be literally translated.[13]

There is much confusion in the use of Tamil particles in that their English equivalents seem the same, but the Tamil meanings are different. The basic difference between ஏ *ee* and தான் *taan* (which are often both translated 'only') is that ஏ *-ee* means 'one compared to many' while தான் *taan* means 'one and only one (compared to none)', 'just.' Thus:

(170) இங்கெயே இருக்கு
inge-yee irukku
here-EMPH is

'It's RIGHT HERE (rather than somewhere else)'.

(171) இங்கெ தான் இருக்கு
inge daan irukku
here-EMPH is

[12] By this is meant uttering an element with more force, more volume, higher pitch, etc. than other elements, in order to emphasize it.

[13] But this fact does not prevent many speakers from doing so anyway, as 'only, itself, just' etc.

'It's here (and ONLY here).

Occasionally, both occur, as தானே *taan-ee* , as in

கேட்டா தானே *keeṭṭaa taanee* 'If (he'd) only listened ...'

தான் *taan,* being a word suffix, obeys word-internal sandhi in Tamil, so sometimes the initial consonant is phonetically voiced, and sometimes not. The same rules that apply to this are the rules shown in ∮1.3 on sandhi. தான் *taan* often functions in a discourse to indicate that new information is related to old information; it therefore functions as a communicative device that speakers use to establish solidarity, as in the following discourse:

A நீங்க யாரு? *niinga yaaru?* 'Who are you?'

B நான் தமிழ் ஆசிரியரு *naan tamir̤ aasiriyaru* 'I'm a Tamil teacher.'

A ஓ நானும் தமிழ் ஆசிரியரு தான் *oo, naanum tamir̤ aasiriyaru taan* 'Oh (well, what do you know?) *I'm* a Tamil teacher, *too*!'

Here உம் *um* is used to indicate 'also' but தான் *taan* indicates that new information (B is a Tamil teacher) is related to old information (A is also a Tamil teacher) and establishes solidarity. Without தான் *taan* the sentence would be abrupt and almost confrontational.

ஏ *ee* also has pragmatic uses that are equivalent to English 'of course, as you know' etc.

A: தமிழ் தெரியுமா *tamir̤ teriyumaa?* 'Do you know Tamil?'

B: ஓ தெரியுமே! *oo teriyumee!* 'Why of course I know (Tamil).'

7.8.5.1 Presupposed Knowledge

ஏ *-ee* has another meaning not associated with தான் *taan*, namely, presupposed knowledge. Its use indicates that the speaker thinks that the hearer ought to already know something. A sentence with ஏ *-ee* in this meaning has a special intonation pattern that falls, rises again, then falls on the last syllable.

A: இந்த கடெக்கி நடந்தே போயிடலாம்
inda kaḍekki naḍandee pooyiḍalaam
'Let's walk to the store.'

B: இல்லெ பஸ்லெ போகலாம் *ille, basle poohalaam* 'No, let's take the bus.'

A: பஸ் இந்த பக்கம் வராதே? *bas inda pakkam varaadee*? 'But the bus doesn't come this way (don't you remember?).'

Tamils seem to feel that this use of ஏ *ee* is somehow 'interrogative' and will supply question marks for such sentences. The question, of course, refers to why the other person is acting in such a way, as if they don't remember some presupposed information. The intonation on the last word would be ↘ போ *poo* ↗ கா *haa* → தே *dee*. Without this intonation, the above sentence would simply be 'emphatic': 'The bus simply doesn't come this way at all.'

7.9 The Verb பாரு *paaru* in Various Permutations

The verb பாரு *paaru* 'see' has the basic lexical meaning, 'see, look' but unlike other verbs it can be used in many different ways with special semantic interpretations.

7.9.1 பாரு *paaru* Meaning 'try VERB-ing', 'try to VERB'

7.9.1.1 Verb–INFINITIVE + *paaru*

A verb in the infinitive form plus பாரு *paaru* means 'try to verb.'

- கொழந்தெ நடக்க பாத்தது *koṛande naḍakka paattadu*
  'The child tried to walk.'

7.9.1.2 Verb + AVP + பாரு *paaru*

A verb in the past participle AVP plus பாரு *paaru* means 'try VERB-ing' rather than 'try to VERB.'

- கொழந்தெ நடந்து பாத்தது *koṛande naḍandu paattadu*
  'The child tried walking.'

The difference in meaning is that with this construction one tries something to see what the result will be, i.e. tries to see whether there will be any success, whereas with 'try to VERB', the idea is that the action one tried might not have even have been completed. Thus, with infinitive the meaning is 'The child tried to walk (but wasn't able to do so very well)' while the meaning with AVP might be 'The child tried walking (but didn't stick with it'.)

7.9.1.3 Lexical Combinations

Certain combinations of verb + பாரு *paaru* have English lexical equivalents as follows:

- சொல்லி பாரு *solli paaru* 'explain' (lit. 'try saying')
- சாப்பிட்டு பாரு *saappiṭṭu paaru* 'taste' (lit. 'try eating')

7.9.1.4 Postpositions plus பாரு *paaru*

Unlike most other verbs, பாரு *paaru* can have postpositions prefixed to it to form other lexical items: மேல் *meel* 'above' + பாரு *paaru* 'see' ⟶ 'oversee, supervise'; எதிர் *edur* 'opposite' + பாரு *paaru* 'see' ⟶ 'look forward, expect.'

Nouns can also be prefixed to *paaru* to form a new lexical item: வேலெ *veele* 'work' + பாரு *paaru* 'see' ⟶ '(to) work.'

7.9.2 பாத்து *paattu* Meaning (Direct the Attention) 'at, towards'

Sometimes பாத்து *paattu* is used with certain other verbs such as சிரி *siri* 'laugh', கொலெ *kole* 'bark' to indicate that the attention is directed AT or TOWARD someone. Cf. ∮2.4.4.3.

என்னெ பாத்து சிரிக்குறீங்களா? *enne paattu sirikkriingaḷaa?*
'Are you laughing at *me*?'

7.9.3 பாத்து *paattu* + VERB

paattu preceding another verb means literally 'seeing, having seen' + VERB: பாத்து போங்க *paattu poonga* 'go while seeing; watch where you go.' The general notion with this use of பாத்து *paattu* is 'deliberately, intentionally, purposefully, carefully'.

அரசாங்கம் எதாவது பாத்து செய்யணும்
arasaangam edaavadu paattu seyyaṇum
'The Government ought to take DELIBERATE action.'

7.9.3.1 பாத்து *paattu* with Time Expressions

When பாத்து *paattu* is used with time expressions, the idea is 'What a bad time for X! Of all the times for X to happen!'

- இண்ணெக்கி பாத்து வந்தாங்க
  iṇṇekki paattu vandaanga
  'They came TODAY of all days; (they deliberately came today when I didn't want them to!)'

- இப்ப சினிமாவுக்கு போகலாம்ண்ணு இருக்குறான், அப்பா மெட்ராஸ்லெருந்து வர்ற நாளா பாத்து *ippa sinimaavukku pookalaam-ṇṇu irukkraan, appaa meḍraaslerundu varra naaḷaa paattu*! 'He wants to go to the movies NOW, of all times, when Father is just about to arrive from Madras.'

Sometimes போயி *pooyi* 'having gone' is also present in such sentences:

> இண்ணெக்கி போயி கதெ எழுதுறாரே பணம் வர்ற நாளா பாத்து
> *iṇṇekki pooyi kade ezuduraaree, paṇam varra naaḷaa paattu* 'He's going to (go and) write a story TODAY, of all days, when money is on its way!'

Note that these sentences tend to end, not with the finite verb clause, but with the clause containing பாத்து *paattu* EXTRAPOSED after the finite verb, for emphasis; extraposition emphasizes the speaker's sense of INDIGNATION or OUTRAGE at the behaviour of the person being described.

7.9.3.2 The Concessive of பாரு *paaru* with Interrogative எப்ப *eppa*

When the concessive form of பாரு *paaru* (பாத்தாலும் *paattaalum*) is used with interrogative எப்ப *eppa*, the meaning literally is 'whenever s.o. sees; no matter when s.o. sees/looks.' Its illocutionary force, however, is that of a reproach or an impatient commentary; its general meaning therefore is 'all the time, day in and out, every time you turn around, ad nauseam.' எப்ப பாத்தாலும் *eppa paattaalum* has therefore become a phrase meaning, at best, 'repetitiously, annoyingly, incessantly, habitually.'

> அவன் எப்ப பாத்தாலும் சினிமாவுக்கு போவான்
> *avan eppa paattaalum sinimaavukku poovaan*
> '(Every time you see him,) he's always going to the movies.'

Chapter 8

LT Equivalents of ST Paradigms

Table 8.1: Sample Imperative Forms, Three Verbs: LT Version of Table 3.1

	Sg. non-polite	**Sg. polite**	**Plural/polite**
Stem [zero]	-உம், *um* -ரும் *rum*	ங்கள் *ngaḷ*	
உட்கார் *uṭkaar*	உட்கார் *uṭkaar* 'come'	உட்காரும் *uṭkaarum*	உட்காருங்கள் *uṭkaarungaḷ*
போ *poo*	போ *poo* 'go'	போரும் *poorum*	போங்கள் *poongaḷ*
படி *paḍi*	படி *paḍi* 'read'	படியும் *paḍiyum*	படியுங்கள் *paḍiyungaḷ*

Table 8.2: Strong Verbs; LT Versions of Table 3.3

	Stem	Gloss	Infinitive	Present	Past	Future
1.	எடு *eḍu*	'take'	எடுக்க *eḍukka*	எடுக்கிற்- *eḍukkir̲-*	எடுத்த்- *eḍutt-*	எடுப்ப்- *eḍupp-*
2.	நட *naḍa*	'walk'	நடக்க *naḍakka*	நடக்கிற்- *naḍakkir̲-*	நடந்த்- *naḍand-*	நடப்ப்- *naḍapp-*
3.	கட *kaḍa*	'cross'	கடக்க *kaḍakka*	கடக்கிற்- *kaḍakkir̲-*	கடந்த்- *kaḍand-*	கடப்ப்- *kaḍapp-*
4.	கல *kala*	'mix'	கலக்க *kalakka*	கலக்கிற்- *kalakkir̲-*	கலந்த்- *kaland-*	கலப்ப்- *kalapp-*
5.	மற *mara*	'forget'	மறக்க *marakka*	மறக்கிற்- *marakkir̲-*	மறந்த்- *marand-*	மறப்ப்- *marapp-*

Table 8.3: Examples of Weak Verbs, with Tense Markers கிற்/இன்/வ;
LT Versions of Table 3.4

Stem	Gloss	Infinitive	Present	Past	Future
1. சொல்லு *sol(lu)*	'say'	சொல்ல *solla*	சொல்(லு)கிறேன் *solluhir̲een*	சொன்னேன் *sonn̲een̲*	சொல்லுவேன் *solluveen̲*
2. பேசு *peesu*	'speak'	பேச *peesa*	பேசுகிறேன் *peesuhir̲een̲*	பேசினேன் *peesin̲een̲*	பேசுவேன் *peesuveen̲*
3. போ *poo*	'go'	போக *pooha*	போகிறேன் *poohir̲een̲*	போனேன் *poon̲een̲*	போவேன் *pooveen̲*
4. வாங்கு *vaangu*	'buy, acquire, get, fetch'	வாங்க *vaanga*	வாங்குகிறேன் *vaanguhir̲een̲*	வாங்குனேன் *vaangin̲een̲*	வாங்குவேன் *vaanguveen̲*

Table 8.4: Strong Verbs, Graul's Class IV; LT Versions of Table 3.5

	Stem	**Gloss**	**Infinitive**	**Present**
1.	சாப்பிடு *saappiḍu*	'eat'	சாப்பிட *saappiḍa*	சாப்பிடுகிறேன் *saappiḍuhir̲een̲*
2.	போடு *pooḍu*	'place, put,' 'serve (food)'	போட *pooḍa*	போடுகிறேன் *pooḍuhir̲een̲*
3.	போட்டுக்கொள் *pooṭṭukkoḷ*	'put on, wear'	போட்டுக்கொள்ள *pooṭṭukkoḷḷa*	போட்டுக்கொள்கிறேன் *pooṭṭukkoḷhir̲een̲*
	Stem	**Gloss**	**Past**	**Future**
1.	சாப்பிடு *saappiḍu*	'eat'	சாப்பிட்டேன் *saappiṭṭeen̲*	சாப்பிடுவேன் *saappiḍuveen̲*
2.	போடு *pooḍu*	'place, put,' 'serve (food)'	போட்டேன் *pooṭṭeen̲*	போடுவேன் *pooḍuveen̲*
3.	போட்டுக்கொள் *pooṭṭukkoḷ*	'put on, wear'	போட்டுக்கொண்டேன் *pooṭṭukkoṇḍeen̲*	போட்டுக்கொள்ளுவேன் *pooṭṭukkoḷḷuveen̲*

Table 8.5: Graul's Class V; LT Version of Table 3.6

Verb stem	**Present**	**Past**	**Future**
நில் 'stand' *nil(lu)*	நிற்கிறேன் *nir̲kir̲een̲*	நின்றேன் *nin̲r̲een̲*	நிற்பேன் *nir̲peen̲*
உண் 'eat' *uṇ*	உண்கிறேன் *uṇgir̲een̲*	உண்டேன் *uṇḍeen̲*	உண்பேன் *uṇbeen̲*
என் 'quote' *en̲*	என்கிறேன் *en̲gir̲een̲*	என்றேன் *en̲r̲een̲*	என்பேன் *en̲been̲*
கேள் 'ask' *keeḷ*	கேட்கிறேன் *keeṭkir̲een̲*	கேட்டேன் *keeṭṭeen̲*	கேட்பேன் *keeṭpeen̲*
காண் 'see' *kaaṇ*	காண்கிறேன் *kaaṇgir̲een̲*	கண்டேன் *kaṇḍeen̲*	காண்பேன் *kaaṇbeen̲*

Table 8.6: Paradigms of வா *vaa* 'come', All PNG; LT Versions of Table 3.7

PNG	**Present**	**Past**	**Future**
1 SG	நான் வருகிறேன் *naan̲ varuhir̲een̲*	நான் வந்தேன் *naan̲ vandeen̲*	நான் வருவேன் *naan̲ varuveen̲*
2 SG	நீ வருகிறாய் *nii varuhir̲aay*	நீ வந்தாய் *nii vandaay*	நீ வருவாய் *nii varuvaay*
3 SG M	அவன் வருகிறான் *avan̲ varuhir̲aan̲*	அவன் வந்தான் *avan̲ vandaan̲*	அவன் வருவான் *avan̲ varuvaan̲*
3. SG F	அவள் வருகிறாள் *avaḷ varuhir̲aaḷ*	அவள் வந்தாள் *avaḷ vandaaḷ*	அவள் வருவாள் *avaḷ varuvaaḷ*
3 SG N	அது வருகிறது *adu varuhir̲adu*	அது வந்தது *adu vandadu*	அது வரும் *adu varum*
1 PL*exclusive*	நாங்கள் வருகிறோம் *naangaḷ varuhir̲oom*	நாங்கள் வந்தோம் *naangaḷ vandoom*	நாங்கள் வருவோம் *naangaḷ varuvoom*
1 PL*inclusive*	நாம் வருகிறோம் *naam varuhir̲oom*	நாம் வந்தோம் *naam vandoom*	நாம் வருவோம் *naam varuvoom*
2 PL (POL)	நீங்கள் வருகிறீர்கள் *niingaḷ varuhir̲iirhaḷ*	நீங்கள் வந்தீர்கள் *niingaḷ vandiirhaḷ*	நீங்கள் வருவீர்கள் *niingaḷ varuviirhaḷ*
3rd PL(pol)	அவர் வருகிறார் *avar varuhir̲aar*	அவர் வந்தார் *avar vandaar*	அவர் வருவார் *avar varuvaar*
3 PL NON-POL & F POL	அவர்கள் வருகிறார்கள் *avarhaḷ varuhir̲aarhaḷ*	அவர்கள் வந்தார்கள் *avarhaḷ vandaarhaḷ*	அவர்கள் வருவார்கள் *avarhaḷ varuvaarhaḷ*
3 PL N	அவைகள் வருகின்றன *avaihaḷ varuhin̲r̲an̲a*	அவைகள் வந்தன *avaihaḷ vandan̲a*	அவைகள் வரும் *avaihaḷ varum*

Table 8.7: Paradigms of போ *poo* 'go', all PNG; LT Versions of Table 3.8

PNG	**Present**	**Past**	**Future**
1 SG	நான் போகிறேன் *naan̲ poohir̲een̲*	போனேன் *poon̲een̲*	போவேன் *pooveen̲*
2 SG	நீ போகிறாய் *nii poohir̲aay*	போனாய் *poon̲aay*	போவாய் *poovaay*
3 SG M	அவன் போகிறான் *avan̲ poohir̲aan̲*	போனான் *poon̲aan̲*	போவான் *poovaan̲*
3. SG F	அவள் போகிறாள் *avaḷ poohir̲aaḷ*	போனாள் *poon̲aaḷ*	போவாள் *poovaaḷ*
3 SG N	அது போகிறது *adu poohir̲adu*	(போனது) போயிற்று *(poon̲adu) pooyir̲r̲u*	போகும் *poohum*
1 PL EXCL	நாங்கள் போகிறோம் *naangaḷ poohir̲oom*	போனோம் *poon̲oom*	போவோம் *poovoom*
1 PL INCL	நாம் போகிறோம் *naam poohir̲oom*	போனோம் *poon̲oom*	போவோம் *poovoom*
2 PL(POL)	நீங்க போகிறீர்கள் *niingaḷ poohir̲iirhaḷ*	போனீர்கள் *poon̲iirhaḷ*	போவீர்கள் *pooviirhaḷ*
3rd PL (POL)	அவர் போகிறார் *avar poohir̲aar*	போனார் *poon̲aar*	போவார் *poovaar*
3 PL NON-POL	அவர்கள் போகிறார்கள் *avarhaḷ poohir̲aarhaḷ*	போனார்கள் *poon̲aarhaḷ*	போவார்கள் *poovaarhaḷ*
& F POL	அவர்கள் போகிறார்கள் *avarhaḷ poohir̲aarhaḷ*	போனார்கள் *poon̲aarhaḷ*	போவார்கள் *poovaarhaḷ*
3 PL N	அவைகள் போகின்றன *avaihaḷ poohin̲r̲an̲a*	போயின *pooyin̲a*	போகும் *poohum*

Table 8.8: Graul's Verb Class System;
LT Versions of Table 3.9

Class	Present	Past	Future
LT 1	-கிற்- [-kiṟ-]	-த்- [-d-]	-வ- [-v-]
LT 2	-கிற்- [-kiṟ-]	-ந்த்- [-nd-]	-வ- [-v-]
LT 3	-கிற்- [-kiṟ-]	-இன்- [-iṉ-]	-வ- [-v-]
LT 4	-கிற்- [-kiṟ-]	-ட்ட்- [-ṭṭ-]	-வ- [-v-]
LT 5	-கிற்- [-kiṟ-]	-ன்ற்- [-ṉṟ-]	-ப்- [-v-]
LT 5b	-கிற்- [-kiṟ-]	-ற்ற்- [-ṟṟ-]	-ப்- [-b-]
LT 5c	-கிற்- [-kiṟ-]	-ட்ட்- [-ṭṭ-]	-ப்- [-b-]
LT 6	-க்கிற்- [-kkiṟ-]	-த்த்- [-tt-]	-ப்ப்- [-v-]
LT 7	-க்கிற்- [-kkiṟ-]	-ந்த்- [-nd-]	-ப்ப்- [-pp-]

Table 8.9: Tamil Verb Classes, LT: Typical Examples;
LT Versions of Table 3.10

Class	Verb Stem	Present	Past	Future
1	அழு 'weep'	அழுகிறேன்	அழுதேன்	அழுவேன்
	aṛu	*aṛuhiṟeeṉ*	*aṛudeeṉ*	*aṛuveeṉ*
2	உட்கார் 'sit'	உட்காருகிறேன்	உட்கார்ந்தேன்	உட்காருவேன்
	uṭkaar	*uṭkaaruhiṟeeṉ*	*uṭkaarndeeṉ*	*uṭkaaruveeṉ*
2b	உடை 'break'	உடைகிறது	உடைந்தது	உடையும்
	uḍai (INTR)	*uḍaikiṟadu*	*uḍaindadu*	*uḍaiyum*
2c	வா 'come'	வருகிறேன்	வந்ததேன்	வருவேன்
	vaa	*varuhiṟeeṉ*	*vandeeṉ*	*varuveeṉ*
3	வாங்கு 'buy'	வாங்குகிறேன்	வாங்கினேன்	வாங்குவேன்
	vaangu	*vaanguhiṟeeṉ*	*vaangiṉeeṉ*	*vaanguveeṉ*
3b	போ 'go'	போகிறேன்	போனேன்	போவேன்
	poo	*poohiṟeeṉ*	*pooṉeeṉ*	*pooveeṉ*
3c	சொல் 'say'	சொல்லுகிறேன்	சொன்னேன்	சொல்லுவேன்
	sollu	*sol(lu)hiṟeeṉ*	*soṉṉeeṉ*	*solluveeṉ*
4	போடு 'put'	போடுகிறேன்	போட்டேன்	போடுவேன்
	pooḍu	*pooḍuhiṟeeṉ*	*pooṭṭeeṉ*	*pooḍuveeṉ*
5	உண் 'eat'	உண்கிறேன்	உண்டேன்	உண்பேன்
	uṇ	*uṇgiṟeeṉ*	*uṇḍeeṉ*	*uṇbeeṉ*
	என் 'quote'	என்கிறேன்	என்றேன்	என்பேன்
	eṉ	*eṉgiṟeeṉ*	*eṉṟeeṉ*	*eṉbeeṉ*
5b	கேள் 'ask'	கேட்கிறேன்	கேட்டேன்	கேட்பேன்
	keeḷ	*keeṭkiṟeeṉ*	*keeṭṭeeṉ*	*keeṭpeeṉ*
5c	காண் 'see'	காண்கிறேன்	கண்டேன்	காண்பேன்
	kaaṇ	*kaaṇgiṟeeṉ*	*kaṇḍeeṉ*	*kaaṇbeeṉ*
6	பார் 'see'	பார்க்கிறேன்	பார்த்தேன்	பார்ப்பேன்
	paar	*paarkkiṟeeṉ*	*paartteeṉ*	*paarppeeṉ*
6b	சமை 'cook'	சமைக்கிறேன்	சமைத்தேன்	சமைப்பேன்
	samai	*samaikkiṟeeṉ*	*samaitteeṉ*	*samaippeeṉ*
7	நட 'walk'	நடக்கிறேன்	நடந்தேன்	நடப்பேன்
	naḍa	*naḍakkiṟeeṉ*	*naḍandeeṉ*	*naḍappeeṉ*

Table 8.10: Examples of Strong Verbs (Graul's Classes VI and VII); LT Versions of Table 3.11

	Stem	**Gloss**	**Infinitive**	**Present**	**Past**	**Future**
1.	எடு *eḍu*	'be located'	எடுக்க *eḍukka*	எடுக்கிற்- *eḍukkiṟ-*	எடுத்து- *eḍutt-*	எடுப்ப்- *eḍupp-*
2.	படு *paḍu*	'lie'	படுக்க *paḍukka*	படுக்கிற்- *paḍukkiṟ-*	படுத்த்- *paḍutt-*	படுப்ப்- *paḍupp-*
3.	கொடு *koḍu*	'give'	கொடுக்க *koḍukka*	கொடுக்கிற்- *koḍukkiṟ-*	கொடுத்த்- *koḍutt-*	கொடுப்ப்- *koḍupp-*
4.	வை *vai*	'put, keep'	வைக்க *vaikka*	வைக்கிற்- *vaikkiṟ-*	வைத்த்- *vaitt-*	வைப்ப்- *vaipp-*
5.	படி *paḍi*	'study, read'	படிக்க *paḍikka*	படிக்கிற்- *paḍikkiṟ-*	படித்த்- *paḍitt-*	படிப்ப்- *paḍipp-*
6.	சமை *samai*	'cook'	சமைக்க *samaikka*	சமைக்கிற்- *samaikkiṟ-*	சமைத்த்- *samaitt-*	சமைப்ப்- *samaipp-*

Table 8.11: Paradigms of பார் *paar*, 'see', all Tenses and PNG;
LT Version of Table 3.12

PNG	**Present**	**Past**	**Future**
1 SG	பார்க்கிறேன் *paarkkir̲een̲*	பார்த்தேன் *paartteen̲*	பார்ப்பேன் *paarppeen̲*
2 SG	பார்க்கிறாய் *paarkkir̲aay*	பார்த்தாய் *paarttaay*	பார்ப்பாய் *paarppaay*
3 SG M	பார்க்கிறான் *paarkkir̲aan̲*	பார்த்தான் *paarttaan̲*	பார்ப்பான் *paarppaan̲*
3 SG F	பார்க்கிறாள் *paarkkir̲aaḷ*	பார்த்தாள் *paarttaaḷ*	பார்ப்பாள் *paarppaaḷ*
3 SG N	பார்க்கிறது *paarkkir̲adu*	பார்த்தது *paarttadu*	பார்க்கும் *paarkkum*
1 PL	பார்க்கிறோம் *paarkkir̲oom*	பார்த்தோம் *paarttoom*	பார்ப்போம் *paarppoom*
2 PL & POL	பார்க்கிறீர்கள் *paarkkir̲iirhaḷ*	பார்த்தீர்கள் *paarttiirhaḷ*	பார்ப்பீர்கள் *paarppiirhaḷ*
3rd PL (POL)	பார்க்கிறார்கள் *paarkkir̲aarhaḷ*	பார்த்தார்கள் *paarttaarhaḷ*	பார்ப்பார்கள் *paarppaarhaḷ*
3 PL NON-POL & F POL	பார்க்கிறார்கள் *paarkkir̲aarhaḷ*	பார்த்தார்கள் *paarttaarhaḷ*	பார்ப்பார்கள் *paarppaarhaḷ*
3rd PL (N)	பார்க்கின்றன *paarkkin̲r̲an̲a*	பார்த்தன *paarttan̲a*	பார்க்கும் *paarkkum*

Table 8.13: Paradigms of இரு *iru* 'be located', all Tenses and PNG; LT Version of Table 3.13

PNG	**Present**	**Past**	**Future**
1 SG	இருக்கிறேன் *irukkir̲een̲*	இருந்தேன் *irundeen̲*	இருப்பேன் *iruppeen̲*
2 SG	இருக்கிறாய் *irukkir̲aay*	இருந்தாய் *irundaay*	இருப்பாய் *iruppaay*
3 SG M	இருக்கிறான் *irukkir̲aan̲*	இருந்தான் *irundaan̲*	இருப்பான் *iruppaan̲*
3. SG F	இருக்கிறாள் *irukkir̲aaḷ*	இருந்தாள் *irundaaḷ*	இருப்பாள் *iruppaaḷ*
3 SG N	இருக்கிறது *irukkir̲adu*	இருந்தது *irundadu*	இருக்கும் *irukkum*
1 PL	இருக்கிறோம் *irukkir̲oom*	இருந்தோம் *irundoom*	இருப்போம் *iruppoom*
2 PL (& POL)	இருக்கிறீர்கள் *irukkir̲iirhaḷ*	இருந்தீர்கள் *irundiirhaḷ*	இருப்பீர்கள் *iruppiirhaḷ*
3rd PL (& HON)	இருக்கிறார் *irukkir̲aar*	இருந்தார் *irundaar*	இருப்பார் *iruppaar*
3rd PL (NON-POL)	இருக்கிறார்கள் *irukkir̲aarhaḷ*	இருந்தார்கள் *irundaarhaḷ*	இருப்பார்கள் *iruppaarhaḷ*
F POL	இருக்கிறார்கள் *irukkir̲aarhaḷ*	இருந்தார்கள் *irundaarhaḷ*	இருப்பார்கள் *iruppaarhaḷ*
3rd PL (N)	அவைகள் இருக்கின்றன *avaihaḷ irukkin̲r̲an̲a*	அவைகள் இருந்தன *avaihaḷ irundan̲a*	அவைகள் இருக்கும் *avaihaḷ irukkum*

Table 8.14: Paradigms of சாப்பிடு: All Tenses and PNG; LT Version of Table 3.14. (Note: for neuters, usually a different verb, தின் *tiṉ* is used.)

PNG	**Present**	**Past**	**Future**
1 SG	சாப்பிடுகிறேன் *saappiḍuhiṟeeṉ*	சாப்பிட்டேன் *saappiṭṭeeṉ*	சாப்பிடுவேன் *saappiḍuveeṉ*
2 SG	சாப்பிடுகிறாய் *saappiḍuhiṟaay*	சாப்பிட்டாய் *saappiṭṭaay*	சாப்பிடுவாய் *saappiḍuvaay*
3 SG M	சாப்பிடுகிறான் *saappiḍuhiṟaaṉ*	சாப்பிட்டான் *saappiṭṭaaṉ*	சாப்பிடுவான் *saappiḍuvaaṉ*
3. SG F	சாப்பிடுகிறாள் *saappiḍuhiṟaaḷ*	சாப்பிட்டாள் *saappiṭṭaaḷ*	சாப்பிடுவாள் *saappiḍuvaaḷ*
3 SG N	சாப்பிடுகிறது *saappiḍuhiṟadu*	சாப்பிட்டது *saappiṭṭadu*	தின்னும் *tiṉṉum*
1 PL	சாப்பிடுகிறோம் *saappiḍuhiṟoom*	சாப்பிட்டோம் *saappiṭṭoom*	சாப்பிடுவோம் *saappiḍuvoom*
2 PL (& POL)	சாப்பிடுகிறீர்கள் *saappiḍukiṟiirhaḷ*	சாப்பிட்டீர்கள் *saappiṭṭiirhaḷ*	சாப்பிடுவீர்கள் *saappiḍuviirhaḷ*
3rd PL (& HON)	சாப்பிடுகிறார் *saappiḍuhiṟaar*	சாப்பிட்டார் *saappiṭṭaar*	சாப்பிடுவார் *saappiḍuvaar*
3rd PL (NON-POL)	சாப்பிடுகிறார்கள் *saappiḍuhiṟaarhaḷ*	சாப்பிட்டார்கள் *saappiṭṭaarhaḷ*	சாப்பிடுவார்கள் *saappiḍuvaarhaḷ*
F POL	சாப்பிடுகிறார்கள் *saappiḍuhiṟaarhaḷ*	சாப்பிட்டார்கள் *saappiṭṭaarhaḷ*	சாப்பிடுவார்கள் *saappiḍuvaarhaḷ*
3rd PL (N)	சாப்பிடுகின்றன *saappiḍuhiṉṟaṉa*	சாப்பிட்டன *saappiṭṭaṉa*	தின்னும் *tiṉṉum*

Table 8.15: Paradigms of வாங்கு ‘buy, fetch, get’, all tenses and PNG; LT Version of Table 3.15

PNG	**Present**	**Past**	**Future**
1 SG	வாங்குகிறேன் *vaanguhiṟeeṉ*	வாங்கினேன் *vaanginṉeeṉ*	வாங்குவேன் *vaanguuveeṉ*
2 SG	வாங்குகிறாய் *vaanguhiṟaay*	வாங்கினாய் *vaangiṉaay*	வாங்குவாய் *vaanguvaay*
3 SG M	வாங்குகிறான் *vaanguhiṟaaṉ*	வாங்கினான் *vaangiṉaaṉ*	வாங்குவான் *vaanguvaaṉ*
3. SG F	வாங்குகிறாள் *vaanguhiṟaaḷ*	வாங்கினாள் *vaangiṉaaḷ*	வாங்குவாள் *vaanguvaaḷ*
3 SG N	வாங்குகிறது *vaanguhiṟadu*	வாங்கினது *vaangiṉadu*	வாங்கும் *vaangum*
1 PL	வாங்குகிறோம் *vaanguhiṟoom*	வாங்கினோம் *vaangiṉoom*	வாங்குவோம் *vaanguvoom*
2 PL (& POL)	வாங்குகிறீர்கள் *vaanguhiṟiirhaḷ*	வாங்கினீர்கள் *vaangiṉiirhaḷ*	வாங்குவீர்கள் *vaanguviirhaḷ*
3rd PL (& HON)	வாங்குகிறார் *vaanguhiṟaar*	வாங்கினார் *vaangiṉaar*	வாங்குவார் *vaanguvaar*
3rd PL (NON-POL)	வாங்குகிறார்கள் *vaanguhiṟaarhaḷ*	வாங்கினார்கள் *vaangiṉaarhaḷ*	வாங்குவார்கள் *vaanguvaarhaḷ*
F POL	வாங்குகிறார்கள் *vaanguhiṟaarhaḷ*	வாங்கினார்கள் *vaangiṉaarhaḷ*	வாங்குவாங்க *vaanguvaarhaḷ*
3rd PL (N)	வாங்குகின்றன *vaanguhiṉṟaṉa*	வாங்கின *vaangiṉa*	வாங்கும் *vaangum*

Table 8.16: Paradigms of படி, all Tenses and PNG; LT Version of Table 3.16

PNG	**Present**	**Past**	**Future**
1 SG	படிக்கிறேன் *paḍikkiṟeeṉ*	படித்தேன் *paḍitteeṉ*	படிப்பேன் *paḍippeeṉ*
2 SG	படிக்கிறாய் *paḍikkiṟaay*	படித்தாய் *paḍittaay*	படிப்பாய் *paḍippaay*
3 SG M	படிக்கிறான் *paḍikkiṟaaṉ*	படித்தான் *paḍittaaṉ*	படிப்பான் *paḍippaaṉ*
3. SG F	படிக்கிறாள் *paḍikkiṟaaḷ*	படித்தாள் *paḍittaaḷ*	படிப்பாள் *paḍippaaḷ*
3 SG N	படிக்கிறது *paḍikkiṟadu*	படித்தது *paḍittadu*	படிக்கும் *paḍikkum*
1 PL	படிக்கிறோம் *paḍikkiṟoom*	படித்தோம் *paḍittoom*	படிப்போம் *paḍippoom*
2 PL (& POL)	படிக்கிறீர்கள் *paḍikkiṟiirhaḷ*	படித்தீர்கள் *paḍittiirhaḷ*	படிப்பீர்கள் *paḍippiirhaḷ*
3rd PL (& HON)	படிக்கிறார்கள் *paḍikkiṟaarhaḷ*	படித்தார்கள் *paḍittaarhaḷ*	படிப்பார்கள் *paḍippaarhaḷ*
3rd PL (NON-POL)	படிக்கிறார்கள் *paḍikkiṟaarhaḷ*	படித்தார்கள் *paḍittaarhaḷ*	படிப்பார்கள் *paḍippaarhaḷ*
3rd PL (N)	படிக்கின்றன *paḍikkiṉṟaṉa*	படித்தன *paḍittaṉa*	படிக்கும் *paḍikkum*

Table 8.17: Paradigms of Transitive உடை *uḍai* 'break (something)', all tenses and PNG; LT Version of Table 3.17

PNG	Present	Past	Future
1 SG	உடைக்கிறேன் *uḍaikkir̲een̲*	உடைத்தேன் *uḍaitteen̲*	உடைப்பேன் *uḍaippeen̲*
2 SG	உடைக்கிறாய் *uḍaikkir̲aay*	உடைத்தாய் *uḍaittaay*	உடைப்பாய் *uḍaippaay*
3 SG M	உடைக்கிறான் *uḍaikkir̲aan̲*	உடைத்தான் *uḍaittaan̲*	உடைப்பான் *uḍaippaan̲*
3 SG F	உடைக்கிறாள் *uḍaikkir̲aaḷ*	உடைத்தாள் *uḍaittaaḷ*	உடைப்பாள் *uḍaippaaḷ*
3 SG N	உடைக்கிறது *uḍaikkir̲adu*	உடைத்தது *uḍaittadu*	உடைக்கும் *uḍaikkum*
1 PL	உடைக்கிறோம் *uḍaikkir̲oom*	உடைத்தோம் *uḍaittoom*	உடைப்போம் *uḍaippoom*
2 PL (& POL)	உடைக்கிறீர்கள் *uḍaikkir̲iirhaḷ*	உடைத்தீர்கள் *uḍaittiirhaḷ*	உடைப்பீர்கள் *uḍaippiirhaḷ*
3rd PL (& HON)	உடைக்கிறார்கள் *uḍaikkir̲aarhaḷ*	உடைத்தார்கள் *uḍaittaarhaḷ*	உடைப்பார்கள் *uḍaippaarhaḷ*
3rd PL F POL	உடைக்கிறார்கள் *uḍaikkir̲aarhaḷ*	உடைத்தார்கள் *uḍaittaarhaḷ*	உடைப்பார்கள் *uḍaippaarhaḷ*
3rd PL (N)	உடைக்கின்றன *uḍaikkin̲r̲an̲a*	உடைத்தன *uḍaittan̲a*	உடைக்கும் *uḍaikkum*

Table 8.18: Neuter Paradigm of உடை *uḍai* 'break (INTR)'; LT Version of Table 3.18

PNG	Present	Past	Future
3 SG N	உடைகிறது *uḍaihir̲adu*	உடைந்தது *uḍaindadu*	உடையும் *uḍaiyum*

Table 8.19: Tamil Modal Verbs; LT Version of Table 3.19

English	Tamil	Negative	Other negatives
can; be able	முடி *muḍi*	முடியவில்லை *muḍiyavillai* 'wasn't able, couldn't'	முடியாது *muḍiyaadu* 'can't, isn't able'
may; let's	லாம் *laam*		கூடாது 'should not' *kuuḍaadu*
must, should, ought	வேண்டும் *veeṇḍum* 'must; should'	வேண்டியதில்லை *veeṇḍiyadillai* 'wasn't necessary to, didn't have to'	வேண்டாம் *veeṇḍaam* 'need not'
let; may	அட்டும் *aṭṭum* 'let (it be)'	கூடாது *kuuḍaadu* 'don't let; forbid it'	வேண்டாம் *veeṇḍaam* 'doesn't have to'

Table 8.20: Inventory of Aspectual Verbs; LT Version of Table 3.21

AM	Meaning	Example	Gloss
விடு *viḍu*	COMPLETIVE For sure' 'definitely,	வந்துவிடுங்கள் *vandu-viḍu-ngaḷ*	'be sure to come'
		போய்விடலாம் *pooyviḍalaam*	'one may go **along**'
		பார்த்துவிட்டேன் *paarttuviṭṭeen̲*	'I **definitely** saw'
இரு[1] *iru*	PERFECT tense, CURRENT RELEVANCE	வந்திருக்கிறேன் *vandirukkir̲een̲* போயிருந்தப்போது *pooyirundappoodu*	'I **have** come (and am still here)' 'When (x) went and **stayed**'
இரு[2] *iru*	STATIVE	பார்த்திருக்கவேண்டும் *paarttirukkaveeṇḍum*	'(x) must **have** seen̲
இரு[3] *iru*	SUPPOSITIONAL	மழை பெய்திருக்கிறது *maṛai peydirukkir̲adu*	'it **seems** to have rained'
கொண்டிரு *koṇḍiru*	DURATIVE	பேசிக்கொண்டிருக்கிறோம் *peesikkoṇḍirukkir̲oom*	'we have **been** speak**ing**'
		வந்துகொண்டிருப்பேன் *vandukoṇḍiruppeen̲*	'I will be com**ing**'
கொள் *koḷ*	REFLEXIVE SELF-BENEFACTIVE	வாங்கிக்கொள்ளுங்கள் *vaangikkoḷḷungaḷ*	'buy **for yourself**'
	SIMULTANEOUS	போட்டுக்கொண்டு *pooṭṭukkoṇḍu*	'**while** wear**ing**'
ஆயிற்று *aayir̲r̲u*	FINALITY EXPECTED RESULT	வந்தாயிற்று *vandaayir̲r̲u*	'It **finally** came'
போடு *pooḍu*	MALICIOUS INTENT COMPL	எழுதிபோட்டான் *er̤udipooṭṭaan̲*	'He wrote it **off**'
		கொன்று போட்டார்கள் *kon̲r̲upooṭṭaarhaḷ*	'They killed (s.o.) **in cold blood**'
தள்ளு *taḷḷu*	DISTRIBUTIVE, COMPL	(x) கொடுத்து தள்ளினார் *koḍuttu taḷḷin̲aar*	'He gave (s.t.) **away**'
தொலை *tolai*	IMPATIENCE, DISGUST, (COMPL)	போய் தொலை! *pooy tolai!*	'Go **get lost**!'
வை *vai*	FUTURE UTILITY, (IN RESERVE)	குடித்து வைப்போம் *kuḍittuvaippoom*	'We'll **tank up** on (s.t.)'
போ *poo*	COMPLETIVE CHANGE OF STATE	உடைந்துபோகும் *uḍaindupoohum*	'It'll **get** broken'

Table 8.21: Paradigms of Dative-Stative Verbs, all Tenses and PNG; LT Version of Table 3.22

	பிடி *piḍi* 'like'	புரி *puri* 'understand'	தெரி *teri* 'know'	கிடை *kiḍai* 'be available'	வேண்டு *veeṇḍu* 'want, need'
INFINITIVE:	பிடிக்க *piḍikka* 'to like'	புரிய *puriya* 'to understand'	தெரிய *teriya* 'to know'	கிடைக்க *kiḍaikka* 'to be available'	வேண்டிய *veeṇḍiya* 'to be wanted'
HABITUAL:	பிடிக்கும் *piḍikkum* 'is liked'	புரியும் *puriyum* 'is understood'	தெரியும் *teriyum* 'is known'	கிடைக்கும் *kiḍaikkum* 'is available'	வேண்டும் *veeṇḍum* 'is wanted'
NEG. HABITUAL:	பிடிக்காது *piḍikkaadu* 'isn't liked'	புரியாது *puriyaadu* 'isn't understood'	தெரியாது *teriyaadu* 'isn't known'	கிடைக்காது *kiḍaikkaadu* 'isn't available'	வேண்டாம் *veeṇḍaam* 'isn't wanted'
PAST, NON-HABITUAL	பிடித்தது *piḍittadu* 'liked'	புரிந்தது *purindadu* 'understood'	தெரிந்தது *terindadu* 'knew'	கிடைத்தது *kiḍaittadu* 'was available'	வேண்டியது *veeṇḍiyadu* 'was needed'
NEG PAST, NON-HABITUAL	பிடிக்கவில்லை *piḍikkavillai* 'wasn't liked'	புரியவில்லை *puriyavillai* 'wasn't understood'	தெரியவில்லை *teriyavillai* 'wasn't known'	கிடைக்கவில்லை *kiḍaikkavillai* 'wasn't available'	வேண்டியதில்லை *veeṇḍiyadillai* 'wasn't wanted'

Table 8.23: Structure of Finite Verbs; LT Version of Table 4.1

Stem	Tense marker	PNG	Gloss
இரு *iru* 'be located'	க்கிற் *kkir̲* 'present'	ஏன் *een̲* '1 SG'	
நான் இருக்கிறேன் *naan irukkireen̲*			'I am located'
வா/வர் *vaa/var* 'come'	ந்த் *nd* 'past'	ஆர் *aar* '3 HON'	
அவர் வந்தார் *avar vandaar*			'he came'
போ *poo* 'go'	வ *v* 'future'	ஈர்கள் *iirhaḷ* '2 PL/POL'	
நீங்கள் போவீர்கள் *niingaḷ pooviirhaḷ*			'you will go'

Table 8.24: Pronouns and PNG-markers; LT Versions of Table 4.2

Person	Singular	Pronoun	English	PNG
I		நான் *naan̲*	'I'	ஏன் *-een̲*
2	(NON-POL)	நீ *nii*	'you'	ஆய் *-aay*
3	M	அவன் *avan̲*	'he'	ஆன் *-aan̲*
	F	அவள் *avaḷ*	'she'	ஆள் *-aaḷ*
	M HON	அவர் அவர்	'he, she*' (polite)	ஆர் *-aar*
	F HON	அவர்கள் *avarhaḷ*	'she' (POL)	ஆர்கள் *-aarhaḷ*
	N	இது/அது *idu/adu*	'it'	அது *adu**
Person	**Plural**	**Pronoun**	**English**	**PNG**
I	PL EXCL	நாங்கள் *naangaḷ*	'we (EXCL)'	ஓம் *-oom*
	PL INCL	நாம் *naam*	'we (INCL)'	ஓம் *-oom*
2	PL	நீங்கள் *niingaḷ*	'you (POL)'	ஈர்கள் *-iirhaḷ*
3	PL	அவர்கள் *avarhaḷ*	'they' (ANIM)	ஆர்கள் *-aarhaḷ*
3	PL N	அவைகள் *avaihaḷ*	'they' (INANIM)	அன *-an̲a*

Table 8.25: Pronouns and Oblique Forms; LT Version of Table 4.3

Person	Pronoun	Gloss	GENITIVE	DATIVE
1 SG	நான் *naan̲*	‘I’	என் *en̲*	எனக்கு *enakku*
2 SG	நீ *nii*	‘you (SG)’	உன் *un̲*	உனக்கு *un̲akku*
3 M	அவன் *avan̲*	‘he’	அவன் *avan̲*	அவனுக்கு *avan̲ukku*
3 F	அவள் *avaḷ*	‘she’	அவள் *avaḷ*	அவளுக்கு *avaḷukku*
3 M HON	அவர் *avar*	‘he (POL)’	அவர் *avar*	அவருக்கு *avarukku*
3 F HON	அவர்கள் *avarhaḷ*	‘she (POL)’	அவர்கள் *avarhaḷ*	அவர்களுக்கு *avarhaḷukku*
3 N	இது/அது *idu/adu*	‘it’	இது/அது * *idu/adu*	இதுக்கு/அதுக்கு *idukku/adukku*
1 PL EXCL	நாங்கள் *naangaḷ*	‘we (EXCL)’	எங்கள் *engaḷ*	எங்களுக்கு *engaḷukku*
1 PL INCL	நாம் *naam*	‘we (INCL)’	நம் *nam*	நமக்கு *namakku*
2 PL	நீங்கள் *niingaḷ*	‘you (POL)’	உங்கள் *ungaḷ*	உங்களுக்கு *ungaḷukku*
3 PL	அவர்கள் *avarhaḷ*	‘they’ (ANIM)	அவர்கள் *avarhaḷ*	அவர்களுக்கு *avarhaḷukku*
3 PL N	அவைகள் *avaihaḷ*	‘they’ (INANIM)	அவைகளின் *avaihaḷin̲*	அவைகளுக்கு *avaihaḷukku*

Table 8.26: Structure of Demonstrative Pronoun Sets; LT Version of Table 4.4. Note: the form எவர்கள் *evarhaḷ* is usually replaced by யார் *yaar*

Proximate இ *i*	Distant அ *a*	Interrogative எ *e*
இது *idu* 'this thing'	அது *adu* 'that thing'	எது *edu* 'which thing?'
இவர் *ivar* 'this person'	அவர் *avar* 'that person'	யார் *yaar* 'which person? who?'
இவள் *ivaḷ* 'this (FEM)'	அவள் *avaḷ* 'that (FEM)'	எவள் *evaḷ** 'which (FEM)'
இவன்) *ivan̲* 'this male'	அவன் *avan̲* 'that male'	எவன் *evan̲** 'which male'
இவர்கள் *ivarhaḷ* 'these persons'	அவர்கள் *avarhaḷ* 'those persons'	எவர்கள் *evarhaḷ** 'which persons?'
இவர்கள் *ivarhaḷ* ('this woman (POL)')	அவர்கள் *avarhaḷ* ('that woman (POL)')	எவர்கள் *evarhaḷ** ('which woman (POL)?')

Table 8.27: Structure of Demonstrative Adjectives and Other Deictic Sets; LT Version of Tables 5.1 and 5.2 (Note: forms marked with asterisks are grammatically possible but not common, and usually replaced by யார் *yaar*.

Proximate இ *i*	Distant அ *a*	Interrogative எ *e*
இந்த *inda* 'this'	அந்த *anda* 'that'	எந்த *enda* 'which?'
இப்போது *ippoodu* 'now'	அப்போது *appoodu* 'then'	எப்போது *eppoodu* 'when?'
இவ்வளவு *ivvaḷavu* 'this much'	அவ்வளவு *avvaḷavu* 'that much'	எவ்வளவு *evvaḷavu* 'how much?'
இங்கே *ingee* 'here'	அங்கே *angee* 'there'	எங்கே *engee* 'where?'
இன்றைக்கு *inr̲aikku* 'today'	அன்றைக்கு *anr̲aikku* 'that day'	என்றைக்கு *enr̲aikku* 'which day?'
இவர் *ivar* 'this person'	அவர் *avar* 'that person'	யார் *yaar* 'which person? who?'
இவர்கள் *ivarhaḷ* 'these persons'	அவர்கள் *avarhaḷ* 'those persons'	எவர்கள் *evarhaḷ** 'which persons?'
இவைகள் *ivaihaḷ* 'these things'	அவைகள் *avaihaḷ* 'those things'	எவைகள் *evaihaḷ** 'which things?'
இத்தனை *ittan̲ai* 'this many'	அத்தனை *attan̲ai* 'that many'	எத்தனை *ettan̲ai* 'how many?'

Table 8.28: Basic Tamil Cardinal Numerical Morphemes; LT Version of Table 5.3

ஒன்று	*on̲r̲u*	'one'	நூறு	*nuur̲u*	'hundred'
இரண்டு	*iran̲ḍu*	'two'	ஆயிரம்	*aayiram*	'thousand'
மூன்று	*muun̲r̲u*	'three'	இலக்ஷம்	*ilakṣam*	'lakh'
நான்கு	*naangu*	'four'	கோடி	*kooḍi*	'crore'
ஐந்து	*aindu*	'five'			
ஆறு	*aar̲u*	'six'			
ஏழு	*eer̤u*	'seven'			
எட்டு	*eṭṭu*	'eight'			
ஒன்பது	*on̲badu*	'nine'			
பத்து	*pattu*	'ten'			

Table 8.29: Oblique or Adjectival Forms of Numerals; LT Version of Table 5.4

Basic form of numeral			**Oblique or adjectival form**
ஒன்று	*on̲r̲u*	'one'	ஒரு *oru*
இரண்டு	*iraṇḍu*	'two'	இரு *iru-*, ஈர் *iir-*
மூன்று	*muun̲r̲u*	'three'	மூ *muu-*, மு *mu-*
நான்கு	*naangu*	'four'	நா *naa-*
ஐந்து	*aindu*	'five'	ஐ *ai-*, ஐம் *aim-*
ஆறு	*aar̲u*	'six'	அறு *ar̲u-*
ஏழு	*eer̤u*	'seven'	எழு *er̤u*
எட்டு	*eṭṭu*	'eight'	எண் *eṇ-*
ஒன்பது	*on̲badu*	'nine'	(no special form)
பத்து	*pattu*	'ten'	பதி *padi-*, பத *pada-*
நூறு	*nuur̲u*	'hundred'	நூற்று *nuur̲r̲u*
ஆயிரம்	*aayiram*	'thousand'	ஆயிரத்தி *aayiratti*
இலக்ஷம்	*ilakṣam*	'lakh'	(no special form)
கோடி	*kooḍi*	'crore'	(no special form)

Table 8.30: Regular and Irregular Combined Forms of Numerals

'Teen' Forms		
பதினொன்று	*padinon̲r̲u*	'eleven'
பன்னிரண்டு	*panniraṇḍu*	'twelve'
பதின்மூன்று	*padin̲muun̲r̲u*	'thirteen'
பதினான்கு	*padin̲aangu*	'fourteen'
பதினைந்து	*padin̲aindu*	'fifteen'
பதினாறு	*padan̲aar̲u*	'sixteen'
பதினேழு	*padin̲eer̤u*	'seventeen'
பதினெட்டு	*padin̲eṭṭu*	'eighteen'
பத்தொன்பது	*patton̲badu*	'nineteen'
Multiples of Ten		
இருபது	*irubadu,*	'twenty'
முப்பது	*muppadu*	'thirty'
நாற்பது	*naar̲padu*	'forty'
ஐம்பது	*aimbadu*	'fifty'
அறுபது	*ar̲ubadu*	'sixty'
எழுபது	*er̤ubadu*	'seventy'
எண்பது	*eṇbadu,*	'eighty'
தொண்ணூறு	*toṇṇuur̲u*	'ninety'

Table 8.31: Multiples of Hundreds and Thousands

Hundreds		
எரனூறு	*eranuuru*	'200'
முன்னூறு	*munnuuru*	'300'
நானூறு	*naanuuru*	'400'
ஐனூறு	*ainuuru*	'500'
அறுனூறு	*arunuuru*	'600'
எழுனூறு	*er̤unuuru*	'700'
எண்ணூறு	*eṇṇuuru*	'800'
தொள்ளாயிரம்	*toḷḷaayiram*	'900'
Thousands		
ரெண்டாயிரம்	*reṇḍaayiram*	'2,000'
மூவாயிரம்	*muuvaayiram*	'3,000'
நாலாயிரம்	*naalaayiram*	'4,000'
அஞ்சாயிரம்	*anjaayiram*	'5,000'
ஆறாயிரம்	*aaraayiram*	'6,000'
ஏழாயிரம்	*eer̤aayiram*	'7,000'
எட்டாயிரம்	*eṭṭaayiram*	'8,000
ஒம்பதாயிரம்	*ombadaayiram*	'9,000

Table 8.32: Nominalized Adjectives and Adverbials; LT Version of Table 6.1

	NOMINALIZED ADJECTIVES	ADVERBIAL
1.	இந்த வீடு புதியது *inda viiḍu pudiyadu* 'This house is new.'	இந்த வீடு புதியதாக இருக்கிறது *inda viiḍu pudiyadaaha irukkir̲adu* 'This house is new at present.'
2.	இது சரி *idu sari* 'This is okay.'	இது சரியாக இருக்கிறது *idu sariyaaha irukkir̲adu* 'This is okay now.'
3.	இது நல்லது *idu nalladu* 'This is (a) good (thing).'	இது நன்றாக இருக்கிறது *idu nan̲r̲aaha irukkir̲adu* 'This is good now.'
4.	இந்தக் காலம் மிக மோசம் *inda kaalam miha moosam* 'This climate is very bad.'	இந்தக் காலம் மிக மோசமாக இருக்கிறது *inda kaalam miha moosamaaha irukkir̲adu* 'The weather is bad now.'

Table 8.33: Cleft and non-Cleft Sentences; LT Version of Table 7.2

NON-CLEFT SENTENCES	CLEFT SENTENCES
நான் மார்க்கெட்டுக்கு போகிறேனா? *naan̲ maarkeṭṭukku poohir̲een̲aa*? 'Am I going to the market?'	நான் மார்க்கெட்டுக்கு போகிறதா? *naan̲ markeṭṭukku poohir̲adaa*? 'Is it that I am going to the market? Am I supposed to go to the market?'
துணியைக் கொண்டுவந்தாயா? *tuṇiyai koṇḍuvandaayaa?* 'Did you bring the laundry?'	துணியைக் கொண்டுவருகிறதா? *tuṇiyai koṇḍuvaruhir̲adaa*? 'Is it that you have brought the laundry? Is it the laundry you've brought?'
நான் எதைச் செய்கிறேன்? *naan̲ edai seyhir̲een̲?* 'What will I do?'	நான் எதைச் செய்கிறது? *naan̲ edai seyhir̲adu?* 'What is it that I will do? What am I supposed to do? What's to be done?'
நான் கூப்பிடுகிறேன் *naan̲ kuuppiḍuhir̲een̲* 'I am calling.'	இது ராம் கூப்பிடுகிறது *idu raam kuuppiḍuhir̲adu* 'This is Ram calling.'

Table 8.34: Ordinary Sentences and Doubt-Marked Sentences; LT Version of Table 7.3

ORDINARY SENTENCES	DOUBT-MARKED SENTENCES
அம்மா இருக்கிறார்களா? *ammaa irukkir̲aarhaḷaa*? 'Is (your) mother there?'	அம்மா இருக்கிறார்களோ? *ammaa irukkir̲aarhaḷoo*? 'I wonder if maybe (your) Mother is there?'
துணியைக் கொண்டுவந்தாயா? *tuṇiyai koṇḍuvandaayaa?* 'Did you bring the laundry?'	துணியைக் கொண்டுவந்தாயோ? *tuṇiyai koṇḍuvandaayoo*? 'Have you (perhaps) brought the laundry (or what)?'
வருவாரா வரமாட்டாரா? *varuvaaraa varamaaṭṭaaraa* 'He'll either come or he won't.'	வருவாரோ வரமாட்டாரோ *varuvaaroo varamaaṭṭaaroo* 'He might come, and then again he might not.'

References

[1] Andronov, M. 1962. *Razgovorny tamil'ski yazyk i ego dialekty.* [The Colloquial Tamil Language and its Dialects.] Moscow: Nauka.

[2] Andronov, M. 1975. 'Problems of the National Language in Tamilnad.' *Anthropos* 70:180-193.

[3] Annamalai, E. (n.d.) 'Notes and Discussions; the Standard Spoken Tamil—some Observations.' (ms.)

[4] Annamalai, E. 1985. *Dynamics of Verbal Extension in Tamil.* Trivandrum, Kerala : Dravidian Linguistics Association of India.

[5] Annamalai, E. 1997. *Adjectival Clauses in Tamil.* Tokyo: Institute for the Study of Languages and Cultures of Asia and Africa and Tokyo University of Foreign Studies.

[6] Arden, A. H. 1942 (rev. 1963). *A Progressive Grammar of the Tamil Language.* Madras: Christian Literature Society.

[7] Arokianathan, S. 1981. *Tamil Clitics.* Trivandrum: Dravidian Linguistics Association.

[8] Asher, R. E. 1982. *Tamil.* LINGUA DESCRIPTIVA SERIES. Amsterdam: North-Holland Publishing Company.

[9] Britto, Francis 1986. *Diglossia: A Study of the Theory with Application to Tamil.* Washington, D.C.: Georgetown U. Press.

[10] Burrow, T. and M. B. Emeneau 1961. *A Dravidian Etymological Dictionary.* Oxford: the Clarendon Press.

[11] Chidambaranatha Chettiar, A. (ed.) 1961. *English-Tamil Dictionary.* Madras: University of Madras.

[12] Dale, Ian Randall Hampton 1975. *Tamil Auxiliary Verbs.* Unpublished School of Oriental and African Studies PhD Thesis.

[13] Firth, 1934. 'Phonetics of Tamil' (in Arden 1934, 1942).

[14] Hopper, Paul J. and Sandra A. Thompson, (eds.) 1982. *Studies in Transitivity.* New York: Academic Press.

[15] Hopper, Paul J., and Elizabeth Claus Traugott 1993. *Grammaticalization.* Cambridge and New York: Cambridge University Press, 1993.

[16] Hymes, Dell 1971 *Pidginization and Creolization of Languages.* London and New York: Cambridge University Press.

[17] Labov, William 1971. 'The notion of "System" in Creole Studies.' In Hymes 1971.

[18] Malten, Thomas. 1989. *Reduplizierte Verbstämme im Tamil.* BEITRÄGE ZUR SÜDASIENFORSCHUNG. BD. 127. Stuttgart: Steiner Verlag.

[19] McAlpin, David 1976. *A Core Vocabulary for Tamil.* Department of S. Asian Regional Studies, University of Pennsylvania. Final Report, USOE Contract 300-75-0314.

[20] Paramasivam, K. 1979. 'Effectivity and Causativity in Tamil.' *International Journal of Dravidian Linguistics* 8(1):71-151.

[21] Percival, Peter 1861. *A Dictionary, English and Tamil.* Madras: Madras School Book and Literature Society, 1935.

[22] da Proença, Antam. *Vocabulario Tamulico com a significaçam Portugueza. Na impremssa Tamulica da Provincia do Malabar, por Ignacio Aichamoni impressor della.* 1679. 247 fo. New edition, *Antão da Proença's Tamil-Portuguese dictionary, A.D. 1679.* Kuala Lumpur: University of Malaya, 1966.

[23] Rajaram, S. *English–Tamil Pedagogical Dictionary.* 1986. Thanjavur: Tamil University.

[24] Ramanujan, A. K. and E. Annamalai 1967 *Preliminary Studies for a Reference Grammar of Tamil.* Chicago: University of Chicago Dept. of Linguistics (unpublished ms.)

[25] Schiffman, Harold F. 1968. 'Morphophonemics of Tamil Numerals.' In Asher, R. and X. Thani-Nayagam (eds.), *Proceedings of the First International Conference-Seminar of Tamil Studies.* Kuala Lumpur: University of Malaya Press.

[26] Schiffman, Harold F. 1979 *A Grammar of Spoken Tamil.* Madras: Christian Literature Society.

[27] Schiffman, Harold F. 1980: 'The Tamil Liquids.' In Proceedings of the Berkeley Linguistics Society, 6:100-110. (EMENEAU FELICITATION VOLUME). Berkeley: Department of South and Southeast Asian Languages.

[28] Schiffman, Harold F. 1993: 'Intervocalic V-deletion in Tamil: Its Domains and its Constraints.' *Journal of the American Oriental Society* 113(4):513-528.

[29] Schiffman, Harold F. 1998: 'Standardization and Restandardization: the case of Spoken Tamil.' *Language in Society*, 27(3) 1-27.

[30] Steever, Sanford B. 1983. *A Study in Auxiliation: The Grammar of Indicative Auxiliary Verb System of Tamil.* Unpublished U. of Chicago Linguistics dissertation.

Index

73066633R00143

Made in the USA
Lexington, KY
06 December 2017